Changing Places of Work

Alan Felstead,
Nick Jewson and Sally Walters

palgrave
macmillan

First published 2005 by
PALGRAVE MACMILLAN
Houndmills, Basingstoke, Hampshire RG21 6XS and
175 Fifth Avenue, New York, N.Y. 10010
Companies and representatives throughout the world

PALGRAVE MACMILLAN is the global academic imprint of the Palgrave Macmillan division of St. Martin's Press, LLC and of Palgrave Macmillan Ltd. Macmillan® is a registered trademark in the United States, United Kingdom and other countries. Palgrave is a registered trademark in the European Union and other countries.

ISBN-13: 978–0333–94907–8 hardback
ISBN-10: 0–333–94907–2 hardback
ISBN-13: 978–0333–94908–5 paperback
ISBN-10: 0–333–94908–0 paperback

This book is printed on paper suitable for recycling and made from fully managed and sustained forest sources.

A catalogue record for this book is available from the British Library.

Library of Congress Cataloging-in-Publication Data

Felstead, Alan, 1963–
　　Changing places of work / Alan Felstead, Nick Jewson and Sally Walters.
　　　　p.　cm.
　　Includes bibliographical references and index.
　　ISBN 0–333–94907–2 (cloth) – ISBN 0–333–94908–0 (pbk.)
　　　1. Office layout.　2. Work environment.　3. Technological innovations.
　　4. Organizational effectiveness.　I. Jewson, Nick, 1946–　II. Walters, Sally, 1973–
　　III. Title.

HF5547.2.F45　2005
658.2′3 – dc22

　　　　　　　　　　　　　　　　　　　　　　　　　　　　　　　　2004063662

10　9　8　7　6　5　4　3　2　1
14　13　12　11　10　09　08　07　06　05

Printed in China

Contents

List of Tables

Acknowledgements

We would like to acknowledge the support of the Economic and Social Research Council with respect to two research projects, under the Future of Work Programme, from which the original qualitative and quantitative data in this book are derived ('Working at Home: New Perspectives' [L212252022] and 'Transforming Places of Work' [L212252051]). We are grateful to our transcribers for their excellent work. We are also indebted to Marilyn Jewson for reading, and commenting on, the final draft. Last but not least, our thanks must go to our respondents, who generously gave of their time and attention, and to whom this book is respectfully dedicated.

1

Themes and Issues

Few organizational researchers are seriously studying the material and symbolic contests over the physical spaces of organizations. These include struggles regarding size, location, and quality of physical premises, equipment, and furniture, the personalization of individual and group workscapes (and the countertendency to reappropriate this space from employees through hot-desking and teleworking), and the creation of no-go areas for superiors through a variety of subordinate activities.

(Gabriel 1999: 197)

Introduction

A recent article in the *Guardian* described the 'work space' of Tony Barker, sales and marketing director of President Office Furniture (Deeble 2003). Tony relies on his mobile phone, laptop and wireless headset. These constitute the tools of his trade and his virtual work space. Wherever he is in the world, he can check his e-mail and get onto the office network. He 'dials' by pressing a headset button and speaking the number he wants – his mobile phone stays in his bag. Co-workers access his diary and book appointments for him, while he can remotely download from the internet and intranet. Wireless technology enables him to move from office to car to sofa to gym to home, while staying connected with colleagues, customers and the business. Face-to-face meetings in the office to update on sales, quotations or specifications are no longer necessary. This can all be done electronically, saving time and enabling deals to be closed more quickly. 'Dead time' – previously wasted in airports, taxis or waiting for appointments – has become work time harnessed to the benefit of the company. These developments promise increases in productivity and cost savings. Tony, an enthusiast for these ways of working, is described as: 'in control of his work and his life'. However, he strikes a note of caution: 'We've got this technology that if we're not careful is going to drive us to perdition. With a 24-hour day we'll all go crazy'. He goes on to say that it is crucial for staff to learn how to manage their own

1

working lives for themselves; for example, by setting their own pace
of work. He concludes: 'We need to rewrite the rule book for working in
a mobile way'.

Tony Barker's lifestyle incorporates advanced technology but in terms
of the way he organizes his working space and time it is not unusual. Profound changes are currently under way in the places where paid work is
conducted, and these developments are having a particular impact on the
lived experiences of professional and managerial workers. Tony Barker is
in the vanguard of changes that are transforming the meaning and experience of employment. The world of work that is fading is one in which the
spaces and times of employment were clearly delineated from the rest of
life, work time was spent in specialized sites such as offices, and workers
were designated specialized cubes of space that comprised their personal
workstations. This pattern of life shaped the familiar rhythms of 'going to
work' and sitting in an office, or at a desk, with a name-plate on it. The
emerging new landscape of employment is one in which the spaces and
times of work and non-work are not clearly separated, work time is spent
in a variety of locations, many of which are not specifically set aside for
job-related tasks, workers are required to construct their own sequences
and sites of activities, and personal space in the labour process is absent,
problematic or contested. We no longer go to the office but, instead, the
office comes with us, every where and every when.

Professional and managerial workers are particularly likely to experience
these changes because of their high levels of mobility, heavy use of expensive office space, involvement in long-hours occupational cultures and
extensive use of information and communication technology (ICT). Their
jobs cover a wide range of activities but typically entail generating, evalu-
ating and presenting data that relate to a variety of contexts – such as market
movements, personnel performance, client demands and technological
functions. Sometimes those who perform such tasks are referred to as
'knowledge workers'. Arguably, this term captures an important aspect of
their working lives: that is, the application of esoteric bodies of knowledge,
acquired in formal and informal learning situations, to the solution of work
problems. However, it can be argued that all forms of employment entail
some degree of application of skill and knowledge in the solution of problems. Moreover, the term 'knowledge worker' has become associated with
a particular view of the development of the advanced societies – towards a
'knowledge economy' and 'knowledge society' – that is contentious. For
these reasons, we shall avoid using the term.

The next section will provide an overview of our argument, outlining
a series of issues that will be explored in later chapters. This serves, therefore, as a summary of what is to come. The chapter then describes the
range of original quantitative and qualitative empirical data that inform

our analysis. The last section comprises a brief review of the themes developed in each of the subsequent chapters.

The Exploding Workplace

It is a sociological truism that industrialization created two distinct spheres of social life – home and work – that had previously been undifferentiated and interwoven. The landscape of factories and offices became an aspect of the regulation of workforces through control over space (Marglin 1976; Baldry *et al.* 1998; Baldry 1999; Felstead *et al.* 2003a). Employers and managers discovered that threats to material security, productivity and process co-ordination could be greatly attenuated by allocating individual workers to specific locations in which they were required to remain while performing their tasks. This geography of work made possible processes of monitoring, observation and surveillance, with their associated disciplines and opportunities for regulation (Foucault 1977). The panoptican is, above all, a building. Workplaces became social technologies of control.

These developments are often discussed in relation to assembly workers. However, in office buildings, too, managerial control was built into the spatial relations of employment. Regulation of office-based employees depended on the allocation of workers to specific fixed places and the visual inspection of their activities in those spaces. Elsewhere we have referred to these attributes of managerial control as 'presence' and 'visibility' (Felstead *et al.* 2003a).

The highly disciplinary environments of early industrialization shaped the subjectivities of workers. Employees acquired a sense of identity and selfhood partly as a result of the physical organization of workstations and workplaces. An office constituted a personal location in the place of work. It might take the form of a walled cell (cellular office) or, particularly from the 1960s onwards, a desk within an 'open plan' floor plate ('Bürolandschaft'). Either way, workers were allocated their own cube of space, dedicated to their use (sometimes called 'veal pens'; Zelinsky 1997: 141). Staff not 'in the office' were, by definition, not 'at work' and were not eligible for payment. Equally, staff who 'put in the hours' in designated locations were deemed worthy of reward. Employers purchased the time of their employees within specific places determined by the employer (Thrift 1990; M. Harvey 1999).

The cubes of space occupied by office workers were never, of course, their personal property. Capitalist employment relations are based on the alienation of wage labourers from the means of production. Hence, white-collar employees could not buy or sell their workstations, nor could they pass them on to their heirs. Indeed, they only exercised tenuous control over their allocation, which was ultimately a managerial prerogative. Nevertheless, they often developed a strong sense of personal identification with 'their' office. Office workers were frequently allowed to personalize their working environment with pictures, plants, photographs, souvenirs and other memorabilia. Although they had no legal entitlement, they were able symbolically to colonize the space of their employment.

The visibility and presence of office workers were, therefore, double-edged weapons in the armoury of management. Offices and desks were devices of managerial regulation, control and disciplinary gaze. At the same time, by symbolically personalizing their designated cubes of space, office workers were differentiating themselves from other members of the workforce and projecting aspects of their individual and private identities into the impersonal world of employment relations. Visibility and presence were transformed into claims of status and autonomy.

It should be acknowledged that, even during the classic era of office and factory-based production, there always remained some ways of earning a living that did not entail attendance at a workplace. Some members of the sales force – 'commercial travellers' or 'road warriors' – visited customers (Spears 1995). Many self-employed people, and some of their staff, worked in premises where they lived, including small hotels, corner shops, guest houses and pubs (Hawkins and Radcliffe 1971; Honsden 1984). Similarly, some farmers and rural labourers lived on the land where they worked (Newby 1977, 1979). Industrial homeworkers, in low-paid manual and clerical jobs, continued to be employed at home (Boris and Daniels 1989; Boris 1994; Boris and Prügl 1996; Felstead and Jewson 1996, 2000). However, these were not typical. Their numbers were limited compared with those who commuted to and from a workplace to conduct their daily tasks at a designated workstation. Furthermore, their way of life was regarded neither as the norm nor as ideal. They were not profiled in broadsheet newspapers as cutting-edge models of the future of work, nor as exemplars to be emulated by others.

The central tenet of this book is that the social order embedded in the workplaces of early capitalist industrialization is giving way to new spatial and temporal relations of employment. In the twenty-first century, the technologies of professional and managerial work no longer require staff to be present in designated buildings over long periods of time. Work can be conducted using electronic technologies that make possible communication – in word, image and speech – with co-workers and clients who are geographically remote. Mobile phones, e-mail, laptops and the internet – not to mention faxes, video conferencing, text messaging, web cams and a multitude of other devices – mean that increasingly we can work at any time or place. For senior white-collar staff in particular, work increasingly entails participation in a network of electronically mediated processes of information exchange. As long as they are in contact with this 'electronic envelope', their jobs no longer require them to 'go into the office'.

It is true that not all aspects of employment relations can be conducted in this way. There remains a crucial role for face-to-face interaction in the form of formal meetings and informal social contacts (Boden and Molotch 1994). Nevertheless, a large proportion of managerial and professional work tasks can be achieved by these means. The potential implications for the organization and experience of work are enormous – and are already apparent in the lives of people like Tony Barker. There is no inevitability about how these potentialities will be manifested in any particular context; the advent of new technology does not determine exactly what will happen. Nevertheless, ICT does make possible ways of working that are profoundly different from those that dominated mid-twentieth century workplaces. In particular, the idea that some spaces and times are ring-fenced for work and others for non-work is already being swept away.

It is now possible to work in a hotel, motorway service station or airport lounge; while in transit on a train, plane or car; or at home. It is possible to 'log on' at any time – weekends and evenings, holidays and festivals, family celebrations and dinner parties with friends. Thanks to 'Wi-Fi' (wireless web connections), we can take a moment while chatting in the pub or strolling down the street to check our e-mail. We can break into our vacation without leaving the resort to deal with that urgent mobile phone call. Indeed, it becomes increasingly misplaced to talk about 'breaking into' non-work times and places. The times and places of employment can now weave their way into and through the nooks and crannies of our lives. The relationship between spaces and times of work and non-work are no longer sequential, linear and chronological but, instead, are becoming a dispersed mosaic of ubiquitous connections that are always available. For those who are part of this exploding workplace, the everyday rhythms of life undergo fundamental transformations.

These developments generate options; in any given time or space, it is possible to be working or not working. Decisions have to be made. Such choices are hedged around by a variety of pressures. Some locations and times suit particular work tasks better than others. Some household and family relationships restrict involvement in job tasks. Some work demands are of overriding importance. One of the aims of this book is to explore these constraints. Nevertheless, it is also our objective to highlight the degree of self-management and self-organization required by this way of working. In principle, it becomes possible for workers to create their own distinctive and individualized sequence of activities in time and space. No longer corralled in a single site for fixed hours, individual employees can plan for themselves their movements between a diverse range of locations.

The many possible places in which work can be done may conveniently be grouped into three main categories, each representing a distinctive socio-spatial context. We refer to these as 'working in collective offices', 'working at home', and 'working on the move'.

In collective offices there is an absence of personal or individual space. Employment tasks are conducted at collective facilities – such as 'hot-desks', 'booked offices' and 'touchdown areas' – that are shared with others. Workers are required, under their own initiative, to move around the building to find the facilities they need and to move between work-stations as their tasks change. The absence of personal space makes it possible for employers to achieve considerable savings in costs of land, buildings and equipment. At the same time, however, mobility under-mines the presence and visibility of workers within designated locations, features of workplaces that have long been central aspects of managerial supervision. Thus, collective offices are characterized by strategies of cost control that entail high levels of spatial mobility of staff and strategies of productivity control that seek to find ways of compensating for the dimin-ished visibility and presence of the workforce.

Working at home involves undertaking employment-related tasks within a residential dwelling or household premises. Home-located workers may occupy a variety of contrasting spaces within their place of residence. However, the distinguishing characteristics of working at home are, on the one hand, close physical proximity to the private and personal worlds of domestic relationships and, on the other, geographical distance from colleagues, co-workers and managers. The challenge for home-located workers is to find socio-spatial arrangements in the home that address both these issues. In some respects, they enjoy considerable autonomy in deter-mining their personal working timetables, routines and environments. However, making their choices into practical arrangements draws them into potentially challenging negotiations with other household members over the distribution of time, space and resources in the home. Distance from line managers can enhance independent decision-making and even evasion of managerial controls. However, home-located workers can experience a sense of isolation from the flow of information and support provided by col-leagues and superiors.

Working on the move comprises occupational tasks conducted while in transit from one location to another as well as those done at temporary stopping points along the way. It thus includes not only work done on cars, trains and planes but also that undertaken at motorway service stations, airport lounges, railway stations and hotel lobbies. The distinguishing feature of working on the move is the combination of close physical proximity to the formal interactions of impersonal public arenas with geographical distance from most colleagues, co-workers and managers.

The increasing importance of these three sites of work leads to major shifts in the balance of personal and non-personal space and time in working life. The 'personal office' of the old order put workers in their place but it also gave them a place in which to be, although the imposition of working hours and schedules minimized the opportunity to personalize time. In the emerging landscape of multiple workstations in diverse sites, the opportunity symbolically to personalize space is both reduced and changed in character. However, the necessity for workers to devise their own sequences of activities enhances their opportunity to personalize time.

In the collective office, a desk cannot legitimately become personal territory; it is a collective facility provided for the use of many. It does not, and cannot be permitted to, carry the symbolic trace of an individual user; it is as anonymous as a seat on public transport. Attempts to monopolize or recolonize collective facilities and spaces – 'stalling' in Goffman's terms (1971) – are regarded as unacceptable by management because they restrict the availability of facilities to others. Instead employees are expected to roam through the building, temporarily settling at the desk of their choice but shifting between workstations as and when required (this arrangement is known as 'hotdesking'). They cannot legitimately colonize office spaces; they must plan sequences of movement between them. They may not stall but they must flow. Nevertheless, as will be seen in later chapters, workers often do attempt to capture space for their personal use – leading, in turn, to management interventions aimed at 'stall busting'.

In the collective office, command over personal space is diminished or eradicated. However, increasingly work is conducted at home, which is a personal space *par excellence*. Our evidence will show that the numbers of people who work at home most of the time are low (although growing) but that the numbers who occasionally utilize home as a workplace, as one element in a collection of diverse sites, are far larger. Home is the personal territory of named individuals and may be their legally owned property. Hence, in as much as job tasks become home-located, workers experience an increased capacity to personalize their working spaces and to resist intrusions from management. Furthermore, when working at home, staff often have a high degree of discretion over their timetables. However, working at home entails introducing the anonymous public world of wage labour into the personal and private space of the domestic dwelling. Other household members may resist this intrusion. Employees may be drawn into delicate negotiations with their families to secure control over part of the household for their occupational activities. Children and partners may find themselves subjected to new disciplines and curtailments. In addition, support and advice from managers and colleagues may be attenuated. For some staff, there may be a sense of distance and isolation from co-workers and embattled engagement with family members.

In addition to working in collective offices and at home, workers also typically find themselves working on the move. Here, space is usually the legal property of neither employer nor worker. Planes and trains, railway stations and motorway services, are public spaces that are difficult to personalize. Although some are being upgraded, many of these locations have not been designed as places of work. Hence, working on the move entails generating a temporary bubble or capsule of functional, and possibly personalized, space within the context of anonymous public encounters. The car, an important site of mobile working, is slightly different in that it frequently has closer personal associations with the worker than, say, a railway carriage. Cars also offer a greater degree of time flexibility and discretion to the traveller than the fixed schedules of public transport, although the scope of choice is necessarily limited by the contingencies of road-based travel. Car travel, therefore, incorporates elements of both working at home and on the move.

The overall picture, then, is one of diversity and fragmentation, transitions and flows. Movements within and between the working locations of office, home and travel enable workers to mix and match sites and schedules, tasks and experiences, supervision and self-direction, freedoms and constraints. Places of work are no longer singular but have become multiple. Working hours are no longer fixed but stretch throughout the day, week and year. Work becomes an activity not a place.

These changes have enormous implications for transferable skills and tacit knowledge. The boundaries between work and non-work are no longer given but have to be constructed, negotiated and defended by individuals for themselves. Solutions are likely to differ according to individual relationships, circumstances, resources, personalities and experiences – and will shift as situations change over time. These processes of personal choice are reminiscent of the reflexive, discursive and narrative-based constructions of individual identity-making and self-invention that a number of authors have suggested are characteristic of contemporary societies (Giddens 1991, 1992; Craib 1998; Bauman 2000; Holstein and Gubrium 2000; K. Woodward 2002).

This book is not primarily concerned with the drivers of these changes. It is, rather, focused on their implications for the lived experience of workers and the strategies of control adopted by managers. However, an awareness of their sources emphasizes the likelihood that ever greater numbers of professional and managerial workers will find themselves navigating these diverse, ubiquitous and insidious times and places of employment.

There is no shortage of architects, designers and management gurus who argue that these developments represent more productive and innovative ways of working as well as more autonomous and family-friendly lifestyles (Smith and Kearney 1994; Becker and Steele 1995; DEGW and BRE 1996; Duffy 1997; Raymond and Cunliffe 1997; Worthington 1997; Zelinsky 1997, 2002; Turner and Myerson 1998; Laing *et al.* 1998; Horgen *et al.* 1999; Myerson and Ross 1999; A. Law 1999, 2001). Moreover, organizations often justify the introduction of new ways of working by invoking such professional discourses. However, although these accounts may legitimize changes, in themselves they rarely constitute the main driving force behind expenditure of resources and effort on radical transformations in established assets, skills and ways of working.

Popular accounts often cite ICT as a prime mover. Computers, mobile phones and similar devices are, indeed, essential to the effectiveness of working across and moving between multiple and remote sites. However, these are necessary rather than sufficient explanations for the change. ICT opens up a range of possibilities but it does not determine how they are realized.

Our own, and other, research indicates that the crucial driver is cost saving. By eliminating down-time and stretching working hours, 'exploding offices' offer another way of intensifying work. They also make possible major savings in the provision of office space. Traditional office buildings are inflexible and expensive assets that do not respond quickly to the ups and down of the business cycle. Furthermore, surveys regularly demonstrate that conventional offices remain unoccupied for long stretches of time. Removing personal space in offices, combined with encouragement to work in remote sites, makes it possible for employers to reduce the ratio of office space to staff, concentrate workforces in fewer buildings and reap windfall benefits from property sales. These developments thus introduce a new and lucrative realm of spatial flexibility (Rifkin 2000).

Sources of Data

This book draws on original research findings generated by two studies of professional and managerial workers, funded by the Economic and Social Research Council (ESRC) as part of the Future of Work Programme. The first focused on working at home; the second on the implications of working on the move and in collective offices. These projects generated three broad categories of evidence: results derived from the analysis of secondary and primary quantitative surveys; qualitative data derived from case studies of selected organizations; and qualitative and quantitative data derived from interviews with individual workers.

Quantitative Data Sets

Both projects mined existing data sets that asked questions about the spatial location of work, including the Labour Force Survey, the Workplace Employee Relations Survey and the Census of Population. These provided data on the extent, growth and characteristics of people who work in a variety of locations. We also collected original quantitative data in both projects. Two separate telephone polls of large organizations were conducted in 1999 and 2002. The 1999 poll focused on working at home. The 2002 poll (Location of Work Survey (LWS)) investigated the perceptions of senior facilities/property managers in large organizations in Britain about current and future changes to the physical layout of workplaces and offices (including the use within their organizations of hot desks, touchdown desks, office redesign, working at home and working in a variety of places). The sample comprised the largest private sector companies domiciled in the UK (by capital employed) together with local authority employers in England (county councils, London borough councils and metropolitan district councils). Some 128 out of a possible 185 organizations were successfully interviewed.

Organizational Case Studies

Organizational case studies were also a feature of both projects. These enabled us to interview managers and employees about the impact of changes in the spatial location of work on the dynamics of their organizations.

In the first project we studied 13 public and private sector organizations known to provide opportunities for employees to work at home. Two were small to medium sized enterprises (a virtual law firm and a travel company), some were larger in scale (two local authorities, a university, a consultancy company, a charity, an advisory service and a virtual call centre) and four were multinationals (two financial institutions, a telecommunications company and a pharmaceutical company). Interviews were conducted with 82 respondents, 71 of whom were directors, policy makers, facilities managers, property planners or line managers. The remainder were trade union officers or representatives, some of whom also exercised managerial responsibilities. Interviews covered a range of topics (including organizational structure, the character of the labour process, overall managerial strategies and the history of the enterprise) as well as specific questions about respondents' experiences of managing home-located workers, the drivers of and support for home-located working within the organization. Interviews took place between April 1999 and May 2001.

The second project included case studies of ten organizations, derived from the telephone polls, trade press, media coverage and existing contacts. Seven of the ten were selected because they had radically redesigned their office spaces (an advertising agency; a public sector agency; a telecommunications company; a pharmaceutical retailer; an airline; a county council; and a multinational bank). A total of 72 semi-structured interviews were conducted with key informants in these enterprises, exploring drivers of change, managerial strategies of control and workers' lived experience. In one of these organizations we took several hundred photographs and made a video film. These visual materials provided a unique record of the use of workstations and communal spaces within this workplace. A further three case study organizations were selected because they supplied working facilities to staff 'on the move'. They included firms offering: 'hotelled' office space; office facilities at motorway service stations; and facilities for working on the train. In total, 26 directors and senior middle managers were interviewed in these three organizations.

Interviews with Workers

With the co-operation of the 13 case study organizations studied in our first project, we were able to construct a sample of employees who worked at home for some or all of the time. Only those who were home-located for at least 40 per cent of their working week were included in the sample. However, this was a minimum and most worked at home for longer periods. Between April 1999 and May 2001, we interviewed 60 professional and managerial employees who worked at home (37 men and 23 women) and their partners (120 interviewees in total). In ten cases it transpired that the partner/spouse also worked at home. Interviews explored household characteristics and formation, individual biographies, patterns of home-located working, spatial and temporal divisions between home and work, household decision making, the domestic division of labour, experiences of managerial control and relationships with colleagues and, where applicable, clients. Respondents were interviewed in their own homes and, whenever possible, partners were interviewed separately.

In our second project, a group of 11 workers based in a collective office participated in a photo-elicitation study carried out over seven days. We decided to concentrate these interviews in one of our seven employer case study organizations – Cool Marketing plc – as it had made the most radical and complete transformation of the workplace. Respondents were given disposable cameras, a schedule for photographing their working environments, and asked to make written notes on their movements. They produced 297 pictures and were subsequently interviewed, in late 2002, about their visual diaries. Interviews were tape-recorded and transcribed. In addition, two employees participating in the photo-elicitation study agreed, in December 2002, to shoot a video diary of working life in the organization, generating some four hours of footage. These, and other, materials were used to create an exhibition about the 'new' office, displayed at two venues in central London during 2003.

Two of the supplier case study organizations that participated in our second project offered us access to their clients. The company providing office facilities at motorway service stations allowed us to spend three weeks at three of their sites in April 2002. Questionnaires were administered to 57 users as they booked on-site facilities (such as meeting rooms, internet connections, computers and printers). A main-line rail operating company provided us with free first-class travel for one month in September 2002, enabling us to interview business travellers in transit about their use of the train as a place of work. This generated 60 completed questionnaires. These approaches proved highly effective in gaining rapport with respondents and generated three further research activities. First, 46 respondents (25 encountered at service stations and 21 on board trains) agreed to participate in detailed semi-structured interviews, lasting 40–60 minutes. Secondly, seven of these agreed further to participate in a photo-elicitation study of working on the move. They were asked to photograph locations where they worked and the devices used to do their jobs, over a seven-day period, generating 115 images. Subsequently, they were interviewed (60–90 minutes) about the significance and meaning of their photographs. Thirdly, ten respondents encountered on trains and service stations (five male and five female) agreed to be shadowed for between one and two working days. Shadowing entailed travelling with respondents to observe their working practices, tape-recording respondents' conversations with co-workers and researchers, making extensive field notes, and researchers taking photographs. In summary, then, we collected original questionnaire data from 117 workers on the move, conducted in-depth interviews with 46 of these and completed intensive case studies (using shadowing and visual research methodologies) with 17.

Outline of the Book

This section provides a brief overview of the chapters that follow. Chapter 2, 'Conceptual Framework', is devoted to explicating the main theoretical themes and frameworks that inform the book as a whole. The first half outlines an intellectual toolkit of concepts that we deploy throughout our analysis; in particular, the terms 'workstation', 'workplace' and 'workscape', as well as 'personal office' and 'collective office'. The second half of the chapter explores three ideal-type models of the socio-spatial relationships entailed in working at home, working on the move and working in different types of offices.

Chapter 3, 'Transforming Locations of Work', presents some background context to processes of change in places of work and provides quantitative evidence of their extent. The first three sections outline major developments that, historically, have shaped the possibilities and experience of working in offices, at home and on the move. The last, and longest, part of the chapter comprises a review of up-to-date quantitative data that offer an overall picture of current processes of change in locations of employment.

Chapter 4, 'Working in Collective Offices', explores the social and spatial relationships characteristic of offices where staff do not have personal space or opportunities to personalize space. It begins by examining the implications for the movement and flows of workers within office buildings. It argues that, although collective offices generate high levels of mobility within workplaces, they also generate forces that encourage workers unofficially to colonize space. Such attempts are, typically, met by managerial interventions that seek to prevent 'stalling' of this kind. The chapter goes on to describe the implications for conventional managerial strategies based on visibility and presence. As the opportunities for panoptical surveillance diminish, other strategies of control come to the fore. Prominent among these, we argue, are those associated with the distinctive aesthetic of collective offices, which create embodied experiences that foreground commitment to change, openness to observation by others, serendipitous interactions and totalizing 'buddy' group cultures.

Chapter 5, 'Working at Home', examines the uncertainty and unpredictability generated for home-located workers by, on the one hand, their proximity to private domestic relationships and, on the other, their distance from managers, supervisors and co-workers. The first part of the chapter examines the household element of this equation. It argues that the erosion or blurring of boundaries between home and work calls forth a range of responses from home-located employees, prominent among which are attempts to re-establish conventional spatial and temporal divisions under the domestic roof. In this context, we examine the way in which workers and other household members construct boundaries of time, space and activity within the home. The second part of the chapter identifies a series of managerial initiatives that seek, in various ways, to compensate for the absence of visibility and presence of home-located workers.

Chapter 6, 'Working on the Move', examines the experience of working in a variety of public, semi-public and semi-private sites while in transition between places. It provides insights into workers' experience of various states of mobility, including periods of movement (e.g. in the car or on the train), semi-mobility (e.g. on the move but caught in traffic) and intentional stasis (e.g. in motorway service stations). The chapter analyses how those working on the move take corrective action to cope with the deficiencies of these environments as places of work and mould their work activities around what is possible and acceptable behaviour in different locations. It also examines the texts, disciplines and devices deployed by managers to compensate for the loss of worker visibility and to facilitate interaction among peers and others in the organization. It ends by identifying ways in which workers on the move attempt to avoid, subvert and defy these interventions.

Chapter 7, 'Conclusion', does not provide a summary of the analysis presented elsewhere in the book but, instead, highlights a series of underlying themes that are developed throughout the text. These all relate to transformations in employment relations and the experience of work that are generated by changing places of work.

2

Conceptual Framework

One of the most powerful ways in which social space can be conceptualised is as constituted out of social relations, social interactions, and for that reason, always and everywhere an expression and a medium of power.

(Massey 1995: 284)

Introduction

This chapter outlines the conceptual framework we have employed in analysing processes of change in the spaces and places of work. It is divided into two sections. First, we elucidate terms and concepts that appear throughout the book and explore issues raised by these distinctions. Second, we outline three ideal-type models that identify key aspects of the socio-spatial relations of employment characteristic of working in collective offices, at home and on the move.

Terms and Concepts

Although discussions of working time regularly appear in textbooks, working space features much less frequently if at all. Since the Hawthorne experiments of the 1920s, students of work organization have assumed that they can disregard the physical environment in their analyses (Baldry 1999). Recent years, however, have witnessed a 'spatial turn' in social science, generating renewed interest in both the spatial constitution of social relations and the social construction of spaces. There is an emerging awareness of workplaces as symbolic and material relations of power, status, surveillance, management, investment and marketing (Marglin 1976; Stimson 1986; Markus 1993; Baldry et al. 1998; Baldry 1999).

A key distinction, employed in this book, is that between workstations, workplaces and workscapes. *Workstations* we take to refer to the immediate locations within which employment tasks are conducted, such as a desk, meeting room, car interior, seat in a railway carriage, or computer terminal in a spare bedroom at home. Workstations are constituted around bodily faculties and functions – such as reach, touch, sight and hearing – that are mobilized in operating devices utilized in the execution of work tasks. The concept of workstation, thus, is a reminder that work is an embodied process, an aspect of the labour process that is often ignored (Witz *et al.* 2003).

We use the term *workplaces* to designate buildings, or other physical constructions, that contain and support one or more workstations. Workplaces include office blocks and factories but, in certain circumstances, may encompass railway trains, domestic homes, motorway service stations, airport lounges or any other container of permanent or temporary workstations.

We have developed a third term – *workscapes* – to refer to the total network of workplaces and workstations that are occupied by individuals or groups in the course of their employment. Workscapes comprise the specific sites in which individuals or groups conduct work tasks and, crucially, the channels of communication and transportation that link them. Thus, for example, the workscape of a university lecturer typically includes not only particular locations (such as lecture theatres, seminar rooms, meeting rooms, libraries and desks) but also interstitial places (such as corridors, stairways, coffee bars, bookshops, stationery cupboards, lifts, car parks and pigeonholes).

The significance and lived experience of any particular site or activity within a workscape is determined by its location in the overall network of relations. Thus, for example, workscape connections may be maintained in many different ways, including the use of face-to-face meetings, technological devices, formal rulebooks, training programmes, informal social 'get togethers', and so on. These practices are significant in as much as they are embedded within the totality of workscape relationships, entailed in the execution of specific work tasks conducted in particular workstations and workplaces. Workscape is a relational concept.

Although there is a long history of network analysis in social science, the concept of flows between sites within networks has acquired increasing prominence in recent years (Castells 2000a, 2000b; Urry 2000a, 2000b). However, there is a danger, exacerbated by some forms of socio-metric analysis, of conceptualizing networks as static and solid structures. Actor-network theory, in contrast, emphasizes processes of network formation, the vulnerability of network alliances and connections, and the need to reproduce and maintain networks on a continuous basis (Law and Hassard 1999). It speaks of social order*ing* and social organiz*ing*, in order to emphasize the on-going, contingent and fragile qualities of network ties. In this view, different combinations and alliances of actors or agents struggle to mobilize and organize people and objects in order to create and sustain networks of relationships – in our case workscapes. These net-works permit individuals and groups to achieve their objectives, but they are often contested by others, or alliances of others, seeking to subvert established networks or create new ones altogether. The powers, charac-teristics and attitudes of actors are a product of their shifting positions within these endlessly evolving network constructions. Inanimate objects and artefacts – such as maps, cars, books, telephones, computers, trains – become aspects of networks, acquiring their significance because they enable groups and individuals to exercise control over others in and through workscapes. Thus, power is not conceived as an attribute of indi-viduals or objects, but is derived from the organization of people and things in networks of relations. Dominant individuals and alliances are able to develop hegemonic stories and narratives that characterize and justify their actions, thereby tying in other members. To exercise power is to be able to generate and disseminate stories that prevail at the expense of those told by others in the network. The contesting of network ties, the incorporation of artefacts and the weaving of legitimating narratives are all processes that will be explored in the chapters that follow.

Working in the 'collective office', 'at home' and 'on the move' may be thought of as three *clusters* of network connections, incorporated into workscapes in various combinations. Any particular individual or group may include some or all of these, to a greater or lesser extent, in their working lives. Each of these clusters comprises a distinctive combination of workstations and workplaces and may be thought of, in Goffman's terms (1959), as a region of performance. Channels between clusters within workscapes often constitute particularly uncertain network con-nections, subject to poor communications and weak controls. Seen from the point of view of workers, the propensity of bridges between network clusters to falter may, at different times, represent a threat to productivity, a shelter from competing demands or a welcome opportunity to avoid managerial gaze.

Even relatively simple workscapes typically comprise different daily combinations of workstations and workplaces. There are several potential routes that can be taken in navigating around the network. Our university lecturer, for example, might make her way to the bookshop by the shortest route, or via the pigeonholes and departmental secretary's office, or via the library and her researcher's office, or via the telephone and internet. There are choices to be made among multiple potential ways of making connec-tions. A variety of constraints direct her to follow one trajectory rather than another. She might be motivated by pressures to engage in multi-tasking, to avoid conflict by steering clear of antagonistic co-workers, or to gener-ate team camaraderie by maximizing informal social contacts. Although such decisions face all workers, as workscapes incorporate a variety of different sites and spatially differentiated regions, navigational choices become more complex. There are many more ways of getting around. We use the term *pathways* to refer to the sum of potential trajectories and *routes* to refer to the favoured directions routinely taken. A study of workscapes thus leads into investigation of the ways in which people perceive pathways and construct routes. These processes are often embedded within narratives constructed in making network connections.

In this book we are interested in the emergence of workscapes associated with high levels of mobility within and between workplaces and workstations. A useful distinction, therefore, is between *singular workscapes* and *plural workscapes*. The difference between singular and plural workscapes is best conceived as a continuum. At one extreme, singular workscapes comprise just one workstation located in one workplace. A factory worker confined to a single lathe, a call centre worker operating one telephone, or a shop assistant stationed at one checkout are all examples. In contrast, at the other end of the scale, plural workscapes incorporate many workstations and workscapes. They require movement between a multiplicity of sites. This book is an investigation into the social relationships and lived experiences of professional and managerial workers who occupy plural workscapes.

A further distinction can be drawn between different types of plural workscapes. Some comprise multiple workstations contained within just one workplace. Thus, for example, during the course of a working week a university lecturer might write an article in her office, make presentations in lecture theatres, conduct small group teaching in seminar rooms and attend examination boards in committee rooms – all without leaving the university campus or even one building. Her workscape includes several workstations but only one workplace. These socio-spatial arrangements are in contrast to those of an executive who has a London office in corporate headquarters (HQ), uses hot desks in satellite buildings in Manchester and Glasgow, word-processes on trains when travelling between these sites, and also works at home one day a week. This book is particularly interested such individuals who occupy several workstations in several workplaces.

Plural workscapes – particularly those comprising multiple workstations and multiple workplaces – make possible complex and shifting combinations of time, space and task. Similar activities may be done in different types of spaces and different tasks in the same place. These decisions in part reflect the suitability and acceptability of different locations for tasks. A crowded railway carriage full of rowdy football supporters is probably a poor location for phone calls to ingratiate oneself with clients or to report to the boss. However, decisions about what to do where and when may also reflect personal preferences and aptitudes. Thus, plural workscapes enable workers to order their lives in different ways. The executive referred to above might have a colleague in a similar position who has devised a quite different pattern of working, generating a contrasting lived experience. Yet another might elect to chop and change, never settling for one way of organizing transitions between workstations and workplaces.

Singular workscapes impose spatial and temporal routines that are fixed and unchanging whereas plural workscapes permit variety and diversity. However, the choices afforded by plural workscapes bring their own demands. Although they do not face the imposed regimes of singular workscapes, workers in plural workscapes are required to invent their own routines. They are forced to choose. This entails allocating tasks to slots of time and space – and capturing or adapting times and spaces for particular tasks. This calls for qualities of self-motivation, self-mobilization and self-discipline. It also requires the capacity to motivate, organize and control others who may have different objectives and plans. In this book, we are interested in exploring how workers cope with the choices and constraints inherent in plural workscapes, the options they choose and how they acquire skills in managing themselves and others.

In constructing plans to carry out work tasks in a series of different workstations and workplaces, workers are engaged in a process of *assembly*. Assembly refers to the planned sequencing of space and time in the execution of work tasks. It entails a mixture of repetitive mundane routines and one-off tactical decisions. Assembly involves activities such as making appointments, drawing up lists, charging mobile phones, collecting documents, buying tickets, generating PowerPoint slides, practising presentations, and so on. Assembly skills are integral to all workscapes but become more complex and more critical in plural workscapes, where sites are geographically remote and transitions between clusters are vulnerable to disruption.

Along with assembly goes *repair*. Repair refers to the process of responding to disruptions of, and interruptions to, planned sequences of space and time in the execution of work tasks. The best-laid plans go astray – the car gets stuck in traffic, trains are delayed, baggage is lost, an unexpected visitor has to be entertained, the data projector bulb blows, coffee is spilt on the keyboard. Processes of assembly are unravelled by a myriad of contingencies, urgencies and emergencies that frustrate predictability and certainty. Workers are forced either to make new plans or to adjust original arrangements. Repair work of this kind is, once again, a familiar aspect of all workscapes but it is particularly a feature of plural workscapes. When work involves creating and reproducing interconnections between diverse geographically remote workstations and workplaces, the chances of things going wrong are multiplied. Plural workscapes typically call for on-going processes of repair.

Assembly and repair involve the management of objects and artefacts. Our analysis seeks to reveal some of the ways in which tools and technologies feature in the practical accomplishment of these social activities and actions. We are also interested in the extent to which workers personalize machines (such as cars, hot desks and personal computers (PCs)) or seek to exercise individual command over access to key devices or favoured sites (for example, by colonizing hot desks or monopolizing the photocopier). This entails examining the ways in which commonsense skills, practical actions and everyday forms of reasoning are acquired and deployed in a range of situations (Suchman 1987, 1999; Heath *et al.* 2000).

Assembly and repair are prerequisites for the physical and virtual movements involved in negotiating the network of sites and connections that constitute workscapes. *Wayfinding* refers to the knowledge, skills and attitudes required to travel around, communicate in and transmit information through plural workscapes (cf. I. Woodward *et al.* 2002). Some clues about the nature of wayfinding in plural workscapes can be discerned in John Law's (1986) account of the ways in which sixteenth-century Portuguese merchants, seafarers and military controlled lucrative trade, and its attendant warfare, with a remote empire in Goa. He discusses how European imperialists exercised power at a distance through everyday practices, tacit skills and formal knowledge. They employed *texts* (such as, tables of declination, calendars, charts, books of sailing instructions), *devices* or *machines* (such as astrolabes and quadrants) and *systems of social discipline* (such as skills in sailing and course finding). These elements came together to enable networks of communication and action at a distance (see also Thrift 1996: 177 and Heath *et al.* 2000).

To these dimensions of wayfinding should be added *technologies of the self* (Foucault 1988; Rose 1990; Burchell 1993). Technologies of the self 'refer to ways in which people, more or less consciously and reflexively, mobilize and organize their attitudes, practices and feelings in the course of their everyday lives' (Felstead and Jewson 2000: 116). They comprise self-generated, self-imposed and self-policed strategies, tactics and rules of personal behaviour. Technologies of the self enable individuals to conceive of themselves as sovereign and autonomous agents, authors of their own actions and capable of choosing their own destinies. Plural workscapes call for technologies of the self that incorporate individual reflexivity, personalized learning processes, idiosyncratic decision-making and unique performances that reflect the personalities and sense of identity of workers.

Workscapes function across time and space by incorporating a range of texts, devices, social disciplines and technologies of the self. Workscapes are the networks of machines, techniques, organizations, documents and disciplined people through which flows of information, resources, ideas and values are relayed (Urry 2000a; 2000b: 193). The effectiveness of a workscape depends upon the organization of these elements into a functioning whole. However, these systems are never fully effective; there is always an element of indeterminacy, not least as a result of resistance. Thus, the properties of workscapes are not fixed and unchanging. They are contingent outcomes of processes of assembly and repair, which seek to counteract forces that unravel and disrupt network connections. Workscapes have to be worked on. Our analysis will seek to reveal ways in which workers who navigate plural workscapes respond to sources of indeterminacy. It will examine the information, techniques and skills on which they draw. It will also explore the accounts which workers themselves offer of these processes, including their coping strategies, legitimations for intervention and rationalizations of outcomes. Among these are strategies and tactics employed in resisting management controls and reducing workloads.

The lived experience of plural workscapes has to be understood in the context of processes of managerial control within enterprises located in capitalist societies. Having purchased their time and attendance, employers face the problems of organizing and disciplining workers in productive activities that maximize profitable outputs. Plural workscapes – particularly those with multiple workstations and workplaces – pose distinctive challenges for long-standing conventional forms of managerial control. As discussed in Chapter 3, the factories and offices of early industrial capitalism were not merely a product of technological imperatives but also, in their spatial organization, provided employers and managers with greatly enhanced opportunities to regulate the behaviour, and subordinate the activities, of employees. This was achieved by placing workers, both manual and non-manual, within individually designated spaces within the workplace that, in turn, facilitated the inculcation of social disciplines. Systems of managerial control, therefore, rested on the *presence* of workers in specified locations for long periods of time and their *visibility* in those sites. However, plural workscapes undermine both presence and visibility. Workers on the move within and between workplaces and workstations cannot be easily observed and their performances cannot be continuously monitored. Their activities become far more opaque (see Felstead *et al.* 2003a). The workscape, once the solution to problems of managerial control, now becomes a problem.

A corollary of the reduced presence and visibility of workers in plural workscapes is that they also often experience reduced opportunities to occupy *personal space* or, more generally, to personalize the spaces they occupy. Thus, for example, while working on the move, staff are likely to occupy impersonal public or semi-public spaces for at least part of the time, such as railway compartments, hotel rooms or airport lounge seats. Even if they hire temporary facilities – such as so-called 'hotelled' offices – they will only occupy the site for a short period and will have few opportunities to put their personal mark on the environment. Moreover, suppliers of such facilities are keen to maintain spatial anonymity in order to be ready for the next customer. Some modes of transport offer more opportunities for personalizing space than others; the car, for instance, may be decorated with personal souvenirs. However, in general, working on the move entails navigation through many anonymous, temporary and inflexible environments that cannot be easily personalized.

Collective offices not only eliminate personal space but, by definition, prevent workers personalizing locations. In the past, both cellular and open plan offices provided workers with a cube of space that they could symbolically mark out as their territory. These *personal offices* placed workers in fixed sites that they attended every day and which others did not use. However, in *collective offices* workers are no longer assigned fixed and permanent workstations for their sole use. Instead, they move between a range of workstations within the workplace, depending on which are available at any one time. Each workstation is occupied temporarily. When the immediate task is over, it is relinquished to others who, in their turn, eventually move elsewhere. For employers, this arrangement maximizes the time that spaces and facilities are actively in use. For workers, it means that it is no longer possible to put up posters, arrange family photographs or display a selection of cuddly toys.

Resistance to the introduction of collective office space can take several forms, including *stalling*. 'Stalls' are bounded spaces to which individuals lay claim, typically by utilizing various symbolic forms of boundary marking (Goffman 1971). In collective offices, stalling involves attempts by individuals or groups to reclaim office space as 'theirs'. This may be achieved by gradually introducing idiosyncratic territorial markers, signalling others to keep away. If management is serious about maintaining collective office spaces, these attempts to personalize space must be prevented or countered. The reintroduction of personal space will clog up the arteries of mobility and undermine the whole edifice of flexibility. However, 'stall busting' can take a variety of forms, as our case study organizations demonstrate.

The process of stalling is not confined to collective offices. Stalling techniques are widely used by workers on the move to lay claim to particular spaces. For example, places on trains or cafés may be stalled by placing a briefcase or coat on a seat. Stalling also occurs in the home when paid work is introduced into domestic environments. Here, it is often directed towards lodging claims to spaces and times that other family members may wish to use. Home might appear to be one of the more predictable working environments, free from the disruptions of collective offices and public sites as well as distant from the demands of line managers. However, working at home generates its own uncertainties, associated with the presence of other household members.

Three Clusters in Plural Workscapes

The plural workscapes that increasingly characterize managerial and professional workers in the twenty-first century, and which are the subject of this book, comprise three main clusters of relationships: 'collective offices', working 'at home' and working 'on the move'. The remainder of this chapter is devoted to a comparative analysis of the characteristic features of these three clusters, utilizing a series of formal benchmarks. These include:

- Opportunities to personalize work spaces

- Presence of diverse types of workstations

- Presence of multi-functional workstations

- Opportunities to personalize work times

- Participation in the electronic envelope

- Opportunities for informal social interaction

- Susceptibility to visual surveillance

- Opportunities to display status symbols to co-workers

- Boundaries between work and non-work relationships

- Participation in the corporate aesthetic.

A summary of this analysis is contained in Table 2.1.

It should be emphasized that, in this section, we are developing ideal-type models and not reporting the empirical findings of our own or other research investigations. Like all ideal types, the models below comprise one-sided accentuations of key attributes of the social reality under examination. These elements are not to be regarded as an average, or amalgam, of real-world empirical descriptions. Nor are they ideal in any ethical or normative sense. Rather, they represent a theoretical schema that selects and highlights a series of themes that together constitute yardsticks for identifying critical aspects of the socio-spatial relations of employment.

Table 2.1 Clusters in plural workscapes

Features of clusters	Working in the collective office	Working at home	Working on the move
Opportunities to personalize work spaces	Low	High	Medium
Presence of diverse types of workstations	High	Low	High
Presence of multi-functional workstations	Medium	High	High
Opportunities to personalize work times	High	High	Medium
Participation in the electronic envelope	High	High	High
Opportunities for informal social interaction	High	Low	Low
Susceptibility to visual surveillance	High	Low	Low
Opportunities to display status symbols to co-workers	Low	Low	Low
Boundaries between work and non-work relationships	Low	Low	Medium
Participation in the corporate aesthetic	High	Low	Low

Opportunities to Personalize Working Spaces

Collective offices are defined by the elimination of personal space in the workplace. Management removes opportunities for employees to personalize space; for example, by maintaining 'clear desk' and 'clean walls' policies that entail the removal and disposal of any personal items found on display. Facilities are provided collectively and allocated to users on a temporary basis. Hence, during the course of a working day one person may occupy several workstations, and one workstation may be occupied by several people. 'Hotdesking' and related practices call for a system that allocates facilities to users, although this may range from the highly regulated to the largely informal. The personalizing of space is prohibited partly to preserve the aesthetic of the workplace (see below) but also, primarily, to maintain spatial flexibility. Collective provision of facilities allows management to diminish the ratio of floor space to employees, reduce equipment down-time and ensure that locations are used to the maximum. Collective offices, therefore, make possible savings on the provision of expensive office space as well as permitting smooth and rapid responses to ups and downs in workforce headcounts.

In contrast, when working at home, employees have much greater opportunities to personalize space. In general, staff working at home can, with impunity, customize their workstations with personal mementos, family photographs and individual ornaments. They can paint the walls their favourite colours, select their own furniture, keep their desk tidy or chaotic, as they please. However, the source of such freedoms is also a potential obstacle. The home is a place where all household members enjoy high levels of individual autonomy and self-expression. Albeit mediated by class, gender, ethnicity and generation, the home has a unique cultural status as the locus of individual identity formation. Individuals not only have maximum opportunity to express their personal taste but also the expectation that private identities will not be interrupted by institutionalized public performances. Those who work at home may themselves regard job-related activities as an intrusion of the corporate world into the personalized territory of the home. Other members of the household, who are not employees of the organization, may have similar feelings. Boundaries between home and work may become problematic and tense.

Workers on the move are not hemmed in by the impersonal aesthetics of collective offices, nor are they constrained by the presence of domestic space. Furthermore, they may exercise some degree of freedom in personalizing working environments. They may display football stickers in the rear windows of their cars, put family photographs on hotel sideboards and chose personal screensavers on their laptops. Nevertheless, many of the places in which they engage in job tasks are irredeemably bland and beyond personal signature. Motorway service stations, 'hotelled' offices, railway carriages and airport lounges do not offer many chances to impose an idiosyncratic individual style. However, those who successfully work on the move do so by generating an insulated bubble of space/time in the midst of anonymous public spaces. The creation and maintenance of boundaries around these temporary sites call for a variety of assembly and repair skills, which may entail personalizing the immediate environment to some degree. A personalized keyboard or customized bag may constitute cues, for themselves and others, that they are switching into work mode. Thus, those who work on the move enjoy some leeway to construct personal working environments but their opportunities to do so are limited and uncertain.

Presence of Diverse Types of Workstations

In personal offices workers remain stationary and work activities come to them – in the form of files, papers, memos, shorthand typists, meetings with clients, meetings with colleagues, and so on. Personal offices, thus, are required to accommodate a series of different tasks and each has to be equipped to meet the demands of all these activities. In collective offices, in contrast, workers move around the workplace to make use of workstations adapted for different tasks. Individual employees do not have their own items of equipment for their sole use, located in their personal cube of space. As a result, it is possible for management to reduce the provision of equipment and support facilities, on the grounds that at any one time only a fraction of the workforce needs them. A mosaic of specialized workstations emerges, designed with different purposes in mind, requiring workers to move around to meet different needs. Thus, touchdown desks can be used by anyone in the building on a 'first come, first served' basis and are typically used for just a few minutes, while hot desks have to be booked in advance and are typically used for longer periods of time. Management can calculate the optimum number of facilities required by the workforce for each type of task, thereby eliminating wastage. In principle, all items of equipment can be in use all the time without any member of staff having to wait. Workers are, however, required to move at the end of tasks, prior to commencing new ones. Such moves may be frequent and short distance (e.g. going to the printer to collect output several times during the course of a morning) or occasional and long distance (e.g. attending a two-hour meeting in a hot room on another floor of the building). The totality of these movements creates high levels of fleeting interactions and visual observation by others. Both of these are important aspects of collective office spaces discussed below.

Staff working at home frequently spend most of their time at one workstation and the diversity of their workstations is likely to be low. It is true that some people who work at home occupy a series of different places, possibly at different times of the day or according to the nature of the task in hand. Thus, it may be possible to type at a conventional desk, correct proofs on the dining room table and read documents in the bath. The absence of other members of the household during the daytime may facilitate roaming of this kind. However, competition for space from other household members, limited numbers of rooms in domestic dwellings, and the need to avoid disruptions caused by the presence of other household members are all likely to constrain such possibilities. Income, gender and household composition all mediate options to roam.

People who work on the move are likely to find themselves in a wide variety of locations. They may enjoy some level of discretion in stitching together different and contrasting transient workstations and workplaces – such as a car on the move, a car stationary on the roadside, a table in a motorway service station, a rented terminal in a cyber café, and so on. They may be able to vary their working locations further by patronizing different cafés, car parks and country lanes. However, whilst each of these temporary workstations may offer a different ambience and milieu, in practice they are likely to offer similar facilities. Not many provide specialized workstations. The capacity to work on the move depends to a large degree on the ability to generate a capsule of working space/time within a more or less indifferent or recalcitrant environment, and maintaining its viability.

Presence of Multi-Functional Workstations

Collective offices generate specialized workstations. However, paradoxically, they are also characterized by locations that have multiple purposes and functions, fulfilling a range of different tasks and activities. For example, a café in the atrium may, simultaneously, host team meetings, colleagues networking, client greetings, and individuals reading paperwork. Electronic communications may be unobtrusively built into these locations – such as sockets discreetly placed in the floor and 'Wi-Fi' internet connections. Multi-functional locations of this kind are attractive to management for three main reasons. First, by stacking different types of activities in one space, the overall floor plate can be reduced; for example, fewer rooms have to be provided if many meetings take place on comfy chairs in the foyer, or over coffee in the café. Second, multiple-functional spaces generate informal and unplanned interactions between staff, which are perceived to create innovative and serendipitous solutions to business problems. Third, by putting eating and relaxation facilities in the same space as work facilities, the exposure of workers to observation by peers and others is increased.

Those working at home are likely to occupy multi-functional workstations. Pressures of space and requirements of other household members make it unlikely that they will be able, or wish to, construct a range of specialized workstations in the home. They are more likely to occupy one workstation in which they conduct different work tasks. Those who live alone may, potentially, have greater opportunity to spread out, enabling them to conduct different types of tasks in specialized locations within their dwelling. Even here, however, personal preferences and ingrained cultural predispositions may restrict the spaces devoted to work life within the home.

Those working on the move enjoy even fewer opportunities to occupy spaces specifically designed for specialized work tasks and are likely to adapt *ad hoc* multi-functional spaces, whose primary purpose has little or no connection with their employment. There are some exceptions, particularly as more dedicated workplaces begin to appear within places of transition (e.g. internet connections on railway stations, touchdown desks in clients' premises, business centres on aircraft). The emergence of these services may gradually change the character of working on the move, increasing time spent at specialist workstations and decreasing the proportion spent in multi-functional sites.

Opportunities to Personalize Work Times

Collective offices afford many opportunities for individuals to devise idiosyncratic timetables for the execution of work tasks. Opportunities to personalize space are limited but there are many ways in which to personalize time. Workers can navigate their way through the variegated spaces of the office building – both specialized and multi-functional workstations – in an order of their own choosing. They may perform the same task in different places and different tasks in the same place. They vary the sequence on different days. It becomes possible for individuals to match their work location to changes in their mood, the weather, friendship patterns, or many other criteria. This opens up choices but also brings a new realm of decision-making. Whereas the architecture of personal offices dictates time/space sequences, collective offices require self-discipline in the planning and execution of sequences of activities.

Working at home also affords extensive opportunities to develop personal timetables and sequences of activities. Working days may start and finish early or late. Breaks may be taken in the middle of the day – to go shopping, collect the kids from school or just relax – in the knowledge that the hours can be made up later on. Furthermore, the absence of colleagues and co-workers in the home frees up time from the fixed rituals of informal gossip circles and formal meetings. These freedoms may be circumscribed by pressures from managers and colleagues; for example, there may be a requirement permanently to be available at the end of a phone or computer line during office hours. Nevertheless, a well-known attribute of working at home – particularly for those in professional and managerial jobs – is the scope to work outside conventional office hours. Indeed, there is a frequently attested downside to this discretion (Felstead and Jewson 2000). In the absence of the cues and boundaries of conventional work timetables, those who work at home run the risk of becoming 'workaholics'. Ever-present access to work tasks, combined with an absence of formal institutional indicators of when enough is enough, can generate round-the-clock attention to business. This danger highlights the need for specific technologies of the self in working at home, focused on devising and implementing time disciplines.

Working on the move does not completely eradicate personal control over the sequencing of job tasks but it does diminish it substantially. Workers on the move are governed by timetables imposed by systems of transportation. It is true that they can choose which train to catch or which route to drive but, in practice, their options are often limited. Moreover, once having made a selection of a particular transport mode and route, autonomy often swiftly declines thereafter. Official timetables are often disrupted in ways that are beyond control, with limited opportunities for repair work. When in stationary traffic on the motorway, little can be done to speed up the journey. Even here, however, options are not wholly eliminated. Workers caught in traffic switch to other tasks, such as catching up with business phone calls, listening to voicemail messages or dictating letters (Laurier and Philo 1999). Furthermore, the well-known propensity of travel journeys to go awry may provide a useful cover for non-appearances. In general, however, staff moving out of the confines of office or home, and hoping to work whilst in transit, are likely to experience some loss of autonomy in setting their own timetables.

Participation in the Electronic Envelope

The advent of collective offices has only been possible as a result of the recent explosion of ICT in the workplace. Whilst the motivation for collective office spacing is often cost saving, the means that have made it possible are innovations in office technology. This has resulted in the 'reinvention of the workplace' (Worthington 1997). Zelinsky (1997: 4) comments: 'reducing real estate portfolios is a common and major reason for exploring and implementing alternative workplace strategies, but it's the technology that allows it to happen'.

In collective offices, it can be difficult to contact co-workers; they might be sitting anywhere in the building and they may have moved since the last time they were seen. The easiest way to make contact is electronically. ICT is, therefore, crucial to making collective offices a viable possibility. Problems of communication become still more acute when colleagues work at home or on the move. ICT enables individuals to communicate with one another wherever they are located and without necessarily informing one another of their geographical location. Computers – in the form of laptops, remote terminals or touchdown screens – enable employees to access files and e-mails outside the workplace as well as within it. Mobile phones bring a virtual presence across distances and can, among a group of users, establish a virtual community (Myerson 2001).

ICT, then, changes the context – the temporal and spatial order – of workscapes. The spaces and times of the employment now stretch farther and wider than ever before. There is a sense in which the office – thought of as the totality of working time/space – becomes ubiquitous. It has burst out of designated buildings and threatens to overwhelm numerous other social settings. Potential workstations and workplaces are everywhere.

Opportunities for Informal Social Interaction

Collective offices maximize informal social interactions between co-workers. Space is organized in ways that promote unscheduled, unscripted and unpredictable encounters, conversations and meetings. High levels of informal interaction are generated by the absence of personalized working space. Staff come into contact while looking for workstations. It is difficult or impossible to hide from others in defended silos or private cubes of space. A common way of enhancing these tendencies is to centralize the provision of support services, such as photocopiers, printers, faxes, mail, refreshments, resources and so on. This forces people to move through the building and congregate in specific areas, generating serendipitous encounters. These locations are often referred to as the 'hub' and the main avenues of flow leading to them as 'streets' (Becker and Steele 1995: 65). The buzz of interaction in the collective office is predicted, by management theorists and architectural designers, to enhance creativity, synergy, team-building and a sense of corporate belonging. As a result, 'real work' and 'skiving' may be redefined; for example, 'hanging out' with colleagues may become regarded as a necessary and productive activity in its own right (Becker and Steele 1995: A. Law 1999, 2001).

In contrast, working at home is notoriously characterized by isolation from colleagues and line managers. Personal contact and face-to-face interaction with co-workers is difficult to establish, even allowing for the presence of electronic means of communication. Staff may feel left out of office gossip, organizational politics, informal discussions and crisis management. Making contact with co-workers whilst working at home calls for deliberate effort and social skills in establishing rapport via phone and internet. Home-located workers employ a variety of technologies of the self to counter loneliness but it remains a chronic problem (Felstead and Jewson 2000: 134–6).

Workers on the move also frequently experience a sense of isolation. They can deploy a variety of texts, devices and disciplines to create interaction possibilities but these tend to be fleeting, small-scale and easily disrupted. Whereas collective offices are replete with chance meetings, working on the move may require systematic initiatives to create similar kinds of encounters. When working on the move, chance meetings cannot be left to chance but have to be organized and planned.

Susceptibility to Visual Surveillance

Collective offices erode the chance of panoptical surveillance by management. The spaces of collective offices do not comprise a central watchtower with open cells arranged around. Workers are constantly on the move within the building and, therefore, cannot be readily subjected to static centralized monitoring. However, the movement and interaction characteristic of collective offices greatly increases the chances that staff will observe one another. Surveillance is decentralized and involves all members of the workforce as both observers and observed. In Chapter 4, we describe this as the replacement of the panoptican by a polyoptican. Collective offices, thus, render workers highly visible to co-workers, including seniors, juniors and peers. The physical barriers and symbolic markers that typically accompany personal offices are swept away, offering a clear view across the floor plate. The constant flow of people around the building – moving to and fro between workstations – represents a roving surveillance screen. Furthermore, multi-functional workstations, such as cafés and atriums, heighten opportunities to see and be seen by staff at all levels within the organizational hierarchy. In Goffman's terms (1959, 1971), 'personal fronts' and 'fixed territories' of 'settings' within collective offices, comprising intimate expressive equipment and spaces claimed by performers, are eroded or eliminated. This frequently has the additional consequence that 'back regions', where performance masks can momentarily be let slip, are also greatly diminished. Performances have to be more continuous and sustained. If workers are merely engaged in what Hochschild (1983) calls 'surface acting', their credibility is tested by collective office spacing.

In contrast, when working at home, staff are far less visible to managers, co-workers and subordinates. Not only are they geographically distant from their peers but they are also located in one of the most private spheres of social life in contemporary societies. Hence, managers and others are often in an ambiguous or uncomfortable position when seeking to make contact, whether in person or electronically. Visits and phone calls can appear intrusive or impolite, and have to be prefaced with apologies. ICT does make home-located workers more open to surveillance than in the past; for example, it may be possible to monitor their e-mails and telephone calls. However, managers may feel themselves to be guests when entering the territory of their subordinates, whether virtually or in person. Although people working at home frequently engage in work activities outside conventional office hours, it is far less certain that other members of the organization have the right to make direct contact at these times. The home, then, represents a symbolic and physical barrier to worker surveillance. Nevertheless, it should be added that working at home potentially makes employees more visible to other household members. This, in turn, may be one of the reasons most home-located workers prefer to occupy a space within the home that is sealed off from contact with and observation by other residents.

The activities and practices of workers on the move are opaque both to staff back at the office and other members of the household at home. Workers on the move cannot be physically observed by either of these audiences for long stretches of time. As with home-located workers, ICT offers substitute forms of monitoring and surveillance. Moreover, there are fewer boundaries of privacy around working on the move than at home; for example, staff may be regarded as available for contact even outside conventional office hours. However, there are also more contingencies likely to frustrate attempts at communication or disrupt planned work activities. These, in turn, may offer workers on the move opportunities to evade managerial observation and controls.

Opportunities to Display Status Symbols to Co-Workers

Collective offices offer far fewer opportunities than personal offices for staff to display symbols of status and prestige. In collective offices, all grades of staff work alongside one another, using the same equipment and workstations, without visible indicators of rank. Senior staff are not hidden behind high walls or cosseted in prestigious sites, such as penthouse suites or corner offices. All staff make use of common dining, social and hub facilities. Promotions and demotions are not accompanied by reshuffling of office furniture and fittings. Of course, differences of power, wealth and status do actually remain between staff but they are not paraded in bricks and mortar, desks and chairs. This has a number of implications. Senior staff are just as much on display and available for engagement in everyday interaction as juniors. Indeed, they may need to develop social skills or acquire charismatic qualities in order to command respect from subordinates. Collective offices, thus, place a premium on interpersonal skills. Those in command may find it harder to rely on rank as the legitimation for their actions. They may have to perform seniority more proactively, rather than relying on deference sustained by invisibility.

Because those who work at home usually enjoy opportunities to personalize space, they can incorporate into their workstations symbols of rank and prestige. If they wish, they can adorn their desks with expensive pen sets, lean back in executive-style black leather chairs and cultivate banks of prestigious jungle foliage. However, opportunities to display these items to co-workers are few and far between. Nevertheless, there are two other audiences of status displays that should not be forgotten. First, there are other members of the household. Given the tensions that can surround demands on limited domestic space made by home-located workers, clothing workstations in high status décor and furnishings may be a way of legitimizing claims on household resources. The second audience is the home-located workers themselves. It is well known that working at home calls for exceptional levels of self-discipline and self-organization. Creating a lavish working environment may be one way in which workers generate the sense of self required to manage this way of working. Just as people decorate their homes and cultivate their gardens in order to manufacture a sense of personal identity, so too they may design their home offices as markers, cues and stage sets that tell them who they are when they are at work.

Those who work on the move may enjoy a certain amount of freedom to select, decorate or customize the devices they use to conduct their jobs. As a result, they may be able to incorporate status symbols into their workstations. However, since they frequently find themselves in public or semi-public locations, using public or semi-public facilities, the scope is limited. They are often only at these sites for relatively short periods of time, further reducing chances of mobilizing status performances. Although they may sometimes travel with colleagues, they are likely to spend large amounts of time with strangers. However, unlike many workers at home, staff on the move do encounter clients and, to some degree, co-workers in contexts where devices – such as cars, laptops or personal digital assistants – might be taken as indicators of prestige. They also have opportunities to engage in status displays with more generalized others, such as fellow passengers on trains or drivers on motorways. There is evidence, for example, that cars are status markers among business users. Mobile workers on motorways, who have no direct relationship with one another, appear to share codes of deference and etiquette reflecting the size and make of vehicles. These status markers are reflected in the jostling and intimidation of other road users as well as aspects of driving, such as overtaking and giving way (Laurier 2001a).

Boundaries between Work and Non-Work Relationships

Collective offices blur the boundaries between work and non-work relationships by drawing colleagues and co-workers into relationships of friendship and intimacy. Previously autonomous spheres of life, located in institutionally specific contexts, increasingly blend or overlap. Collective offices promote a group-centred way of life where opportunities for individuals to retreat into a private shell are limited. The spatial configuration of the workplace makes participation unavoidable, observation inevitable and fun compulsory. Notions of belonging, participation and involvement with co-workers become the glue that holds organizational practices and structures together. As a result, the locus of socializing shifts markedly towards the workplace. This is often further enhanced by on-site provision of a range of services that are not intrinsic to the performance of work tasks – such as shops, supermarkets, restaurants, clinics, dentists, hairdressers, bars, gyms, sports facilities, and so on. The allure of work-based sociability may be strengthened by semi-official celebrations, away days, fun weekends and carnivals. The boundaries between the times and spaces of 'hanging out', informal team bonding and group conduct of business may be difficult to discern and not one management wishes to draw. An ethic of togetherness surrounds the collective office as it becomes a second home. In this respect, collective offices both reflect and facilitate a shift away from bureaucratic modes of managerial regulation, based on rules and regulations, towards control via the colonization of the subjectivities of workers and the mobilization of informal workgroup cultures.

Working at home removes staff from the social buzz of the office. It makes unlikely 'bumping into', 'hanging out' and other informal connections with co-workers. Nevertheless, in another sense, those who work at home do experience the proximity of the worlds of work and non-work. Two spheres of contemporary social life, both with strong cultural representations and institutional frames, are brought geographically close. Whereas the collective office makes for friendship and intimacy among colleagues, working at home brings those who are already intimate into contact with aspects of employment that are otherwise hidden. Many uncertainties and ambiguities of home-located work arise from the introduction of market-based employment relations into the spaces and times where individualized, private identities are forged around ties of emotion and reciprocity. Among professional and managerial workers, most seek to enforce a clear spatial separation of paid work and domestic life by physically and symbolically sealing off workstations from the rest of the household. A minority attempt to integrate work and non-work spaces and times in a seamless web within the home. Yet others adopt positions between those extremes. Whatever approach is adopted, there is considerable potential for invasion, intrusion and collision of work and home relationships.

Working on the move also tends to isolate staff from co-workers and the hubbub of the collective office. However, there are aspects of working on the move that may lead to an overlap or merging of the times and spaces of work and non-work. Working on the move may enable job tasks to leak into what were once down-times, such as those spent between locations or commuting from home. Workers may be called upon, or take the opportunity, to undertake job tasks while on the move to and from leisure, family or social occasions. Furthermore, devices used when working on the move may, in other contexts, become part of non-work life. Thus, the family car may switch between being a work tool and a domestic facility. Working on the move also may entail short stays away from home, such as at conferences or client meetings, where socializing and networking mingle. Moreover, workers on the move may deliberately co-ordinate movements so as to cross paths or meet up at chosen times and places. With respect to the erosion of boundaries between work and non-work, then, working on the move falls somewhere between the collective office and working at home.

Participation in the Corporate Aesthetic

Office buildings project distinctive aesthetic codes, encrypted in their physical design, eliciting particular performances, subjectivities and inter-actions among staff (Gagliardi 1990, 1996; Strati 1996). The aesthetic of personal offices expresses organizational hierarchy and panoptical sur-veillance from above. The landscape, structure and décor of the personal office communicate awareness of rank and a disciplinary gaze. The aes-thetic of the collective office projects powerful messages about communal belonging, identities rooted in participation in the corporation, and a reified sense of the unitary organization. As Becker and Steele remark about DEGW: 'The whole building showcases the corporate culture: the building *is* the corporate culture' (1995: 32). The aesthetic of collective office space demands proactive performance rather than passive confor-mity. It expresses general values, attitudes and beliefs but articulates them in a way that partially conceals their political significances while enhanc-ing their seductive power. In this way, the aesthetics of collective offices contribute to the construction of subjectivities at work. Moreover, empha-sis on aesthetic experiences at the workplace brings employment rela-tionships in line with other aspects of workers' personal identities as consumers, thereby tapping into the sensibilities that they bring with them to the workplace.

Those who work at home are cut off from the aesthetic of the office, at least temporarily. Corporate aesthetics are weak in the home. However, home-located workers are in very close proximity to a powerful alterna-tive aesthetic order – that of the home. This is, moreover, an aesthetic in which workers are likely to have a high personal stake and in which they are likely to want to participate as individuals along with other household members. Working at home thus raises questions about how people make home and make workplaces, and how they make them together.

Mobile workers are remote from the aesthetic orders of office and home, both of which in their different ways emphasize an exclusive togetherness. Workers on the move spend large amounts of time in public or semi-public spaces and sites where aesthetic codes are likely to be formal, impersonal and low key. They are frequently plunged into environments that make little connection with, and make few concessions to, the corporate landscape. Many spaces of transition, such as airports, are bland and anonymous (Augé 1995; Gottdiener 2001a). Workers on the move, thus, encounter few aesthetic cues that prompt their work performances. They may need to adopt high levels of self-motivation or self-discipline to counter the dispiriting and demoralizing experience of spending large amounts of time in impersonal and stressful locations. They may, therefore, deploy relatively small aesthetic interventions in the environment to generate a sense of order and purpose in their work practices. Briefcases may contain not only instrumental devices but also items of symbolic significance, which contribute to defining and creating an insulated capsule of space and time that constitutes a workstation in a non-working environment.

Conclusion

This chapter has introduced a suite of terms and concepts that are used throughout this book. The most important of these are workstation, workplace and workscape. Examination of the processes characteristic of the networks of connections between workstations and workplaces, that constitute workscapes, led us to identify a series of further concepts that illuminate various aspects of the socio-spatial relations at work. These include: pathways, routes, assembly, repair, wayfinding, presence, visibility and stalling. Drawing on this theoretical framework, we were further able to identify different types of workscapes (such as singular workscapes and plural workscapes), different sectors of workscapes (such as the clusters of workstations and workplaces that comprise collective offices, working at home and working on the move), and different practices that make workscapes possible (such as texts, devices, social disciplines and technologies of the self).

Three clusters are of particular importance within contemporary plural workscapes – the collective office, working at home and working on the move. Our comparative ideal-type analysis highlights their diversity and difference. Each cluster comprises a different combination of attributes and qualities, constraints and opportunities. It is critical to remember that many workers are not confined to one or other of these spatial locations; rather, they switch between these contexts at different times and depending on the work tasks in hand. Contemporary workscapes, thus, require workers to manage transitions between radically different environments, calling for contrasting skills, knowledge and abilities.

3

Transforming Locations of Work

The workplace suddenly becomes a far bigger place than just this building. The workplace suddenly becomes here, the customer, the car, the home. Suddenly the workplace explodes and it isn't just a traditional office any more.

(Anna Connolly, Senior Manager, Development Council)

Introduction

This chapter has two purposes. First, it provides some historical background and contemporary context to the development of the three main places of work that are replacing the 'personal office': that is, the 'collective office', 'working at home' and 'working on the move'. Their rise is examined in the next three sections. Secondly, the chapter goes on to present recent statistical data on the extent of these three ways of working in contemporary Britain.

From Personal to Collective Offices

A key feature of early factories and offices was the spatial distribution of individual workers. The allocation of each person to a place and each place to a person was the foundation of regulation and control embedded in the physical construction of assembly lines and 'personal offices'. 'Placing' workers made the security of materials and regulation of work flows much easier to achieve. More subtly, it made possible the introduction of disciplinary devices associated with panoptical surveillance, the normalizing gaze and the regimentation of time (McKendrick 1962; E.P. Thompson 1967; Gioscia 1972; Reid 1976; Foucault 1977; Joyce 1987). The design of offices played an important role in the emergence of this regime of discipline, policing and control. A cube of space in the workplace (desk, bench or machine) became synonymous with a unit of labour on the payroll. 'The industrial and engineering metaphors of so much organizational theory have been mirrored by the functionalist design dogma of Modernist, hard-edged, rectilinear offices' (Turner and Myerson 1998: 20). Tayloristic management practices were applied in, indeed constituted by, Taylorized buildings (Baldry *et al.* 1998; Baldry 1999). The term 'office', which had once meant a position or function, increasingly was also used to refer to a place. In 'personal offices', an individual worker and a designated space became synonymous.

Personal offices also expressed the status of white-collar workers, both *vis-à-vis* manual workers and others in 'desk jobs'. Offices were distinguished by their location and décor from manufacturing areas, symbolically and sometimes literally looking down on the shop floor. Organizational hierarchies were inscribed in architecture and furnishings. Higher-grade workers were awarded visible symbolic markers of prestige in the form of minor non-utilitarian items of décor, such as carpets and curtains. In some organizations, such as the British civil service, the calculation of these signs could become both elaborate and strictly policed (Bedford and Tong 1997: 67).

In the 1960s and 1970s cellular versions of personal offices, surrounded by walls, were increasingly challenged by 'open plan' designs (Duffy 1992; Laing 1997). Open plan offices frequently rendered the personal cubes of space occupied by workers more readily observable but, typically, did not entail the elimination of personal space. Indeed, workers often responded by defending their personal space against visual intrusion; for example, by using equipment to recreate dividing walls, introducing symbolic territorial markings, and deploying 'civil inattention' (Goffman 1971).

The pace of innovation in office design increased sharply in the 1990s as architects and designers began to explore the implications of ICT in facilitating new ways of working based on different kinds of social interaction. Their proposals were intended to make social encounters in the workplace more varied, unpredictable and fluid. By the beginning of the twenty-first century, numerous radical office designs, and accompanying neologisms, jostled for attention (Becker 1990; Duffy 1990, 1992, 1997; Becker and Steele 1995; Ross 1995; DEGW and BRE 1996; Pelegrin 1996; Raymond and Cunliffe 1997; Turner 1997; Zelinsky 1997, 2002; Laing *et al.* 1998; Holtham 2001). Some of these approaches were only superficially different. Many were based upon a crude spatial or architectural determinism. Others can appear faddish when examined through the lens of social science. In this book, our classification of offices is based upon an analysis of the ways in which space is defined, allocated and controlled within the social relations of production. We contrast offices where space is collectively organized and mobilized (which we refer to as 'collective offices') with those in which space is allocated to individual workers for their sole use and in which they may inscribe space with their personal signatures (which we denote as 'personal offices'). It is our contention that a shift from personal to collective office spaces is not just cosmetic but propels office workers into new ways of relating to colleagues, clients and managers.

Stone and Luchetti (1985) were among the first to challenge the taken-for-granted assumption that each worker should occupy a single specific office space in which to conduct all his or her job tasks. They imagined that office buildings might incorporate a variety of different types of work settings, with individuals moving between them depending on the nature of their tasks. Different locations within the office could, thus, offer different experiences and types of interactions – quiet or busy, confidential or sociable, contemplative or action-oriented. Another author who has made a major contribution to this paradigm is Frank Duffy. As the founder of DEGW, a firm that combines architectural practice and management consulting, Duffy has become one of the leading advocates and designers of what are often referred to as 'new workplaces'. He is perhaps best known for his delineation of four types of working environments that, depending on the mix of tasks characteristic of the enterprise, may be combined within a single building (e.g. DEGW and BRE 1996; Laing *et al.* 1998). The den offers simple settings suitable for teams and interactive groups to work closely but where individuals have relatively low autonomy. The club provides a variety of settings where high skill and autonomous workers can network in multiple ways. The hive comprises cubicles that facilitate iterative work processes, with low levels of autonomy and interaction. The cell is a setting rich in ICT, occupied by those engaged in tasks demanding high autonomy and low interaction with others.

These approaches adopt a task-oriented perspective that explores the fit between specific types of work activity and suitable spatial locations. Although they raise interesting questions, which we address at length, our analysis has a different starting point. It is not only more general but is directed, in the first instance, to power interdependencies within the spatial and social dynamics of employment relationships. We are interested in the social processes by which space is designated, claimed, used and contested within organizations. In subsequent chapters we do, indeed, investigate how workers slot particular types of activity into what they perceive to be appropriate units of time and space. We also examine the ways in which they adapt spaces and times for particular tasks. However, we analyse these processes in the context of a broader examination of changes in the socio-spatial relations of employment. These generate new conceptions of relevant job tasks and the suitability of places for particular activities. Thus, for example, post-bureaucratic organizations may reconfigure their offices spaces in order to promote random, informal, high-intensity interaction among staff as part of an attempt to exercise managerial control by mobilizing group loyalties and individual subjectivities behind company goals. Avoidance of participation in the informal small group culture in order to get on with routine tasks may be perceived as inappropriate. 'Hanging out' in designated times and spaces becomes a legitimate and expected part of the job.

Our approach also makes connections between, on the one hand, the lived experience of particular workplaces and, on the other, the political economy of firms and organizations in capitalist societies. Private sector enterprises are constrained to make profits and declare dividends; public sector organizations to manage budgets and meet service delivery targets. Both are subject to the twin pressures of synchronizing income and expenditures (cost management) and maximizing the output of labour (productivity management). The introduction of collective offices is intended to make a contribution to both these objectives.

Office buildings carry high overheads yet surveys regularly show that they are rarely fully occupied. Staff are away from their desks when visiting clients, consulting colleagues, attending meetings, working at home, looking up information, on holiday and off sick (Zelinsky 1997: 48–56; Turner and Myerson 1998: 70). Some surveys suggest that workstations and offices go unoccupied for as much as two-thirds of a typical working week. When weekends and holidays are factored in, the cost of unused space rises still further. The realization that personal offices are a waste of corporate resources is the launch pad for much of the debate. 'The way in which any new office design solution captures and utilizes this spare capacity is at the heart of environments that support new ways of working' (T. Thompson 1997: 113).

Collective offices address these issues by prioritizing time over space. Costs are reduced if space is provided to office workers only when needed in order to conduct work tasks. This allows organizations to function with less office space or to expand their workforces without investing in new buildings. It also facilitates the regrouping of disparate groups of staff, with attendant economies of scale, elimination of duplication, reduction in overheads and enhanced speed of communication. The sale of redundant buildings may net significant windfall gains. Collective office spacing is, thus, more flexible, responsive and cheaper than personal office spacing.

Advocates of collective offices also argue that they raise productivity by generating more dynamic, innovative and creative patterns of working (Duffy 1990, 1992, 1997; DEGW and BRE 1996; Worthington 1997; A. Law 1999, 2001; Myerson and Ross 1999; Antonelli 2001). They argue that the elimination of personal space generates an interactive and group-orientated office life that promotes innovative solutions to business problems, a sense of corporate belonging and a strong joint work ethic. However, collective offices can also pose managerial problems. In the era of personal offices, managerial strategies of control rested on the presence and visibility of individual workers within designated cubes of space (Marglin 1976; Baldry 1999). The abolition of personal space in the office challenges and undermines this mode of management (Felstead *et al.* 2003a). Collective offices require staff to engage in continual movement between locations within the building, making panoptical surveillance far harder to achieve. In Chapter 4 we examine some of the ways in which managers respond to these challenges.

Bringing Work Home

The conduct of economic activities within dwellings that are also places of residence has a long history. Prior to industrialization, households were simultaneously places of social reproduction and production. Farms, workshops, manor houses and palaces were household economies. As a result, domestic and economic relationships were closely integrated; home and workplace were not separate spheres of social life (Tilly and Scott 1978; Laslett 1979; Anderson 1980; Mitterauer and Sieder 1982). Farmers and rural labourers occupied the same buildings as agricultural machinery and livestock. Apprentices slept beside their benches in artisans' workshops. Relationships within households defined roles and responsibilities within economic life. Participation in the economy was achieved through participation in the household. Thus, women were involved in production of foods, agricultural products and other goods in workshops (Segalen 1983; Bradley 1989; Wiesner-Hanks 2000). Similarly, a range of services were provided within households: educating and disciplining children, for example, were aspects of the regulation and training of the junior workforce. Similarly, the times of work and non-work were closely interrelated, with the festivals of religious and community life closely mirrored in the seasonal rhythms of economic production.

In the early stages of capitalist industrialization, household, family and kinship bonds continued to play an important role in mobilizing workforces and, to some degree, business enterprises. Co-resident families worked as teams in a variety of new industries, such as textiles. Household relationships continued to provide important networks of emotional and material support well into the twentieth century. However, economic growth, institutional differentiation, capitalist labour markets and the emergence of specialist workplaces eventually eliminated most household units of production and family-based work teams (C. Harris 1977; Hall 1982; Hareven 1982, 1993; Roberts 1984; Davidoff 1990). Individuals, rather than co-resident groups, entered the labour market and became wage labourers. Manufacturing technologies became too large and expensive to be provided at home.

Two new relatively autonomous sets of relations had come into being – home, focused on consumption, and work, dedicated to production (Humphries 1982; Boxer and Quataert 2000). Henceforth, most people left home to go to work and, at the end of the working day, left work to return home. The relationship between the times and spaces of work and non-work became linear, sequential and chronological. For most people, household relations ceased to be the direct path into participation in economic production. Indeed, for many women they became an obstacle. The separation of home from the workplace meant work was no longer an integral part of family life but a separate external activity.

Homes gradually changed their character. Notwithstanding class and ethnic variations, home became the site where emotional bonds between parents and children were forged, ideals of romantic love between partners pursued, and processes of leisure-based consumption shared by household members (Gillis 1974; Zaretsky 1976; Stone 1977; Cunningham 1995; Bennett 2002). Increasingly, homes became hedged around with symbolic and physical boundaries. They became popularly perceived as places of freedom from the surveillance and controls embedded in workplaces and as places of individual self-expression manifested in choices of goods, partners and lifestyles (Allan and Crow 1989; Dupuis and Thorns 1998; Chapman and Hockey 1999; Hepworth 1999). Home was portrayed as a place to escape, a sanctuary from the frustrations and pressures of the outside world, 'a haven in a heartless world' (Lasch 1977). Even for those with satisfying jobs, home-based identities became highly desirable forms of selfhood. Home-making, initially seen as a project for women (Davidoff and Hall 1987; Rybczynski 1988), increasingly involved all household members. Aesthetic performances and decorations became intrinsic to these processes (Douglas 1993; D. Miller 2001). Huge industries emerged to serve the popular dream of home-based identity.

There is, clearly, a disjunction between home as imagined ideal and a lived reality. Although popular culture portrays the home as a place of individualized fulfilment, much research and political lobbying has also established that it is a locus of inequality, violence and uncertainty (Dobash and Dobash 1992; Goldsack 1999; Hockey 1999). The home is also a place of unpaid domestic labour that remains unequally divided between male and female members (Gregson and Lowe 1994; Warren 2003). The forms of household relationships found within the home are increasingly diverse, fragmented and fragile, reflected in high numbers of 'broken homes'. Increasingly, people decide to enter, construct and leave homes in terms of their perceived personal interests and desires rather than as dictated by communal codes and ethics. All these trends suggest that, in contemporary societies, the social relationships of home are both of enormous significance as a source of identification and increasingly based on processes of discussion and negotiation between the members (Finch and Mason 1993; Jamieson 2002).

Although the onset of industrialization meant that the majority of workers were engaged in work activities outside the home, the domestic sphere remained an important workplace for a number of occupational groups. For example, lawyers and doctors often conducted their practices in the home. Similarly, some manual jobs continued to take place in the home. For many years home-based workers engaged in routine manual and industrial tasks were a neglected and exploited group (Boris 1994; Boris and Prügl 1996). Official surveys and censuses tended to undercount their numbers, employers paid them rock bottom wages, trade unionists treated them as unwelcome competitors to factory-based workers, and business analysts regarded them as an anomaly in a modern economy. They were an invisible workforce hidden from public view within the private sphere of the home. Many were women with young children. Migrant and ethnic minority communities were also heavily involved (Allen and Wolkowitz 1987; Phizacklea and Wolkowitz 1995; Felstead and Jewson 2000).

In the late twentieth century, popular attitudes towards working at home underwent a sea change (Mirchandani 2000). This can be seen in recent media representations of home-located working which speculate that the fusion of work and home in the same space will once again become the norm. These accounts typically do not portray industrial workers, who are still relatively invisible, but concentrate on professional and managerial staff. They are presented in middle-class domestic settings, surrounded by high quality environments, engaged in work tasks by using ICT. The growth of this kind of home-located work is represented as having many benefits, including the greater involvement of busy parents (particularly fathers) in family life, expanded choice in the times and milieux of employment, greater equality in the domestic division of labour, reduction in congestion and pollution generated by commuting, a revival of the economic and community life of suburban and rural areas, and the erosion of gender differences. The ideology of individual fulfilment in domestic life is mirrored in the freedoms perceived to be entailed in working at home.

As will be seen later in this chapter, there is reliable statistical evidence that increasing numbers of people are working at home for part or all of the time. Moreover, the growth of home-located work has created lucrative markets in equipment, facilities, furnishing and décor. Thus, for example, mass furniture manufacturers and retailers routinely include desks, cabinets and chairs suitable for the 'home office' in their catalogues. Rising numbers of books on the design of offices in the home have been published in the last ten years (Brock 1998; Gaventa 1998; Barrett 2002; Zimmerman 2003). Mobile phone manufacturers advertise their wares as devices to aid home-based work as well as leisure. Indeed, increases in the numbers of people working at home are associated with innovations in ICT. Once workers no longer have to present themselves at specific and designated places of work in order to carry out many of their job tasks, they can work in any number of locations, including home.

Working at home can be a positive experience for all household members. However, the role of the home as a locus of private, personal, negotiated and reflexive identities means that the introduction of the times, spaces and disciplines of employment can be fraught for both worker and others. The affectionate rumpus of normal family life may, for the worker, now be perceived as disruptive and distracting. Disputes and negotiations may surround control over valued spaces in the home. Attempts to combine childcare and domestic labour with work can be highly frustrating. The absence of temporal cues for stopping and starting, combined with the continued presence of the technology of work, may create workaholics who who cannot switch back into home life. The distance of home-located workers from line managers, colleagues and clients may create anxieties, on all sides, about whether the home-located worker is functioning effectively and diligently. Households and individuals create a range of responses to these problems, as will be seen in Chapter 5. Some, probably the majority, favour a complete separation within the home between the spaces and times devoted to work and domestic activities. A smaller number seek to blur the boundaries, attempting some kind of integration between home life and job-related activities. Others fall at various points in between.

Mobile World, Mobile Working

Routine mass travel has a much shorter history than either factory/office work or economic activity within the home. Widespread working on the move – other than by 'commercial travellers' (Spears 1995) – is even more recent.

The history of travel in the last two centuries has been one of increasing speed and flexibility leading to the compression of time and space: that is, it has become possible to travel ever greater distances in a given amount of time (D. Harvey 1989). The two-hundred-year history of the railway as a mode of personal travel has left a strong and enduring imprint on the nature and experience of physical travel today. It provides a point of comparison with other, more privatized, forms of travel – such as the car – which are more commonly used today as vehicles and places to work (Wolf 1996). Journey speeds continued to increase throughout the twentieth century, prompted in particular by the growing and widespread use of the car and plane (Pooley and Turnbull 1999). Despite frequent cries that urban travel speeds have reduced as road traffic grows (e.g. *Guardian* 2003a), the overall picture of the contemporary world is one in which time and space have become ever more compressed and journeys ever longer. Whereas in 1950 the average person in Britain travelled five miles per day, this has now risen to 28 miles – and is forecast to double again by 2025 (Adams 1999a; ONS 2003b). At the same time, the pace of travel has quickened. Car speeds on trunk roads and motorways have increased, rail journey times have shrunk and jet aircraft transport people across the globe in a matter of hours.

Modern travel, then, allows links to be made between places inaccessible in the recent past and in timeframes unimaginable even a few decades ago. However, this has been achieved at the cost of removing the traveller's connections with, and closeness to, the places in between. In the case of rail travel, the landscape between the point of embarkation and destination becomes a swiftly passing series of 'panoramic' views, framed by the carriage window (Schivelbusch 1986). Motorway travel, too, shields the principal places it connects from view. Instead, it relies on roadside signs to announce notable features to travellers, who are confronted with a bland roadscape of traffic lanes, bridges and a myriad of exits and entrances (Edensor 2003). Nevertheless, rail and road travel merely restrict appreciation of the landscape rather than eliminating it altogether. The same cannot, of course, be said of air travel that completely disconnects passengers from the landscapes over which they fly.

In addition to shielding places from view, modern travel insulates passengers from the sounds, smells, tastes and temperatures of the places through which they pass. The private car provides the ultimate means of controlling the senses while in transit. The outside environment is kept at bay by the windows that enclose driver and passengers. Car occupants are cocooned in a private, moving capsule. Inside, temperatures can be accurately controlled, music played, travel and news information gathered and phone calls made – all without intruding on the territories of strangers and without the outside environment impinging on the world within (Graves-Brown 1997; Urry 2000a, 2000b). Stop-over points – such as railway junctions, motels and airport hubs – are experienced as places on the way to or from somewhere else, rather than as places with their own individuality and character. These have been referred to as 'pseudo-places' or 'non-places': that is, places which are easy to understand, familiar, instantly recognized, but which represent pauses in, rather than the beginnings or endings of, journeys (Fussell 1980; Morris 1988; Augé 1995: 75–115). This is reflected in their aesthetic appearance, denoting functionality and commonality. Motorway service stations, station platforms and airport lounges are often adorned with reassuring landmarks – such as familiar company names, logos and styles – which heighten a sense of detachment from a local sense of place and increase feelings of anonymity. However, these places also possess a narrative potential that can, under appropriate circumstances, be shaped by those who use them. Users can mark these non-places with their own identity and personal meaning – such as a convenient mid-way point on the way home, a good place to stop to check e-mails, or a place from which to hide legitimately from others on account of poor mobile phone reception. In the words of Augé (1995: 79) such places: 'are like palimpsests on which the scrambled game of identity and relations is ceaselessly rewritten'. In what ways, how and why these non-places are written and rewritten by workers on the move is considered in Chapter 6.

The anonymity of travel has grown as it has become simpler, cheaper and more popular. At the beginnings of journeys – in waiting rooms, departure lounges and station platforms – and while in transit – whether by train, plane or car – travellers have become more numerous, and visual encounters with strangers more frequent. The tactics employed by early nineteenth century railway passengers in coping with the uneasiness such encounters can generate remain firmly in place today. Reading while travelling grew in significance throughout the nineteenth century and became almost obligatory as 'public' transport (i.e. sharing travelling space with strangers) became widespread. This is reflected in the rise of bookstalls (and even lending libraries) at railway stations, investigations into the medical effects of reading while travelling, and observations of everyday travel practice made by contemporary writers (Schivelbusch 1986).

More recently, 'virtual travel' has become possible. This entails transporting people across geographical boundaries in real time so that they become 'tele-present' in one world while being 'absent but present' in another (Urry 2000a, 2000b; Gergen 2002; Green 2002). The mobile phone offers this possibility, thereby providing a potential antidote to the anonymity of travel. First, the mobile phone facilitates gossip (MORI/Vodafone 2003), stretching the notion of 'being with' across time and space (Myerson 2001). Secondly, mobiles can be used as 'symbolic bodyguards' to be activated when feeling vulnerable and exposed in public places. They allow users to erect barriers around themselves and signal to others nearby that they are not alone (Fox 2001). Thirdly, texting offers a more discreet way of maintaining network bonds and creates brief, frequent and spontaneous virtual encounters. The act of texting itself allows users to avoid the gaze of strangers seated nearby. The laptop, too, can be used as a means of travelling to another world while simultaneously occupying an anonymous place in the midst of strangers. Users can immerse themselves in a familiar environment, disengage from the immediate surroundings of physical travel and transport themselves to a virtual place not shared or experienced by those co-present.

The combination of increased corporeal travel and the ability to travel virtually has provided the possibility for more work to be conducted in unconventional places, such as homes, cars, trains, motorway service stations, hotel lobbies and airport departure lounges. This has benefits and drawbacks. On the one hand, it permits the harnessing of 'dead time', such as that spent travelling between meetings and time spent doing tasks that have become second nature and therefore do not command total attention (Laurier 2001a). These minutes and hours can be used to plan and co-ordinate with others, access information, send/receive messages and draft documents, while remaining within the reach of other network members. On the other hand, respite from employment pressures becomes more difficult to maintain. Legitimate spatial isolation and temporal freedom from work are diminished, to be replaced by an ever-growing list of productive tasks from which there is seemingly no escape. Not so long ago, for example, journeys by plane excused business travellers from maintaining contact with colleagues; for the length of the flight, they were deemed to be incommunicado. However, fax, phone and internet connections now extend vertically for seven miles as well as horizontally around the world. Increasing numbers of long-haul flights, such as those crossing the Atlantic, and short-haul flights will soon offer travellers 'perpetual contact' (Katz and Aakhus 2002). By the same token, the seashore, the end of a waterside jetty and even a mountain-top are not beyond the reach of communications technology and the world of work. With ingenuity and improvisation these exotic places – as well as the more mundane – can function as workplaces. In Chapter 6, we examine how this is done and how this way of working is managed.

Quantitative Evidence of Change

Thus far, this chapter has described the origins and context of the three spatial locations of work that are the subject of this book. As already indicated, a key facilitator in detaching individuals from their personal cubes of space has been the increased use of ICT. This has made it possible for professional and managerial workers to share space and facilities with one another, allow more work to be done at home, and permit work to be carried around and completed wherever and whenever possible. This section, therefore, examines the statistical evidence on the spread of ICT in the workplace. It then goes on to outline the evidence that the potentiality for work to be carried out in these locations is being mobilized and harnessed by employers in Britain today.

Figures for the spread of ICT are startling. The mobile phone, for example, has become a mass consumer product within the space of two decades. Worldwide, in 1990 there were 11 million mobile phone subscribers; by 2001 they had risen to 955 million, with 1329 million forecast by the end of 2003 (ITU 2003). In Britain, ownership of a mobile phone was relatively rare twenty years ago, but by 2000 official figures showed that more than half of the adult British population were users (*Financial Times* 2000; Myerson 2001: 16–17; Dant and Kaisler 2001). By 2002, this had risen to 76 per cent, with 80 per cent of households having access to at least one mobile phone (Crabtree *et al.* 2003: table 1). In the mid-1980s marketing campaigns for mobile phones pictured wealthy businessmen brandishing large, cumbersome 'brick-like' objects, whereas today they are marketed as light, inexpensive fashion accessories. Early models permitted little personalization; today customizable face plates, ring tones, screensavers and games offer users innumerable ways of displaying their individuality (Vincent 2003). The importance of mobile phones to people's work and social lives has also grown. A recent survey reported that almost two-fifths of British adults (38%) said they could not be without their mobile phone. In contrast, one in five (19%) said that they would find it difficult being without their desktop computer, internet access (18%), e-mail (17%) or text messaging (15%) (MORI/Vodafone 2003). This evidence supports the contention that: 'the personal computer was a misnomer. The truly personal digital device today is the [mobile] phone' (*Economist* 2002).

Clearly, mobile phones are used for work as well as pleasure. Unfortunately, it is only recently that surveys have asked specific questions about this aspect of their use. Nevertheless, a randomly conducted survey of 2466 workers in 2000 found that around half of all professionals and managers used a mobile phone in the course of their work (R. Taylor 2002a: table 7). Data series which chart the use of ICT for work purposes more generally, however, are available. They strongly suggest that there has been a rapid increase in the use of computers at work. In 1986, two-fifths (40.3%) of employees reported that they used computerized equipment in the course of their daily activities. By 1992 the proportion had risen to over half (56%) and by 2001 it was almost three-quarters (73.7%). Furthermore, by 2001 it was very rare for non-manual workers to report that they did not use computers at all in their work. Indeed, their use was regarded as 'essential' to the conduct of non-manual work activities by over a half of those surveyed (Felstead *et al.* 2002c: 56–66, tables 5.1, 5.2 and 5.5).

As with the fixed-line telephone, the computer too became mobile with the invention of the laptop. These developments opened up the possibility for office workers to do their jobs in a much wider variety of locations and times. There is no technical necessity for most non-manual workers to be in a particular building, office or desk for most of the time. This is not to suggest that we are entering the era of the paperless office or the virtual meeting; there are circumstances where presence in a designated place is desirable and/or required. However, the number of such instances is drastically reduced by the mobile phone and the laptop (Worthington 1997; Zelinsky 1997).

There is so much media interest in the development of the collective office that piecemeal changes to buildings are often enough to warrant feverish press activity. For example, the introduction of 'hot desks' in GCHQ (Government Communication Headquarters) in 2001 and in the Greater London Authority's City Hall in 2002 both attracted broadsheet attention (*Guardian* 2003b, 2003c). These examples remain at the level of anecdote and do little to establish whether, in general, office workers are becoming detached from personal desks and offices. For this kind of evidence, we have to rely on national surveys of employers and workers. Unfortunately, surveys that carry questions on the location of work are few. Moreover, data collection processes lack subtlety and may not always detect the fine-grain changes to people's working lives that the mobile phone and laptop unknowingly bring. However, in what follows we try to piece together currently available data.

One source of evidence is the Change in Employer Practices Survey (CEPS). This survey was carried out between July and September 2002 and comprised telephone interviews with 2000 senior human resource/industrial relations managers in a nationally representative stratified random sample of workplaces in Britain. The CEPS covered all sectors of the economy and was constructed to collect evidence from both large and small establishments provided they employed at least five workers. Around two-thirds of managers approached took part in the survey, with interviews lasting around 30 minutes (R. Taylor 2002b). The survey was designed to assess recent changes in employer practices and indicate expected changes in the near future. Respondents were accordingly asked to report on 'change over the last three years' and plans for change 'over the next 12 months'. The topics covered included numbers and types of employees, promotion and recruitment, staff working conditions, employee involvement, the use of information technology, the legal and regulatory environment and, last but not least, the management of space at work. With respect to the last, respondents were asked: 'Over the last three years have any of the following things happened at your establishment?'. Options included: 'Increased use of open plan offices', 'The use of hotdesking' and 'The reorganization of equipment and machines to release space'. They were also asked: 'Are you planning to introduce/extend use of [each practice] during the next 12 months?'

In this survey, around one in six establishments reported an increase over three years in the use of open plan offices (17.4%) and hotdesking (15.6%) (hotdesking was defined in the survey as the situation where 'staff have no fixed personal workspace and use any available desk as needed'). A third (35.3%) reported carrying out a 'reorganization of equipment and machines to release space' during the previous three years (see Table 3.1). A smaller, but still sizeable, number of managers said they intended to extend or introduce such changes in the next twelve months. For example, as many as a fifth (22.1%) said they planned to extend or increase the reorganization of equipment in order to release more space inside the establishment. These proportions are sizeable and are indicative of substantial changes to the physical layout of offices and factories. In reviewing this evidence, one commentator, who is in general sceptical of claims that employment relations are dramatically changing, was moved to concede that 'we are going through a radical transformation in the physical shape of offices and plants' (R. Taylor 2002b: 12).

CEPS was an establishment-level survey. The Location of Work Survey (LWS) was conducted at an organizational level. The LWS polled the views of 128 senior facilities/property managers in large organizations in the first six months of 2002 (see Felstead *et al.* 2003b, 2005). The information gathered provides a high-level organizational view across many establishments of past, current and future changes to the physical layout of workplaces and offices in particular. Organizations participating in the LWS employed, on average, 20,320 workers spread across many estab-

Table 3.1 Moves towards the collective office, 2002

Collective office arrangements	*Percentage of establishments*	
	Increased use over last three years	*Increased use expected over next twelve months*
Open plan offices	17.4	8.0
Hotdesking	15.6	6.3
Reorganization of equipment and machines	35.3	22.1

Note: To provide a representative picture of changing working practices in establishments, the survey results presented here are weighted to reflect the size and sector profile of the workplace population. Unless stated otherwise, a similar approach has been adopted in the other CEPS tables.

Source: Own calculations from the Changing Working Practices Survey, 2002 (Felstead *et al.* 2005, table 3).

lishments. This does mean that organizations are more likely to report change occurring in at least one establishment under their ownership, even though this change may only affect a small proportion of the total workforce.

LWS respondents were asked at the beginning of the interview to think 'about the staff that work for your organization in the UK' and to answer a series of questions. These included: whether they had introduced a number of new ways of reconfiguring office space, the extent to which these internal changes to the layout of their offices had occurred over the last five years, and whether they had plans to roll out these changes throughout the organization's offices. The results suggest that many large organizations have already experimented with some reshaping of their office estates. The penetration of collective office arrangements was high and almost half of large employers expected to institute these changes in other offices under their control in the near future. For example, 'hot desks' (that is, 'desks which workers have to book in advance to use') were present in three out of ten (31.3%) large organizations, rising to almost two out of five (39.6%) large private sector employers (see Table 3.2, panel a). However, the extent of their use was quite modest – in almost all cases less than 5 per cent of office staff were actually reported to be hotdesking. Nevertheless, a sizeable proportion (30%) of hotdesking employers had a formal policy or guidelines on the use of bookable desk space which, in many cases, they were willing to share with the research team. Further-

Table 3.2 Past, current and future use of collective office arrangements, 2002

Collective office arrangements	*Percentage of organizations*		
	All	*Private*	*Public*
(a) Hot desks			
Increased use over the last five years	27.8	32.7	24.3
Currently used	31.3	39.6	25.3
Greater use planned	44.6	36.0	50.0
(b) Touchdown desks			
Increased use over the last five years	29.4	37.3	24.0
Currently used	43.3	61.5	30.7
Greater use planned	43.9	40.8	46.0
(c) Redesigned office space			
Issue under consideration	64.6	76.9	56.0
Plan to redesign office space	47.2	44.0	49.3

Source: Own calculations from the Location of Work Survey, 2002 (Felstead *et al.* 2005, table 4).

more, backward- and forward-looking questions suggest that hotdesking has recently become of interest to large employers. A quarter (27.8%) reported increased use over the last five years; nearly half (44.6%) plan to make greater use of hotdesking in the near future. A similar, if slightly more pronounced, picture emerges with regard to the use of 'touchdown desks' (that is, 'desks that are set aside for drop in use by anyone in the organization'). According to the LWS this arrangement was used to some extent, albeit in only a limited way, in two-fifths (43.3%) of large organizations. Many expected to roll out their use even further in the next few years (see Table 3.2, panel b). Comprehensive redesign of office space was also being considered by almost two-thirds (64.6%) of the organizations surveyed. Almost half of these organizations (47.2%) had plans in place at the time of the interview. Respondents explained in some detail what these redesigns entailed. They ranged from equipping particular areas such as restaurants, cafés and breakfast bars with internet access and laptop plug-in points, through to wholesale reviews of space usage and identification of ways in which space per office worker could be reduced (see Table 3.2, panel c).

Respondents who reported that the organization had changed the location of work in the last five years, or planned to do so in the future, were asked to indicate the main drivers behind these decisions. Two factors were prominent: the need to economize on property costs, and the desire to promote greater work flexibility and social interaction. The latter was cited by over half of respondents whose organizations had increased or planned to increase use of touchdown desks. This reflects other research findings that suggest the further apart people sit and the greater the physical barriers between them, the less likely they are to interact. In personal office environments workers are four times more likely to talk to someone sitting six feet away than they are with someone sitting 60 feet away; any further away and they are unlikely to interact at all. Similarly, personal offices reduce the likelihood of chance meetings taking place – research suggests that two people working on different floors in the same building where individuals are allocated their own desk space have only a one per cent chance of meeting in the course of a day (Nathan and Doyle 2002). The need to save on property costs was also a strong factor driving the introduction of collective office arrangements, particularly among respondents who reported recent increases or planned extensions to their hotdesking programmes. Almost a half of these respondents cited property costs as one of the main drivers behind such programmes.

Although the removal of personal desk and office space may bring management benefits, in terms of increased knowledge-sharing within the organization and savings on property costs, surveys also suggest that employees still hanker for their own space. In 2001, a telephone survey of a random sample of 404 non-manual workers, conducted by the Indus-trial Society (now the Work Foundation), found that having a desk or office allocated for personal use was more than twice as popular as having to use collectively owned space reserved only when required. For a third of respondents, personal space was the most important aspect of their working environment, compared to 14 per cent who gave their highest rating to collective space (Nathan and Doyle 2002: 20–1). This evidence suggests that hotdesking and touchdown desks remove an aspect of work highly cherished by office workers. Other surveys generate similar find-ings and conclude that most people, given the choice, would prefer to have a cellular office (e.g. Anjum 1999). Indeed, it would seem that the urge to personalize is relentless. A recent survey by Office Angels – a recruitment agency specializing in supplying secretarial and office support staff – found that three-quarters of 1500 office workers admitted to marking rulers, staplers, pens and hole-punchers with their names. Over a third (38%) always used the same mug and a half (49%) even had a favourite toilet cubicle (Office Angels 2001). Where such practices are frustrated – as in the collective office – a struggle is likely to ensue in which staff set out to bend the rules and develop tactics to colonize space for their own personal use. This is discussed further in Chapter 4.

Fortunately, we are blessed with more historical data on the extent to which work is carried out at home. The two principal sources are the Labour Force Survey (LFS) and the Census. Each LFS contains data on a random sample of individuals throughout the UK. Almost 60,000 house-holds are contacted and information is collected on a total of 150,000 people, of whom around 65,000 are aged 16 and above and are in work at the time of interview. The LFS series benefits from the regularity with which working-at-home data are collected and the addition of follow-up questions. In 1981, the LFS carried its first question on the location of work. Respondents were asked 'do you work mainly' in one of four loca-tions: in your own home, in the same building or grounds as your home, in different places using home as a base, or somewhere quite different from home (OPCS 1982: appendix 2). Despite offering a unique perspec-tive on the location of work, and providing a sift survey for a study of 'home-based' workers (Hakim 1987), eleven years were to pass before the question was repeated. It reappeared in 1992 and has been asked quar-terly in every LFS since. Further questions were added to the Spring 1997 quarter, which identified those who worked at least one full day at home in the week before interview (see Felstead *et al.* 2000: table A1). The decen-nial Census of population has asked about address of work since 1966 (when the first and only quinquennial census was carried out). Among the options available to respondents was that of indicating that they worked at home. However, only since 1981 have these responses been separately coded and the results published and analysed (Felstead and Jewson 1995, 1996; Hakim 1998: ch. 7). We will discuss, in turn, what light each of these data sources sheds on trends in working at home.

Using the LFS to track labour market change has a number of advantages. It is regularly carried out, has a high response rate, comprises a large number of interviews, uses officially recognized techniques and measures, and can be grossed up to give a picture of the UK in terms of both the proportions and the number of people involved. Table 3.3 presents the overall pattern of change from 1981 to 2002. It shows that the numbers working mainly at home have doubled over the 1981–92 period, but since then the numbers have remained flat at around 650,000. They account for one in 40 workers (around 2.5%) and have done so for the last ten years (see Table 3.3, column 1). The LFS also shows that a further 1.2 million workers spend a shorter period of time – one full day of their working week – carrying out paid work at home. This comprised 4.4 per cent of the working population in the UK in 2002, and represented an increase of one-sixth on the 1997 level (see Table 3.3, column 2). However, working at home for periods of less than a full day are not captured nor are several hours over the space of a number of days, even if during the course of a week they amount to a full day's work. As a result, the question's coverage is conservative. Respondents were also asked whether they sometimes worked at home. In 1998, this captured a further fifth (21.8%) of the employed workforce (Felstead *et al.* 2001a). However, there is no indication how often, how long and when this 'sometime' working at home occurred. It is therefore hazardous to draw the conclusion that working at home is rapidly increasing on the basis of adding together the 'mainly', 'one day a week' and 'sometimes' categories. We can only be confident that working mainly at home has increased substantially during the last two decades – but, as we have seen, still only constituted 2.5 per cent of the employed workforce in 2002. However, working one day a week at home is more common – it is almost twice as prevalent – and it has increased by 17 percentage points between 1997 and 2002. Overall, the LFS data suggests that approaching 2 million of the employed population work on a regular basis at home and that the proportion doing so is increasing.

Census results for 1981, 1991 and 2001 paint a picture of more rapid change. The Census records the number of respondents who ticked the 'works mainly at home' box when asked about the means by which they usually travelled to work. According to this evidence 708,430 people (3.4%) in England and Wales worked mainly at home in 1981, by 1991 this number had risen to 1,063,317 (4.9%) and by 2001 it had reached 2,170,547 (9.2%) (see Table 3.4, first row). The disjuncture between LFS estimates and Census counts is at its most pronounced for the 1991–2001 period. While the LFS saw little change in the numbers reporting that they worked

Table 3.3 LFS estimates of working at home and working on the move, 1981–2002[1]

	Working mainly 'in own home'[2] (1)	Working mainly elsewhere but also working at least one full day 'in own home' (2)	Working mainly 'in different places using home as base' (3)
1981	345920 (1.5)	NA	641900 (2.8)
1992	660793 (2.7)	NA	1201102 (4.8)
1993	618605 (2.6)	NA	1358326 (5.7)
1994	641702 (2.6)	NA	1497994 (6.2)
1995	616955 (2.5)	NA	1571158 (6.4)
1996	628533 (2.5)	NA	1565887 (6.4)
1997	611835 (2.4)	1066386 (4.0)	1552859 (6.2)
1998	642746 (2.4)	934231 (3.5)	1828318 (6.8)
1999	609366 (2.2)	1025766 (3.8)	1979600 (7.3)
2000	634312 (2.3)	1113308 (4.0)	2006683 (7.3)
2001	637387 (2.3)	1211999 (4.4)	1958528 (7.1)
2002	672949 (2.4)	1242383 (4.4)	2130458 (7.6)
Percentage change, 1981–2002	+94.5	NA	+231.9
Percentage change, 1981–92	+91.0	NA	+87.1
Percentage change, 1992–2002	+1.8	NA	+77.4
Percentage change, 1997–2002	+10.0	+16.5	+37.2

Notes:

[1] This table is based on the spring Labour Force Survey for each of the years which carried the work location question. Data have been weighted by the appropriate variable to compensate for differential response rates to the survey, only those aged 16 or over and in paid employment have been selected and percentages are based on those who gave valid responses to the question (unlike Hotopp 2002, and Felstead 1996, reallocations of these responses have not been carried out). These data sets are Crown Copyright, made available by the Office for National Statistics through the Data Archive, and have been used by permission.

[2] The rows for each year show absolute numbers of people involved, with proportions shown in parentheses. The denominator for column 2 is smaller than the other columns since it refers to a sub-set of the 16 and over employed sample (i.e. those mainly working outside of the home).

Source: Own calculations from the spring Labour Force Survey for the years 1981 and 1992–2002 (Felstead *et al.* 2005, table 1).

Table 3.4 Census counts of working at home and working on the move, 1951–2001

	1951 (%)	1961 (%)	1966 (%)	1971 (%)	1981 (%)	1991 (%)	2001 (%)
'Work mainly at home' (in response to question on daily journey to work)	Question not asked	Question not asked	Home not separately coded	Home not separately coded	708 430 (3.4)	1 063 317 (4.9)	2 170 547 (9.2)
'No fixed place' (in response to question on address of place of work)	476 107 (2.3)	675 730 (3.2)	979 900 (4.4)	1 291 590 (5.7)	1 431 140 (6.7)	1 394 625 (6.4)	Not available at time of writing
Coverage	England and Wales, all those in employment the week before the census and aged 15 or over.	England and Wales, all those in employment the week before the census and aged 15 or over.	England and Wales, all those in employment the week before the census and aged 15 or over.	England and Wales, all those in employment the week before the census and aged 15 or over.	England and Wales, all those in employment the week before the census and aged 16 or over.	England and Wales, all those in employment the week before the census and aged 16 or over.	England and Wales, all those in employment the week before the census and aged 16–74.

Notes	The 'no fixed place' includes only those who reported that they had 'no fixed place' of work when asked to provide their workplace address. Estimates are based on a full count.	The 'no fixed place' includes only those who reported that they had 'no fixed place' of work when asked to provide their workplace address. Estimates are based on a full count.	Under the 1920 Census Act quinquennial censuses can be held. This provision has only been used once – in 1966 when a 10% Sample Census was held.	The 'no fixed place' estimate also includes a small proportion (about 6% according to the 1966 Sample Census) of respondents who gave no answer.	The 'no fixed place' estimate also includes a small proportion (about 6% according to the 1966 Sample Census) of respondents who gave no answer.	These estimates (like 1961, 1966, 1971 and 1981) are based on a 10% coding. To take account of the under-enumeration in 1991, the 10% counts have been multiplied by 10.21.	The published results have been adjusted to account for under-enumeration.
Source	General Register Office, 1956: table 6	General Register Office, 1966: table 1	General Register Office, 1968: table 1	OPCS, 1974: 1	OPCS, 1984: tables 1A and 7	OPCS, 1994: 17	ONS, 2003a: table S119

mainly at home, Census results point to a major shift towards the home as a location of work. According to the 2001 Census, almost one in ten of those employed had no need to travel to work since they were 'in work, at home' (Felstead and Jewson 2000), double the proportion reporting home as their place of work in 1991. At the time of writing, full results for the 2001 Census have not been published and researchers have not yet had access to the raw data. However, there is some reason to believe that in 2001 the 'works mainly at home' category may have been artificially inflated by conflation of the 'works at home' and 'works from home' categories, and a reordering of the daily-journey-to-work options which gave more prominence to the home as a location of work than in the past (ONS 2000). Having said this, it is unlikely that all of the recorded increase in the numbers working at home can be put down to artefacts of the data collection process. Census results, therefore, suggest that the public world of work is more frequently invading spaces reserved for the private worlds of emotions, affection and gift-giving between family members. Chapter 5 considers how these two worlds are reconciled by those who work at home and others in the household.

As indicated earlier, the contemporary world is becoming increasingly mobile. The richest segment of the world's population is travelling more often, over longer distances and at greater speed than ever before (Adams 1999a, 1999b). While other forms of land travel such as walking and cycling are on the decline, car travel is predicted to grow at a remarkable rate – tripling between 1990 and 2050 (Urry 2003). A similar story can be told for air travel. Every day at least four million people catch a plane – more than 1.6 billion a year. Every year, there are more than 600 million international passenger arrivals and each year half a million hotel rooms are built to accommodate them worldwide (Doyle and Nathan 2001). These figures are all the more astounding when they are put in the context of a world in which technological devices – such as the mobile phone, e-mail and internet access – might have been expected to substitute for corporeal movement or at least quell our appetite for travel.

Many of these journeys are business-related. Figures suggest that those in managerial and professional occupations register more than double the travel miles of manual workers, with most of the difference the result of differences in job demands. Those routinely working on the move are likely to be among the most travelled – clocking up thousands of miles in cars, trains and planes – and spending large amounts of time in places shared with others and used for a multiplicity of purposes – such as service stations, hotels, airports and cafés. How numerous, then, are these kinds of workers in Britain? Both the LFS and the Census can provide some insights into this question. However, the measures used are far from perfect. For example, one of the allowable responses to the LFS question on location of work is 'in different places using home as a base'. This is intended to pick up those workers who have no fixed place to carry out their work but who instead travel from one destination to another. It is likely that these individuals spend some of their time working at home – arranging schedules, making preparations, doing paperwork – but most of their activities, such as visiting clients and colleagues, are carried out away from the home in a variety of different places. These LFS results are useful but are unlikely to give a complete picture of working on the move. The home-centric nature of the question means that it fails to capture individuals who use their employers' premises as a drop-in centre from which to carry out tasks in a variety of locations. Nevertheless the picture of change they paint is striking. The number of people using their home in order to work in a variety of places has more than tripled over the last two decades. Moreover, similar rates of change have been posted in the 1980s and 1990s. Remarkably, the proportion of workers using their home as a base of work has increased almost every year during this period. By 2002, 7.6 per cent of workers carried out their work in a variety of places using their home as a base. This accounted for around 2.1 million people in the UK in 2002 (see Table 3.3, column 3).

Census counts are based on an entirely different method of determining where people work. Heads of households are asked to complete forms that record, *inter alia*, the address of each household member's place of work. This data series suggests that the numbers of people with 'no fixed place of work' has been on the increase since 1951, tripling within three decades and accounting for 6.7 per cent of the employed population of working age by 1981 (see Table 3.4, second row). The increase stopped in 1991 and, at the time of writing, figures for 2001 have not been released. Nevertheless, Census results coupled with those emerging from the LFS suggest that work is becoming increasingly detached from a particular place and is being carried out a variety of locations. Company surveys also bear this out. For example, a recent AT&T (American Telephone and Telegraph) global survey of 237 senior executives (AT&T 2003) found that big increases in the proportions of staff working independently of any particular location were expected. In 2003, 19 per cent of companies expected half of their staff to be 'on the road at any one time' and 32 per cent expected half of their staff to be location-independent by 2005. Key to this was the provision of laptops. In 2003, they were distributed to all employees in 14 per cent of companies surveyed, but over a quarter (26%) of companies anticipated being in this position by 2005.

Despite evidence suggesting increasing numbers of people are working on the move, we know relatively little about where they actually work. Accordingly, we collected information on the work locations of 57 car-based users of business facilities provided by a motorway service station operator during a three-week period in spring 2002. We collected similar information from 60 first-class passengers surveyed as they travelled on an inter-city route into and out of London in autumn 2002. Both surveys reveal the multiplicity of locations that are used as places of work. Those surveyed in motorway service stations tended to work in places connected to the car. They regularly used their homes, employers' and clients' premises, and stop-over points *en route* (such as hotels) as places of work. Places associated with other modes of transport, such as railway stations and airport lounges, were less frequently used by these respondents. Two-fifths (42.9%) reported that they often used hotel bedrooms as places of work compared to around one in ten (10.5%) who used airport lounges for similar purposes. Rail users, on the other hand, were less reliant on a single mode of travel and, as a result, their places of work were more varied. Around two-thirds reported sometimes using meeting rooms or bedrooms in hotels for work activities and around a fifth often used the car or plane as a workplace. Nevertheless, we still know relatively little about how workers use these locations as workplaces, what work they choose to do, or where and how they are managed by others in the organization. These questions are addressed in Chapter 6.

Conclusion

It is now almost impossible to 'get away from it all'. There are few places in the world that do not have telephone connections, mobile phone networks and internet access. Some even market themselves as 'no news, no shoes' destinations but even geographically isolated archipelagos, such as the Maldives, are struggling to hold back the juggernaut of connectivity. Even when in transit, connections via mobile phones can still be made. Work can, therefore, seep into the interstices and recesses of our lives. Few, if any, places or times are insulated from the world of employment. Those recorded by the surveys reviewed in this chapter as working in collective offices, at home or on the move are just the tip of the iceberg. There are many more professional and managerial workers who now use the mobile, laptop or internet access to connect to their work. Indeed, it is our expectation that many readers of this book will see some of their own daily work routines mirrored in the stories told by our interviewees in Chapters 4, 5 and 6.

4

Working in Collective Offices

The physical side – I won't say it's the easy part because there is a lot of work to be done in the physical related matters too – but, you know, there's a lot of companies will come to you and say: 'I want to paint my office really zany colours because I want to get my staff more productive.' Well, you know, that just doesn't happen. You can't say that that will lead to that. There's this thing in the middle that happens – and that's the part that people need to focus their minds on.

(Rosemary Laithwaite, Project Manager, Development Council)

Introduction

This chapter explores the implications of movement and stasis within office spaces. It argues that collective offices not only institutionalize the formal principle of mobility within the workplace but, paradoxically, also generate informal pressures to 'stall' or 'colonize' space for personal use. The impulse to stall is, thus, not a product of some atavistic desire for personal territory but rather is generated within the socio-spatial relations of employment.

Whilst conforming to managerial requirements to remain in specified places for specified periods of time, workers can, by stalling, invest their workstations and workplaces with symbols of individual identity and assert claims to a 'position' (that is, a job and a location) in the enterprise. In personal offices in particular, stalling exemplifies the ambiguous and Janus-faced character of much resistance that incorporates both defiance and compliance (Collinson 1992a, 1992b, 1994; Gabriel 1999; Fleming and Sewell 2002). Although visibility and presence have been intrinsic to managerial strategies of control, ironically stalling has, in many work situations, been one of the ways in which workers can resist regulation. Stalling enables workers to narrow or reduce the prerogatives of management, limiting the power of supervisors to reorder their working lives. In collective offices, too, stalling is double-edged since some aspects of the official social order of the workplace encourage stalling even though, at the same time, the formal principles of the office explicitly forbid the personalizing of space. Nevertheless, stalling runs counter to the flexibility at the heart of the collective office, threatening to jeopardize its economic benefits. As a result, collective offices are characterized by managerial interventions designed to prevent individuals and groups monopolizing or recolonizing workstations. 'Stall busting' can take different forms, illustrated by our case studies, but is intrinsic to the management of collective offices. Some advocates of collective offices suggest that anti-stalling measures are merely temporary or transitional arrangements, to be rendered obsolete once staff have fully understood and entered into the spirit of their new workplaces. However, our analysis suggests that, because stalling is itself a product of the spatial organization of collective offices, the struggle against attempts by individuals and groups to recapture space for their exclusive personal use will be continual.

The chapter goes on to argue that there is an affinity between, on the one hand, the socio-spatial organization of collective offices and, on the other, contemporary trends in forms of managerial control – particularly those emphasizing corporate culture, group bonding, individual subjectivities and innovative problem-solving. The link between the two, we suggest, is to be found in the aesthetic of collective offices. The aesthetic realm of social life constitutes a mode of social communication in which knowledge, values and normative codes are transmitted via embodied sensual experiences, such as sight, touch and sound. The aesthetics of collective offices generate social relationships that promote and prioritize perpetual change, polyoptical visibility, serendipitous interactions and totalizing participation in the informal social life of the organization. The capacity to perform and portray these aesthetic dimensions of social relationships is acquired and moulded within the workplace. Our case studies illustrate different ways in which this aesthetic, and associated learning processes, are realized in practice.

As outlined in Chapter 1, one of the research projects that informs this book included case studies of seven organizations that are well known, in the architectural and managerial press, as exemplars of the collective office. In this chapter we have highlighted just two of these, referred to by the pseudonyms Development Council and Cool Marketing. They represented the most developed examples of collective office space that we encountered in our case study research. Some organizations with established reputations in this field proved, on examination, either to have rowed back on earlier arrangements or still to be at a relatively early stage of development. Both Development Council and Cool Marketing, in contrast, had fully institutionalized the abolition of personal space within their central offices. They were, however, were quite different in size, ownership and function. The Development Council employed some five hundred people at its HQ, whereas Cool Marketing's staff numbered just over one hundred. Development Council was a public sector organization, funded from government sources. Cool Marketing was in the private sector, operating in fiercely competitive international markets. Development Council offered advice and support to business clients, while Cool Marketing sold advertising, marketing and promotions. Moreover, there were significant differences in the ways in which they managed the elimination of personal space. Development Council was more formal and bureaucratic in its approach, promulgating and enforcing rules of behaviour. Cool Marketing relied on more informal and communal pressures, backed by personal intervention from individual senior managers.

In Development Council, we conducted nine interviews with staff working in a large collective office, including some responsible for commissioning and implementing the office programme, members of the facilities management team and other staff. We also examined various documentary sources. In Cool Marketing we carried out 13 interviews with staff at all levels of seniority and in a wide variety of functions. Eleven of these were photo-elicitation interviews. Respondents were given cameras and asked to take pictures of the places they occupied within the collective office over the course of a week. This proved very effective, generating 297 photographs. Subsequently, respondents were interviewed about their pictures and their experiences of using collective office facilities. Two interviewees also agreed to make a video diary, which generated over four hours of footage. In addition, the researchers themselves took over a hundred still photographs and, with the aid of a professional camera crew, shot a video depicting the socio-spatial organization and working practices characteristic of Cool Marketing.

Organizations, Aesthetics and Space

Collective offices are characterized by an absence of personal space. Staff do not have permanent workstations for their sole use. Instead, they use facilities that are collectively provided and shared with other workers. Workstations are occupied on a temporary basis by whoever requires them. The distinction between personal and collective offices, then, refers to social and spatial relations entailed in the labour process; the mode of allocating and occupying space is integral to the making of social relationships in the workplace.

Our analysis should not be confused with a crude architectural determinism that proposes a one-way relationship between building design and social behaviour. Such connections are sometimes implied, or explicitly formulated, by design professionals. Some of our respondents, responsible for the development of collective offices within their organizations, were critical of simplistic environmental theories and commented that many would-be emulators fell into this trap.

> We have a huge volume of visitors who come and look at this place. And quite often you discover in talking to them that they're confusing open plan, which we are not, with flexible working, which we are. Open plan is just everybody sitting at desks in a big open space . . . But flexible working is they come in each day with a clear view as to what they are doing that day and what kind of facility they need – and that could be anywhere in the building.
>
> (Bruno Jones, Director, Development Council)

> It's not just the buildings . . . It's seeing how people work in the building. It's talking them through the way of working in the building. It's not about the building itself, *per se*. It's about how people use it.
>
> (Vanessa Frank, Consultant, Cool Marketing)

Another respondent, quoted at the start of this chapter, described the relationship between office décor and employee behaviour by saying: 'there's this thing in the middle that happens'. Our contention is that 'this thing in the middle' is the reconfiguration of social relationships that occurs when individualized and fixed cubes of personal space are eliminated. Changes in office design that alter the look of a workplace without disturbing these fundamental elements in social relationships have only superficial effects.

Space dedicated to the use of one person and perceived as an expression of their unique identity is an historical emergent, a manifestation of what Elias (1994) terms 'the civilising process'. In medieval Europe there was little personal space in birth, life and death (Aries 1973, 1985, 1987; Elias 1985, 1994). Personal space in the architecture of everyday life emerged with the growth of the middle classes and was still very limited within working-class homes until the twentieth century (Bryden and Floyd 1999). In the workplace, personal space did not become widely institutionalized until the advent of the factory system under early capitalism, which emerged at the same time as other disciplinary institutions.

Weber famously described the legal-rational mode of organization characteristic of modernity, expressed in the ideal-type of bureaucracy, as an 'iron cage' that incarcerated the human spirit in bonds of rules, regulations and specialized functions. He might have added that the growing numbers of officials occupied a multitude of personalized iron cages, called their offices. His vision was graphically realized in the personal offices of the mid-twentieth century. The principles of hierarchy, limited responsibility and functional specialization were incorporated into the physical layout of the office. Workstations and workplaces were demarcated as rigidly as occupational roles. In the twenty-first century, however, increasing numbers of organizations are characterized by delayered tiers of management, semi-autonomous teams and flexible job descriptions. Both practitioners and theorists advocate a shift in the exercise of control away from rules and regulations towards an emphasis on organizational culture and personal motivation. 'Liquid' or 'flexible' forms of contemporary organization prioritize the uncertainty and instability associated with creative responses to global competition and unstable social conditions (Bauman 2000).

These trends represent a new balance of internalized self-discipline and external coercion. On the one hand, managerial strategies are couched in terms of appeals to emotional feelings surrounding corporate culture, group membership and individualized subjectivities. On the other, they impose devices that enhance the visibility of individuals and measure their performance against targets (Sewell and Wilkinson 1992; Casey 1999; Mason *et al.* 2002). Bonds forged in informal workgroups are intended to maintain emotional involvement and normative commitment. Appraisals and other evaluation techniques aim to measure performance and reveal individual errors and omissions. Corporate culture has moved from rule-governed coercion to a more subtle form of normative control; 'one that transforms each employee into a self-regulating, self-policing subject . . . hardworking, flexible and docile' (Gabriel 1999:180). Personality – or perhaps more accurately persona – becomes a crucial stock in trade for workers in such organizations.

Whereas personal offices institutionalized bureaucratic strategies of managerial control, collective offices facilitate flexible or post-bureaucratic modes of organization. 'Cellular offices which are seen to reinforce hierarchies, discipline and individualism are being increasingly replaced by group areas encouraging interaction, co-operation and innovation' (R. Harris 1997: 41). However, the relationship between socio-spatial forms of the office and modes of managerial control is not simple. Personal and collective offices are best thought of as assemblies of practices that may be realized in different ways, reflecting specific organizational, historical and cultural circumstances. Indeed, our two case studies have been selected to illustrate some of these differences. Furthermore, in practice, office spaces – like other sites – are often palimpsests that bear the marks of earlier arrangements and represent an amalgam of contrasting forms. Nevertheless, there are fundamental differences between personal and collective offices that give each an affinity with particular managerial strategies. This chapter will explore the relationships between collective offices and managerial strategies that focus on colonizing the cultures of informal workgroups and the subjectivities of individual workers. Understanding this relationship requires an analysis of aesthetics in, of and as organization (Warhurst and Nickson 2001; Nickson *et al.* 2003; Witz *et al.* 2003).

The notion that aesthetics are of serious interest to students of employment is relatively recent (Gagliardi 1990, 1996; Strati 1996, 1999; Cairns 2002; Strati and de Montoux 2002; S. Taylor 2002; Carr and Hancock 2003). In this book, the term 'aesthetic' is not used in its conventional sense. Rather, we conceptualize the aesthetic realm of social life to comprise all social relationships in which values, beliefs, norms and knowledge are communicated through embodied sensual experiences, principally of sight, sound and touch. The aesthetic, then, is a particular type of social relationship. It represents a powerful form of communication that is transmitted through the medium of bodily experiences. Aesthetic codes appeal to the senses, arouse emotions and stimulate a symbolic apprehension of the world. They mobilize specific images, impressions, styles and sensations in the service of general principles. Understanding and appreciating aesthetic codes sharply defines membership, illuminates identities and highlights social divisions.

Strati (1996, 1999) emphasizes that the aesthetics of an organization do not merely refer to surface decorations. Instead, the aesthetic order of an enterprise saturates all aspects of its functions, from its formal presentation of an official image to the outside world through to the minutiae of routine practices in the labour process. Gagliardi explores this notion further with his concept of the 'corporate landscape' (1996: 570–2), comprising the entire gamut of artefacts, spaces, buildings, grounds, objects and people that are produced, mobilized or deployed by an organization. The assembly of this terrain, he argues, transforms mere land into landscape: that is, an image to be seen. Landscape incorporates an aesthetic code that is written into the material world. It is made to be experienced by the senses and, thereby, convey a view of the world to the beholder (see also Berger 1972; Hirsch and O'Hanlon 1995; Feld and Basso 1996).

A classic illustration of the aesthetic dimensions of organizational life is contained in recent discussions of the office chair (Gagliardi 1996; Strati 1996). Chairs are such ordinary and taken-for-granted items in workplaces that they are hardly ever noticed, let alone analysed. Their design normally focuses on instrumental issues, such as cost, ergonomics and safety. However, an examination of the aesthetic of the chair opens up a realm of sociological understanding that has often been overlooked. A brief comparison of the kind of chairs found in university lecture theatres, hospital waiting rooms, community launderettes, railway carriages, royal palaces and prison cells makes it clear that these objects convey symbolic truths about these locations – and the respective roles of those who use them. Chairs embody power, status, hierarchy, order and deference. They do this through the direct sensual experience of their look, feel, shape, texture and colour. A papal throne, the managing director's Bauhaus monster and the headmaster's frayed armchair in the corner of the staff room are all icons of authority. They signify a place in society and in space, both for the sitter and those at their (literal and metaphorical) feet. They establish a presence, even when no one is sitting there. Indeed, in some contexts, chairs are not viewed as items to sit on at all but as representations of authority and codes of behaviour. As Witz *et al.* (2003) point out, chairs in smart hotel lobbies are not primarily for relaxation but rather constitute a *mise-en-scène*, a device for establishing the style of the establishment, the conduct of the staff and the behaviour of the clientele. 'Chairs' can become almost entirely symbolic with little or no material reality, such as 'a chair at the negotiating table' or a 'professorial chair'. Chairs, then, may become the 'signature of the organization' (Witz *et al.* 2003: 15). Their physical form incorporates aesthetic codes that convey messages to those who see and experience them.

As with chairs, so with the rest of the corporate landscape. The aesthetic codes of corporate landscapes can be powerful instruments of social control that become central to managerial regulation of the workforce. Corporate aesthetics insidiously establish hegemonic notions of appropriate behaviour and collective identity. The aesthetics of an organization are produced and consumed by employees and clients, who are both actors in and audiences of their own performances. Aesthetic labour is frequently thought of as an attribute of service work that entails direct contact with clients. However, aesthetic performances are characteristic of all labour processes and are addressed to co-workers as well as clients (Warhurst and Nickson 2001; Nickson *et al.* 2003).

The next section of the chapter will explore the impact of the abolition of personal space on the lived experience of office workers. It will highlight struggles between workers and managers over the social reproduction of collective space, including attempts at stalling by employees and counter measures adopted by management. Following this discussion, we shall examine the aesthetic of collective offices, with particular reference to the implications for group and individual identities. It will be seen that, by maintaining the aesthetic of order of collective offices, stall-busting is a critical aspect of managerial regulation.

Moving and Stalling

Collective offices require workers to move around the workplace to find vacant workstations – described by one of our respondents as 'looking for somewhere to perch'. Some workstations offer specialized facilities designed for particular kinds of tasks, others are multi-functional. All are available on a shared, collective basis. Staff may not know precisely when they will have to find a new workstation or whether a suitable one will be available. Although, as will be seen, there are countervailing pressures that encourage workers to limit their mobility, collective offices institutionalize movement.

> You are constantly moving around, you float.
> > (Polly Chan, Account Manager, Cool Marketing)

> I roam, I just go anywhere.
> > (Declan O'Dea, Planner, Cool Marketing)

> Sometimes I walk up and down the agency all day looking for a spot . . . almost like driving round a typical car park. Just go round and round and round.
> > (Paresh Kapadia, Account Manager, Cool Marketing)

The extent and unpredictability of movement depends, in part, on the ratio of workstations to staff; when staff numbers are low, for example, competition for workstations is less intense. In both case study organizations there had been periods when this was the case. However, both had also experienced rapid increases in numbers of staff accommodated within collective office buildings, mainly as a result of business growth and the centralization of scattered workforces. The numerical flexibility of collective offices had been clearly demonstrated.

Breaking the link between individual workers and personal cubes of space allows floor plates to be reconfigured and the provision of specialist facilities to be rationalized. Under-used equipment and facilities can be eliminated. Multi-functional spaces can be created – such as lobbies, atria, cafés and soft seating areas – that serve several purposes simultaneously and where staff engage in a range of activities. In Cool Marketing the principle of multi-functioning extended to almost all the parts of the building. It was not unusual for staff to greet clients in the same rooms that others were holding meetings, writing documents or making telephone calls. Thus, whilst personal offices typically comprise ranks of identical cells (which may or may not be surrounded by physical walls), collective offices usually contain a mosaic of contrasting locations and places, each with distinctive functions, facilities and milieux.

It follows that whereas personal offices impose a single and unvarying relationship between space, time and tasks, in collective offices there are a range of options open to staff. Indeed, in collective office spaces workers are *required* to make personal decisions about how to match their work tasks and work times to particular spaces. Choices have to be made about what to do, when and where. If personal offices are analogous to one-way streets, which offer few opportunities to deviate from an established order of events, collective offices are comparable to shopping malls where people move around in sequences that differ from day to day and person to person.

All our respondents were able to talk at length about the skills and challenges involved in assembling their working lives. They described how they did different types of work in different types of places, moving to find the appropriate facilities on each occasion. Each day called for the assembly and navigation of paths linking locations in the building, depending upon the particular mix of tasks. Some extracts from our research interviews illustrate respondents' awareness of the significance of processes of assembly.

If I come in and my day is crammed with meetings, then I'll just use a touchdown, plug in, straight onto the system. And I keep returning to that seat and place and tap into my e-mails as the day progresses in between meetings. And that's all I need. If I need to have meetings myself, I book rooms from the meeting suite or hot offices or whatever. Just depends whether it's a small meeting, a large meeting or whatever. And any other time when I think I need a place beyond say touchdown but not a meeting room, then I'll just book a hot desk. If I'm on a touchdown then it's really just a means of accessing my e-mail, keeping on top of things as the day progresses, making phone calls, that kind of thing. If I've booked a hot desk then I've probably got things beyond that that I need to do – whether it is reading material, writing stuff or typing stuff. . . . I have quite a lot of confidential discussions . . . you just book a hot office somewhere in the building.

(Bruno Jones, Director, Development Council)

I look for quiet space when I need it . . . if I really need to write something, I need to concentrate. Then most of the Cool Marketing environment, particularly the [name of team room], is usually not good for that. The [name of team room] is like the default room, that's where I'll go most of the time. Yes, that's my sort of starting point. If I need to have a meeting, I may go somewhere else to have a meeting with someone. If I need to go and work quietly somewhere, then I'll look for somewhere quiet . . . if it's a quick meeting we'll go to the café, if it's a slightly longer meeting we'll look for an empty room that's available. And if it's something where you want to be able to relax and not feel pressurized and just explore a subject, then it's good to get out of the agency.

(Declan O'Dea, Planner, Cool Marketing)

The last quotation also illustrates how collective offices are often linked with other clusters of relationships in plural workscapes, such as working at home and or on the move.

One of the reasons workers in collective offices move around is because their colleagues are on the move too. Tracking down a co-worker may entail cruising the floor plate. However, in our case study organizations probably the main way staff made contact whilst inside the office building was electronically. The most extensively used devices were e-mail and mobile phones; others included fax, desktop video, multimedia programmes, electronic open diaries, answer machines, pagers, text messaging and intranet connections. These were employed for both formal and informal communications. As with working on the move and at home, then, working in collective offices was made possible by portable means of communication independent of fixed locations.

Some respondents regarded collective offices as liberating and empowering, at least for some of the time. They felt free to work in ways that matched day-to-day swings in their mood and changes in job tasks. Each individual was able to evolve their own favoured style of working.

> It's a very pre-industrial way in that we're not regulated by the clock . . . It's much more about meeting over lunch, meeting over coffee . . . it's much more about the natural rhythm of the day than a traditional business timetable. . . . I think it's acknowledging how your body works . . . it's treating time in a more human way. . . . I think what we are good at is helping people to work in the manner that best suits them.
>
> (Declan O'Dea, Planner, Cool Marketing)

However, collective offices were also experienced by some respondents as unpredictable, uncertain and disruptive. Others were ambivalent in their attitudes. There was, however, general agreement that collective offices called for high levels of self-discipline, self-motivation and self-direction (cf the 'technologies of the self' demanded by working at home, Felstead and Jewson 2000: 120–42). These tacit skills were highlighted in both case study organizations but particularly by respondents in Cool Marketing where, as we shall see, navigation processes were less bureaucratized and more informal. There are resonances here with the demands of working on the move, discussed in Chapter 6, which also entail the management of uncertainties generated by mobility.

> I don't think it is as hard to let go of status symbols as the literature might have us believe. I think the harder thing to let go of is just your routine – because it takes more time to build up a new one. It's just a headache you've got to think about when, actually, you just want to focus on getting the work done.
>
> (Rosemary Laithwaite, Project Manager, Development Council)

> It's like giving a free rein . . . you have got to be so much more responsible for yourself. . . . The worst thing is it's difficult to establish routine.
>
> (Polly Chan, Account Manager, Cool Marketing)

It's far less rigid and there's far less structure. It can be quite disorienting.
(Lai Tse, Account Manager, Cool Marketing)

There are days when you feel like a fighter pilot and, you know, you just, you're moving at enormous speed. And there are several different things demanding your attention, you're trying to keep in control of the whole thing. And it's not necessarily very easy.
(Declan O'Dea, Planner, Cool Marketing)

There are, then, powerful forces embedded within the socio-spatial organization of collective offices that generate mobility and flows of staff between workstations within the workplace. There are also, however, countervailing pressures that encourage staff to limit their mobility. These give rise to 'stalling': that is, attempts by individuals and groups to lay claim to exclusive and permanent rights over the use of particular workstations or other locations within collective offices (Goffman 1971). Stalling in collective offices cannot be explained in terms of some innate or primeval urge to mark out territory. Rather, pressures to stall are generated by the practices of collective offices themselves. Prominent among these are: the maintenance of friendships; the demands of team working; the desire to avoid the disruptions associated with particular workstations; the attractions of favourite or habitual spaces; and the inconvenience of transporting documents. The assembly of working space/time by our respondents was constantly unravelling because of these pressures, leading to unscheduled and improvised repair work. Stalling was a way of reducing these uncertainties. It was a coping strategy.

Sometimes stalling occurred simply because friends wanted to be near one another. In Development Council, for example, it was apparent that some staff manipulated the booking system governing access to workstations so that they could sit next to the same people every day.

There's certain areas we could go in and say: 'I knew you would be sitting there, I knew you would be sitting there!' And these are hot deskers.
(Patricia Fine, Senior Team Leader, Development Council)

The desire of friends to sit together is a familiar aspect of workplaces but it is of particular significance in collective offices. We shall argue below that the socio-spatial relations and aesthetic order of collective offices are specifically designed to generate intense social interactions among employees by virtue of high levels of movement. Ironically, the immobility created by friends congregating together frustrates this plan and leads to attempts by management to forbid this expression of buddy group familiarity.

More systematic forms of stalling reflected the prominence of team working in both Development Council and Cool Marketing. Respondents reported that maintaining bonds between team members was a regular cause of stalling. Constant movement between workstations was seen as incompatible with the desire of some teams to establish a territorial base and to huddle together for both symbolic and practical purposes. Some staff felt that collective offices represented a threat to confidentiality and security when project teams were dealing with sensitive materials or developing innovative products that might be leaked to commercial rivals. These concerns found expression in tactics designed to exclude others from workstations.

> There are still a number of people who like to have a team identity. And that sort of stretches to some sort of physical identity – that this is their space and they are the team that are there. And we've kind of resisted this. I personally am not keen on branding every nook and cranny of this building according to who is there, because the whole idea behind the building is complete flexibility. This is corporate space for corporate use.
>
> (Bruno Jones, Director, Development Council)

Often teams wanted to reconfigure office space in ways that ran counter to the aesthetic and social disciplines of collective offices, such as introducing physical or symbolic divisions from other groups and marking out team spaces with signs and symbols.

> Some teams have said that they can only associate, or only form their own identity, if they have some of these visuals around them . . . It's a challenge to us to help them form what they call 'identities' in different ways. Because you can't do that in a building that's predominantly glass; and you can't do that in a building that's predominantly flexible. Because we don't want teams to tailor spaces. That would stop others feeling comfortable going and working in those spaces. . . . You have to nip that in the bud.
>
> (Rosemary Laithwaite, Project Manager, Development Council)

In Development Council some respondents argued that collective offices had increased a sense of involvement with the company as a whole but undermined the sense of membership in task-oriented teams. The inward-looking ethos of teams had been challenged by a broader and more gregarious sense of the organizational 'village'.

> Very much community spirit. But in fact some would say, a *corporate* community sprit – to the disadvantage of, perhaps, the very localized team spirit.
>
> (Anna Connolly, Senior Manager, Development Council;
> respondent's emphasis)

In Cool Marketing the impulse of teams to colonize space was accommodated by the development of project rooms, known as 'client rooms'. Client rooms only lasted for the lifetime of a particular contract. They were not exclusively for the use of one particular team, since other members of staff could work there too. However, team members were expected regularly to congregate in their client room, both for business meetings and more informal bonding. Although not required to work in their client room all the time, they were left in no doubt that they had to be seen there. Client rooms, then, represented an attempt to reconcile the spatial identities of teams with the principles of collective offices.

In Development Council, teams that wanted to be together had to reserve project rooms. These could be booked for short periods or up to three months for longer projects. However, this arrangement was not popular. It was felt that booking represented an additional chore, that it did not allow for spontaneous and unpredictable generation of ideas among people routinely in proximity, and that it did not facilitate the informal social buzz that made for high trust within teams. Building managers responded by suggesting teams made regular bookings of project rooms and by providing guidelines for the use of collective office facilities. They made it clear, however, that it was not acceptable for teams to colonize space.

> What we don't want to do is change back to the team space, physical. Because not only is it not cost effective for us and doesn't reflect the way we work, but also we have achieved this huge sense of belonging with the organization. So I would argue it's equally important to feel part of the big picture as it is to just feel part of the small team.
>
> (Rosemary Laithwaite, Project Manager, Development Council)

Nevertheless, over time, team identity marking appeared to be on the increase.

Our respondents indicated that another source of stalling were attempts to avoid using workstations susceptible to distractions, disruptions and interruptions. Open floor plates and continuous movement of people meant that some workstations were particularly prone to background noise, through traffic, roaming colleagues, and temptations to chat. In these circumstances, stalling was an aspect of assembly: that is, planning to conduct work tasks in suitable sites:

> you're in a room, lot of people, lot of things going on, and trying to have a conversation with a client. And that does get very difficult. That's where having no personal space to withdraw to can be difficult.
>
> (Declan O'Dea, Planner, Cool Marketing)

[A section of the building] becomes the busiest place . . . And it's all moving in and out really fast . . . you want to work there during the day but you know you can't. You can get *nothing* done and you just end up dossing and going for fags.

(Polly Chan, Account Manager, Cool Marketing; respondent's emphasis)

Yet another impulse to stall was that most respondents regarded some locations in the building – particular windows, terminals, hot desks or chairs – as personally more congenial to working than others. In our interviews, a wide variety of idiosyncratic reasons for liking one work-station better than another were offered. It may simply be that the habit of regularly occupying a particular place served as a prompt or cue to concentration.

Storage problems represented another reason to stall. The absence of personal offices and desks in collective offices makes it difficult to consult documents while conducting work tasks. Carrying files and papers all day can be inconvenient and insecure. Although staff in the case study orga-nizations had some storage facilities, in both cases these were minimal. It was, therefore, tempting for them to stall workstations so as to avoid carting work-related baggage around the office.

I'm certainly a nester. Simply because I'm quite disorganized myself. So I know that if I was a nomad then I would tend to lose things and documents.

(Lai Tse, Account Manager, Cool Marketing)

Staff in our case study organizations employed a variety of stalling tactics. Personal items were sometimes used to lay claim to a space. Work-stations were staked out by placing a jacket over the back of the chair, locking the screen or strewing the desk with files and papers. However, such tactics often meet with managerial retaliation. As in our two case studies, it is common for collective offices to operate 'clean desk' policies that forbid personal materials to be left lying around collective spaces, such as hot desks. Such items may be collected and thrown away. Simi-larly, 'clean walls' policies prevent staff from marking territory with posters, pictures, banners or similar items. In our two organizations con-trasting strategies were adopted to counter the spread of stalling. In Cool Marketing stall-busting was informal and *ad hoc*, with enforcement partly communal and partly driven by the personal intervention of senior man-agers. Development Council, however, sought to enforce a corporate code of discipline, that was presented as modern, productive and efficient.

Two deterrents to stalling operated in Cool Marketing: peer pressure – expressed in competition for workstations – and direct instruction by senior managers to specific individuals. Both of these were informal and uncodified. Since there was no effective booking system in Cool Market-ing, workstations were mostly occupied on a 'first come, first served' basis. On occasion, therefore, staff would race to occupy favoured spaces, and groups of friends were said to gravitate together in particular locations. However, some staff regarded this behaviour as – in the words of one of our respondents – 'hogging it', and deliberately attempted to frustrate group bunching; for example, by grabbing the favoured places first. However, client rooms – which were themselves relatively temporary devices that were reconfigured to reflect business demands – were places where project staff were expected to be seen spending a significant amount of time. Stalling could be further complicated by the penchant of staff for treating occupied locations as multi-functional spaces ripe for dual usage.

The other main way in which stalling was frustrated in Cool Market-ing was by idiosyncratic instruction, personally directed by senior man-agers. A high degree of visibility inside the building, combined with the sharing of workstations by all grades of staff, meant that senior managers were fully aware of who was sitting where. The chief executive officer, in particular, strongly believed that constant movement of staff was highly conducive to serendipity and synchronicity, a view he had expressed in a number of semi-autobiographical books. A forceful and charismatic figure, he had no compunction in upbraiding individuals guilty of immobility and ordering them to stop sitting in the same places.

In Development Council, stall-busting took the form of gentle, but firm, enforcement of formal rules of conduct. This was done by a small group of workers – known as the concierge – whose task was to police the use of space in the organization. Access to collective space was regulated by an electronic booking system open to all staff. Large screens distributed throughout the workplace displayed who had booked which facilities, where, when and for what purpose. This was a crucial device in the func-tioning of collective office space in Development Council and was central to official stall-busting strategies. It could reveal the state of the entire spatial system, including the distribution of users, popular hot spots and under-used areas. It provided an overview of the workplace and, at least in principle, identified the location of each person in the building at any particular moment. It was an electronic panoptican. Staff attempted to subvert the booking system in various ways; for example, by not com-pleting all the booking details, thereby making it impossible to trace the individual occupying a particular space or discern whether they were using it in an approved manner. Moreover, to a limited degree, Develop-ment Council staff could obtain workstations without going through the electronic booking system. They might log on at an official touchdown area in the building or they could unofficially squat in a currently unoccupied location. However, both these options were of limited effectiveness. Touchdown areas were designed for short-term use, reflected in their levels of comfort. Unoccupied workstations might be claimed at any moment by those who had made legitimate bookings. The official booking system, then, was the main entry point to the collective office in the Development Council.

The management of the electronic booking system at the Development Council was in the hands of the concierge. Members of the concierge recorded room and desk allocations, toured the building twice daily to check that space was being used correctly, and were empowered to challenge staff not following the prescribed procedures. The internal visibility of the building – characterized by open-plan seating, glass internal walls and a central atrium – greatly facilitated these tours of inspection. The main infringements included hot desks booked out but standing idle, meeting rooms being used by lone individuals, workstations occupied by staff without prior booking, and stalling of workstations. The concierge was expected to enforce a 'clean desk' policy as well as to respond to more general informal breaches of etiquette in a shared environment (e.g. noisy and inconsiderate behaviour). In all these cases, members of the concierge were encouraged by management to advise, re-educate and redirect the culprits. These practices were explicitly referred to as the 'soft policing' function of the concierge.

The social skills of members of the concierge could be tested when dealing with staff in these situations. Most miscreants were more senior than those charged with 'soft policing'. Moreover, in the case of Development Council, the concierge function had been outsourced, making confrontational tactics still less likely. Tact and diplomacy were the order of the day and emphasis was put on appeals for co-operation; as one respondent put it, 'you can't go in with big heavy boots and sort of kick ass'.

Members of the concierge were expected to engage in a subtle process of staff re-education during informal interactions. This included instruction in the procedure for booking workstations, the range of available workstations, the suitability of different workstations for particular tasks, and the codes of etiquette applicable to contrasting locations in the workplace. Concierge were also expected to make staff aware that they should occupy the minimum space adequate for their specific work tasks. More generally, they were expected to encourage staff to anticipate forthcoming work tasks and make bookings accordingly. This called not just for knowledge of procedures but greater self-management.

The 'soft policing' operations of the concierge in Development Council were also intended to instil an ethic of mutual surveillance among staff. Some respondents thought this should be part of a general responsibility exercised by all employees for making collective office spaces work effectively. However, there was reluctance by many to risk directly tackling co-workers. Rather than confront the nuisance themselves, staff were more likely to call the concierge and ask them to discipline people behaving in disruptive ways:

> a lot of people don't want to have to play that role. A lot of people want a media-tor so that they don't have to do that uncomfortable thing.
> (Rosemary Laithwaite, Project Manager, Development Council)

Some problems encountered by the concierge in Development Council were a result of the inattention of staff rather than deliberate sabotage. For example, the members of a meeting that finished early might vacate a booked room without cancelling the unused time via the electronic booking system, thereby freeing it up for others. The concierge would subsequently discover a vacant space that was booked out but unused. However, other problems were the product of more deliberate attempts to stall workstations by circumventing or manipulating the electronic booking system. One tactic was to book out a particular room or desk for the entire five days in advance permitted by the system, thereby stalling the location. This could be repeated week after week. Other staff were said to attempt to negotiate bookings with the concierge inordinately far in advance, even stretching years into the future. Touchdown workstations could be stalled by leaving a laptop running all day, even while the owner was absent.

Concierge, in their turn, deployed various means to frustrate these colonizing strategies; for example, they deployed legitimate bookings in ways that broke up or frustrated the plans of stallers. However, some tactics were difficult to counter and concierge described an on-going struggle to hold back a tide of stalling. Moreover, concierge increasingly found themselves drawn into making sensitive judgements. Thus, for example, one of the accepted grounds on which Development Council staff could lay claim to hot offices – and thus avoid having to use hot desks or open seating areas – was the confidentiality of their work tasks. Concierge found themselves having to judge whether such claims were valid or spurious. Some were clear cut, others more ambiguous. Hence, in reaching their decisions, concierge were required to make delicate enquiries about the grade and general type of work done by particular members of staff. In a similar vein, when pressure on space became intense it could become necessary to reallocate some staff, who had made legitimate bookings, to new locations. In these circumstances, concierge had to make fine judgements about which activities were the most important to the business, and which individuals or groups could be moved with minimum fuss.

It is clear that members of the concierge were pivotal to the effectiveness of collective offices in Development Council. They were engaged in far more than their traditional tasks of materials supply and engineering maintenance. They handled complaints, recorded information, processed data, prepared reports, frustrated stalling and attempted to re-educate staff. Their work entailed social skills, levels of judgement and disciplinary functions not usually associated with junior members of the facilities management team. They were described by a senior manager in Development Council as having a 'huge role'.

> They are not really just about filling the photocopier with paper. They have a far more 'added value' role. . . . The concierge's role is quite crucial to the functionality of the building.
>
> (Anna Connolly, Senior Manager, Development Council)

> The concierge . . . it's such a powerful force! You are going to need it to run the office smoothly, you're going to need it so that everybody's not confused about what's going on, and you're going to need it so that we get these new policies adhered to.
>
> (Rosemary Laithwaite, Project Manager, Development Council)

There was some debate in Development Council about whether the role of concierge was merely transitional. Some managers speculated that, once the disciplines of collective office spaces had been embedded in the organization, the concierge would no longer be needed. However, our research seemed to suggest that their role was increasing rather than diminishing. They mobilized texts, devices and disciplines that were vital in sustaining collective office spaces.

> If there wasn't a concierge my belief is that it will be total anarchy. . . . Definitely. . . . They are behaving themselves at the moment. The place is being monitored, being policed. Take away your monitoring, take away your policing, and the place would go right back to 'this is my desk and nobody else is gonna sit in it'.
>
> (Andy Long, Administrator, Development Council)

Management as an Aesthetic Order

The extent to which corporate landscapes are deliberately designed to achieve specific purposes, and thereby constitute a conscious strategy of aesthetic control, varies from case to case. In some organizations, aesthetic dimensions of the corporate landscape may have evolved gradually and without forethought. In these circumstances, workplace aesthetics function as powerful forms of control but not ones that have been systematically planned. In our case study organizations, however, the corporate landscape was a product of careful forethought, conscious reflection and on-going maintenance. It was for this reason that some respondents were scornful of those who take a less systematic approach:

> it's about the conceptual, it's about the integrated approach. That's what makes this different ... what we're about here is an integrated approach to your workplace and changing in response to your work styles. And it's not just about hotdesking.
>
> (Rosemary Laithwaite, Project Manager, Development Council)

As was apparent in the comments of staff responsible for stall-busting, there was an awareness among respondents of the look, feel and experience of the workplace. A visitor to collective offices may see a certain amount of apparently 'wasted' space devoted to relaxation areas, soft seating, chill-out dens, displays, and so on (Turner and Myerson 1998: 70). When viewed as an aesthetic investment, however, their rationality becomes apparent.

> Not all space has to be productive space. It can be 'thought' space, it can be 'inspiration' space, it can be a place where you wander. . . . It is very aesthetic. What I like about this building is that it's very aesthetic. It's ... much more inspirational. I was trapped earlier, at my last company, in a sea of teak and laminate plastic and tabletops. You know, this— each room has different colour, a different feel, a different vibe. You get different levels of energy.
>
> (Vanessa Frank, Consultant, Cool Marketing)

In both case study organizations, senior management had been heavily involved in the design of the exterior and interior of the workplace. Part of their strategy had been to address the public image of the organization. Development Council respondents were in no doubt that their recently acquired, and boldly designed, building represented a positive setting for their dramaturgical performances with clients (Goffman 1959). It was also apparent that the architectural fame of the premises occupied by Cool Marketing served as a powerful advertisement for the company, projecting an image of radicalism and youth. However, neither of these workplaces had been designed simply to impress outsiders. They were also very clearly intended to shape social relationships *within* the organization.

The aesthetics of personal offices are part of the disciplinary institutions of incarceration and correction characteristic of early modernity (Foucault 1977). They incorporate panoptical surveillance, spatial and temporal disciplines, and the normalizing gaze that were also apparent in the schools, barracks, hospitals and asylums of the period. With the rise of collective office spacing, a new corporate landscape is coming into being. A new aesthetic can be discerned in the professional discourses of designers and architects, architectural magazines, public relations promotions, exhibitions, displays, websites, glossy brochures, coffee-table books and similar outlets. This is a new official spatial discourse, of the kind Lefebvre (1991) designated as 'representations of space'.

Our case studies enabled us to analyse how the aesthetic of the collective office operates in practice and its implications for the exercise of power. We concluded that the lived experience of collective offices focuses around four key dimensions embedded within the aesthetics of this corporate landscape.

- The aesthetics of change
- The aesthetics of visibility
- The aesthetics of serendipity
- The aesthetics of participation.

The Aesthetics of Change

The aesthetic of the collective office emphasizes change over stability, process over structure, mobility over stasis, and uncertainty over predictability. The flexibility and transience of space, thus, conveys general messages about impermanence within the organization. Notwithstanding attempts at stalling, described above, collective offices require individuals to be mobile, adaptable and flexible. The embodied experience of the worker is one of perpetual change. Furthermore, collective offices enable management to reclaim control over the spatial environment of the workforce. The internal arrangements of collective office buildings can be quickly and easily reconfigured to meet developing business needs. With few internal walls – both literally and metaphorically – the claims of individuals in defending their personal territory are readily overcome in the name of stall-busting. Desks can be removed, rooms reorganized, walls reconfigured, spaces redesignated, facilities relocated. Constant adjustments in the distribution, allocation and form of the workplace are intrinsic to collective offices.

Mobility engendered by the socio-spatial organization of the office gradually becomes an ingrained habit or bodily disposition. Our respondents described the process of acquiring the personal skills required to work in this way and an appreciation of its deeper meaning:

> like the first three months . . . when you first start working here you kind of need somewhere to, sort of, be your centre – before you start feeling like it's *cool* to roam . . . especially if you come from a traditional environment where

you're used to filing things and knowing where everything is, umm. . . . And then you gradually learn to . . . you, sort of, start moving rooms.

(Vanessa Frank, Consultant, Cool Marketing; respondent's emphasis)

you are constantly moving around and it— and it engenders this feeling of, 'God I *need* to move around'. You need to move around. You know, if you sit in a place too much [pause], it just gets really heavy and you feel a bit stale. . . . It doesn't suit everybody . . . I think I've become someone that tries to push back and make myself do that.

(Polly Chan, Account Manager, Cool Marketing; respondent's emphasis)

Indeed, in Cool Marketing, to be seen in the same workstation too often was regarded as a reason for managerial reprimand.

I do try and move between [names several areas in the building] so I'm not constantly seen in the same place . . . To get the optimal amount out of [Cool Marketing] I think you'd need to move around at least twice or three times a day. To get that optimal amount from each day in terms of conversations.

(Lai Tse, Account Manager, Cool Marketing)

The aesthetic of change was further heightened in Cool Marketing by a deliberate policy of repeatedly remaking the look and layout of the building; this included internal and external décor, displays and notice boards, furniture and furnishings, and disposition of workstations. Individual members of staff were encouraged to be fully involved in this process; for example, lots were drawn amongst employees to decide who would have the opportunity to redesign the lobby. Winners typically would make big changes from the previous décor, adopting wildly radical designs that promoted their persona within the organization. Hence, the lobby had been home to parrots, opera singers, jungle foliage and erotically funky furniture. It also hosted a continually changing sequence of exhibitions, displays and installations as well as logos, statues, notice boards, fish tanks, newspapers and a tongue-in-cheek screen-based market research poll. All these were threaded in and through functional facilities, such as computer terminals, workstations, phone racks, switchboard and the busy reception area. Moreover, there was no clear separation between the amusing and the practical. Thus, for example, some workstations in the lobby area, which appeared to be the progeny of a Harley Davidson motorcycle and a Star Wars mini-fighter, were actually fully functional and very comfortable computer terminals.

The embodied experience of workers in collective offices is, thus, one of change, impermanence and disorder. Spatial arrangements are temporary, unstable and irregular; the only certainty is that things will not stay the same. The collective office is a 'liquid' building (cf. Bauman 2000).

Liquid. . . . I think of sort of, chemistry, I think of molecules sort of, bouncing into each other. . . . So there's some level of chaos, controlled chaos . . . managed chaos.

(Vanessa Frank, Consultant, Cool Marketing)

This is reflected in hourly movements looking for a 'perch', daily shifts between different paths and navigational routes, and longer-term reconfigurations as the building itself adjusts to changing business needs. The conduct of work itself teaches staff to cope with constant innovation and uncertainty. The parallels with the impermanence and uncertainties of contracts, jobs, teams, projects and careers in contemporary employment relations are striking (Worrall *et al.* 2001).

The Aesthetic of Visibility

Visibility is an embodied experience that shapes subjectivities through surveillance (Sewell and Wilkinson 1992; Lyon 1994, 2001; Ford 1999; Mason *et al.* 2002). The spatial organization of the workplace creates an aesthetic that shapes and moulds workers' awareness of visibility. High levels of visibility in the workplace are not new. However, the transition from personal to collective offices entails a radical transformation in forms of visibility. This can be summarized as a shift from the panoptican to the polyoptican.

The panoptican (Foucault 1977) comprises a central observation post or watchtower from which figures of authority (such as supervisors, guards, medical personnel, teachers) can exercise constant surveillance over the behaviour of subordinates (such as workers, inmates, patients, pupils), who are spatially distributed in fixed locations that maximize their visibility (such as benches, cells, beds, desks). Panoptical surveillance in workplaces, as elsewhere, was not intended simply to reveal who was idling, larking about or under-performing. It was also intended to create a regime of social discipline that would shape the very personality and self-awareness of those subjected to it. The knowledge that authority could see everything the inmate did at any time was expected to inculcate fear, docility and compliance. This managerial regime, then, rested on the presence of workers in fixed places that rendered them highly visible to the centralized gaze of authority (Felstead *et al.* 2003a). The aesthetic of personal office space, and the performance of that aesthetic, embodied those disciplines.

Collective office space fundamentally challenges this mode of control. Collective office space requires workers to circulate between workstations. They are not allocated to fixed points within the workplace. Attempts by workers to create fixed and permanent workstations – that is, stalling –

are actively discouraged by management because they undermine spatial flexibility. As a result, centralized observation posts and watchtower surveillance are rendered obsolete. However, although collective offices render older forms of visibility redundant, they make possible new forms of inspection and monitoring. Indeed, in some ways the visibility of the workforce becomes even greater.

Electronic monitoring – visibility in virtual space – is made possible by the rapid expansion of electronic modes of communication. These devices enable staff to be mobile within the workplace but remain in touch with managers and co-workers more or less instantaneously. In Development Council, as we have seen, electronic monitoring devices additionally included a sophisticated booking system which, when working effectively, provided a comprehensive picture of the location of each individual member of staff and the occupation of each workstation. The electronic envelope, then, enables the panoptical gaze to continue in new contexts. However, in many ways our respondents were more aware of the implications of another mode of visibility associated with collective offices. The polyoptican, as we have called it, incorporates disciplinary powers that supersede those of the panoptican.

Collective offices are typically open spaces with uninterrupted lines of sight. Internal walls are torn down or replaced by glass partitions. Floor plates are clean swept and enable spectators to see clearly in all directions. Buildings have large open areas, such as atriums, cafés and streets. Hot offices have glass walls, hot desks are grouped in bunches or corrals. Channels of movement, such as stairs and lifts, are open and exposed. In Development Council, for example, the main lifts were glass boxes hung in the central atrium, enabling passengers both to be seen and to see into and across all floors. In Cool Marketing movement through the building was only possible via narrow open stairways through the middle of the building, requiring staff to squeeze past or wait on landings to let one another through.

This is all about physical transparency.
(Tanya Grall, Manager, Development Council)

We put in as much glass as we could, in terms of all the rooms. And there was absolutely nothing hidden.
(Anna Connolly, Senior Manager, Development Council)

The sheer opportunity to see what goes on in the organization on any day is just phenomenal.
(Rosemary Laithwaite, Project Manager, Development Council)

Not only do collective offices render inhabitants highly visible, they also create a constant flow of people. Staff are aware that not only can they be seen almost anywhere but also that it is possible that someone will enter their field of vision at any moment. Since staff are visible at a distance across the floor plate, they know that, even when they themselves cannot see someone, they could be under observation from afar.

> It is very open. A lot of people don't like that. . . . a lot of people don't like the fact that the Chief Exec can come up and walk past all the time. I think they just always feel they're looking over their shoulder or whatever.
>
> (Tracey Adams, Administrator, Development Council)

> You don't really know who is round the corner. It could be your senior, it could be your junior.
>
> (Tanya Grall, Manager, Development Council)

> Most of it is deliberately very exposing, you can always see who's in any room . . . you can't hide. There are no ivory towers here.
>
> (Declan O'Dea, Planner, Cool Marketing)

> I know that everyone is watching me.
>
> (Polly Chan, Account Manager, Cool Marketing)

The polyoptican, then, entails the potentiality for all-round, 360-degree, observation by both senior and junior co-workers at all times. Whereas the panoptican institutionalized centralized vision by figures of authority, the polyoptican entails decentralized visibility by all and sundry. As one respondent remarked: 'it's a goldfish bowl'.

In both case study organizations, staff reported that there were ways of escaping the gaze of others, if only temporarily. In Development Council there were back stairs and lifts for those who did not wish to see and be seen. In Cool Marketing there was one room in the building designated as a sanctuary, where staff could shut the door and pull down the blinds. Nevertheless, despite the existence of shelters such as these, by and large staff found themselves highly visible. We were told that, for some, this level of exposure revealed their professional limitations in ways that had not occurred when they worked in personal offices.

> In an open environment like this, these things become far more transparent now. . . . Where people are abusing, misusing or not performing, it just becomes far more visible. That's also why, I would argue, a lot of people have apprehensions about these new work environments. Because if you are one of those few who like to skive a little, then it's a bit more difficult to do and not be noticed, in a space like this.
>
> (Rosemary Laithwaite, Project Manager, Development Council)

Unlike the panoptican, the polyoptican exposes senior as well as junior members of staff. Those in the highest ranks find their daily behaviour and demeanour open to the gaze of those in the lowest posts. Indeed, in collective offices senior managers become known by face to a wide range of staff. Inappropriate chatting, flirting, gossiping or other activities can become common knowledge throughout the workforce. Thus, for both senior and junior employees, in collective office spaces what Goffman (1959) designates as the 'back region' is dramatically reduced. Staff are 'on stage' in the 'front region' for a much higher proportion of their working time.

The Aesthetic of Serendipity

Serendipity comprises beneficial discoveries made through chance encounters. As noted earlier, designers and architects often claim that collective offices generate unplanned interactions that inspire creativity, originality and innovation. Constant mobility and movement in the workplace, it is argued, generate unintended meetings that facilitate productive cross-fertilization of ideas and perspectives. Business gets done quickly, without the need for the wasteful rituals of formal meetings. The design of collective offices, thus, creates the circulation of bodies – and hence an aesthetic of creative coincidences and happy accidents. Several authors have drawn parallels between collective offices and the kind of urban environments advocated by Jane Jacobs in her seminal work on American cities (Jacobs 1965; Gladwell 2000). Jacobs argued that vital, vibrant and safe cities were ones which facilitated unplanned encounters of diverse strangers on streets informally monitored by local residents. Mixing up different institutions and land uses within a neighbourhood, she argued, creates a constant flow of different types of people and, hence, endless serendipitous encounters. Office designers have sought to achieve the same result in collective offices by forcing employees out of their private silos and encouraging through traffic to kitchens, copiers, printers, libraries and other workstations. This view was widely supported by our respondents, many of whom asserted that in collective offices business was done in a spontaneous, informal and flexible manner. In particular, they identified two embodied experiences in collective offices that facilitated these outcomes: 'bumping into' others, and getting to know others by 'osmosis'.

The virtues of 'bumping into' others in the collective office were widely extolled by our interviewees. It was seen as a key aspect of productive work rather than as a distraction or interruption.

> You sort of, bump into people and you have impromptu meetings on the stairs, hanging on the stairwells, sort of half-way, mid between, or at the bottom or

at the top, on the landing. . . . It's because people have to move up and down so much, that's where you bump into people . . . And you find the person that you were looking for at a time that you might not have been looking for them. . . . And you grab the person at that moment and then you get something solved right away as opposed to finding them or e-mailing them or calling them.

(Vanessa Frank, Consultant, Cool Marketing)

I believe in the concept that new ideas come from old ideas rubbing together . . . by people bumping into each other on the stairs. . . . I think that the day is full of little transitions and the stairwells and the corridors and the little narrow spaces are very, very important. The conversations you have there are as important as the conversations you have anywhere else. And I think the more of that the better . . . It's really important.

(Declan O'Dea, Planner, Cool Marketing)

The idea of the hot desk is that you bump into different people, that it will spark off different conversations. And it will, and it does do that.

(Polly Chan, Account Manager, Cool Marketing)

In Cool Marketing, lunchtime was regarded as particularly conducive to 'bumping into' other people in the organization. In a delicious twist on Strati's (1996) analysis of the chair, described above, we were told that seating arrangements in the café had been designed deliberately to promote maximum interactivity.

Our café, it's like school benches . . . you can't sit by yourself because it's a bench and you have to move the bench to sit down and, you actually have to sit with people. . . . It's really hard to just sit on your own. . . . And you have to sit next to, you have to scoot up next to somebody.

(Vanessa Frank, Consultant, Cool Marketing)

what is good is coming down and just having to find a place. And finding out who you end up next to. That's good, I like that. . . . I think it's important. . . . Just trying to find somebody to chill with and . . . maybe talk to an unexpected person.

(Declan O'Dea, Planner, Cool Marketing)

A second form of serendipity in the collective office, described by one of our respondents as 'osmosis', comprises a range of oblique methods of information-gathering. These included unobtrusive overhearing, eavesdropping and observing co-workers, facilitated by movement through the workplace and temporary occupation of workstations in proximity to colleagues who are not close associates. 'Osmosis' was, in effect, the lived experience of the polyoptican.

You kind of get an eavesdropping gossip, like, a lot. Unintentionally working in rooms, you just get things by osmosis . . . things that don't necessarily have any pertinence to you in a traditional working manner, that can spark ideas. . . . You're doing other things but you're, kind of, on the edge of your peripheral vision and hearing, you're sort of picking up things. . . . So you're not left out. . . . I mean, it's a sort of entertaining sidelight. And then sometimes it allows you to have a connection with that person, to have a conversation about something completely different at some other juncture in time. . . . And so you kind of get to know people without actually knowing, having to ask questions to get to know them. You kind of get to know people by osmosis.

(Vanessa Frank, Consultant, Cool Marketing)

Several respondents suggested that the ease and informality of these everyday serendipitous encounters shaped the conduct of more formal and planned business meetings, making them more direct and encouraging staff to talk to seniors without fear.

Let's talk to those people who I can get an answer from. Let's not confuse all this by going through bureaucracy . . . this [office] is a model that better supports that. . . . If I know he is the guy that knows about [name of client], then I just want to talk to him. I don't need to worry about how big his office is, and can I approach him. You are not inhibited – the opposite.

(Rosemary Laithwaite, Project Manager, Development Council)

As a result, staff were said to be more willing to approach their line managers with problems and queries. Ironically, for senior managers this made working at home part of the time more attractive because it shielded them from interruptions.

Having a greater visibility means that they see me, they think they can speak to me. And that's lovely [but] I'm either at formal meetings or I'm caught at my desk in informal meetings. Therefore, where and when do you do formal work? End up doing it in twilight or at weekends . . . so I diary out, for a year in advance, a [day] to be my home working day.

(Anna Connolly, Senior Manager, Development Council)

Although random social interactions could be inspiring, they could also seriously disrupt planned work schedules; 'bumping into' others could be another way of describing a litany of interruptions. Our respondents believed that coping with the distractions of collective offices called for distinctive subjectivities and personality characteristics that revelled in unpredictability and spontaneity, sensing that this was where the career action was to be found.

You tend to follow the noise despite the fact that you've got a lot of work to do. If you really want to work you can hide away . . . but I think conversations are a great part of Cool Marketing. In fact the defining part, I suppose. You have so many different conversations, you're allowed to contribute to so many different ideas and projects in the building.

(Lai Tse, Account Manager, Cool Marketing)

I'm really nosy and inquisitive and I don't like to miss stuff and I like to move around all the time. I see the advantages of doing it within a work environment; in terms of, like, speaking to people and just finding out what's going on. And I know for a fact that . . . you can miss out on doing something or not know about something . . . purely because you weren't sitting with those people.

(Polly Chan, Account Manager, Cool Marketing)

The Aesthetics of Participation

A number of authors have drawn attention to the 'totalizing' qualities of contemporary managerial controls, arguing that they permeate all aspects of workers' identities and awareness of self, leaving no room for dissent (Schwartz 1987a, 1987b; Willmott 1993). Work-based activities, it is suggested, swallow up ever greater proportions of employees' waking hours. Work tasks call for wholehearted involvement in team and corporate culture. All employees, including managers, are subject to surveillance. Workers' core senses of self and identity are, thus, forged within organizational controls. There is an attempt insidiously to mould the ways of thinking, feeling and acting of individuals (Sewell and Wilkinson 1992; Parker 1995; Du Gay 1996; Gabriel 1999, 2002).

The spatial organization of collective offices generates embodied lived experiences that facilitate this kind of worker subjectivity. The aesthetics of collective offices promote 'totalizing' participation within the organization. The mobility, visibility and interaction of collective offices create an atmosphere of heightened social intensity and engender a strong sense of togetherness and identification with others. Individuals are absorbed into the organization, conceived as a transcendent unity. In our case studies, this was a conscious managerial strategy.

Very much wanting it to be an inclusive and integrated organization, and very visible and transparent. . . . In our previous building we had all been just simply so separated, even in one floor. . . . So there was no kind of wrapping around or sharing anything.

(Anna Connolly, Senior Manager, Development Council)

Performing the aesthetics of collective offices does not require mere compliance but calls for fluent command over proactive forms of behaviour (Hochschild 1983). Bureaucratic regulations may be capable of implementation with weary indifference or overt cynicism but the performances of the collective office require a greater degree of vitality and involvement in order to be credible. This is one of the most important – and neglected – ways that corporate cultures become individual identities. Participation in the aesthetic of collective offices colonizes the self.

Absence of back regions, high levels of mutual surveillance and constant fleeting encounters all put a premium on the performance of identity and the presentation of self. The popularity and perceived personality of the worker become crucial work assets. Recognition of identities is a currency that runs through informal interactions and career progress.

> You are a personality and recognized in the agency. And I think people tend to flock to you if you are known for that. And that could lead on to a whole different spectrum of possibilities. . . . Being a personality here at work is very much part of being at Cool Marketing.
>
> (Lai Tse, Account Manager, Cool Marketing)

> Your personality is allowed to shine through much more here than at any other company I've ever been in before.
>
> (Vanessa Frank, Consultant, Cool Marketing)

> You would have to be quite ballsy, I think, socially. I think, you know I think shy people would find it very difficult here. I should think they would disappear.
>
> (Declan O'Dea, Planner, Cool Marketing)

Staff become emotionally vulnerable if they are unable to command acceptance from others.

> It's a bit in your face, overwhelming. . . . You're very exposed emotionally here. Because there aren't hiding places, there aren't. You can't hide behind a job title. You can't get things done just because you're 'X' title. You have to persuade people to get things done. Whoever you are. I don't think you can ever say 'do this because I say so' in here.
>
> (Declan O'Dea, Planner, Cool Marketing)

Establishing a credible persona may require convincing and culturally skilful participation in extra-curricular activities. In our case studies, these ranged from musical performances at group meetings, through organized in-house social events, to organized activities in the outside world. In Cool Marketing in particular, staff meetings entailed a mixture of business agendas, informal socializing, high jinxes and cult rituals.

In highlighting the participative qualities of collective offices, architects and design professionals often invoke the concept of community, frequently in idealized and simplistic ways. They draw analogies between workplaces and villages, utilizing terms such as 'streets', 'neighbourhoods', 'meeting places' and 'village green' to describe locations within the collective office. This terminology was also current among several of our respondents, who emphasized the interactive and all-embracing character of their workplaces.

> I think all of our open spaces are, are sort of streets . . . like our café is the Town Hall . . . then all the stairwells and, sort of, the walking spaces, are sort of our village streets where you kind of bump into people and have conversations.
>
> (Vanessa Frank, Consultant, Cool Marketing)

> For this building the idea was a sense of community. . . . This building for me is a small village. You come in and you've a vertical street. . . . You then have different kinds of spaces. You've got your communal area and café area, which is very pleasant. You have your more dedicated eating area at the back. You have leather sofas and slightly more informal space. You then walk up onto a meeting room floor and you have your boulevard street here, with your trees and the cafés. . . . Your corner shop, where you can go for everything. Very much that philosophy.
>
> (Anna Connolly, Senior Manager, Development Council)

In addition to metaphors of community, our respondents also portrayed the collective office as the home of a corporate family. The idea of the organization as a happy family – sometimes boisterous and belligerent but ultimately loyal and affectionate – has entered corporate idiom and management speak (Casey 1995, 1999; Gabriel 1999). Family metaphors emphasize the depth and breadth of corporate ties – their totalizing grip.

> There are some people you get along with more closely than others. There are distant cousins, there are people you see on a daily basis, there are family members that you're close to that you have a love–hate relationship with – you really respect them but there are times when you actually fight it out. And I think in most organizations outside of this place, people don't fight it out and so the relationships aren't as deep, right? So, if we've never got in an argument and actually hashed something out, and gone to blows with each other, then we have a fairly shallow relationship. . . . Some people have tempers and they shout and they fight. . . . It's just like any relationship, you know, you sort of, you voice your issues.
>
> (Vanessa Frank, Consultant, Cool Marketing)

Familial metaphors acquire greater apparent credibility when, as in collective offices, the aesthetics of home and work are blurred. Hochschild (1997) has described how workplaces increasingly resemble domestic spaces. She highlights ways in which long hours spent with colleagues at work increasingly become reference points in the identities of office workers. In similar fashion, the collective office represented a major point of focus not only within our respondents' workscapes but also within their whole lives.

> I rarely spend the whole day working at home . . . because, you know, you miss the interaction.
>
> (Lai Tse, Account Manager, Cool Marketing)

Aesthetic markers play an important role in this process. In the home, décor and furnishings are sources of meaning and identity (Chapman and Hockey 1999; D. Miller 2001; Bennett 2002). When workplaces become charged with aesthetic messages that imitate and reflect those of home and village, similar processes of psychological identification can take place. A workplace with intense aesthetic appeal, with high consumption values and designer expressions of identity, may become a home from home. It may be experienced not as an economic or political unit but as a symbolic universe, expressing and generating desires and emotions (Gabriel 1999: 190). The *office* becomes a haven in a heartless world (Willmott 1993; Parker 1995):

> you tend to find people staying here until eight, nine o'clock at night, playing pool and table football and just generally chatting. Because it does feel so much like a home environment. And your work colleagues are actually your good close friends. You do so much together. You go out after work together. You have all these bonding experiences after work in the workplace.
>
> (Lai Tse, Account Manager, Cool Marketing)

It is interesting to consider the rise of the office *as* home alongside the emergence of the office *in* the home, discussed in Chapter 5. Ironically, the office in the home frequently incorporates an aesthetic that is reminiscent of a traditional personal office, whereas the office as home draws upon an aesthetic that is derived from attributes of domestic life. Turner and Myerson (1998: 1) argue that: 'Organizations become the family for our working lives, and their physical surroundings become our professional home.' They go on to suggest: 'New fashions in interior design are starting to suggest that the distinctions between the office and domestic domains – in furniture, lighting, materials, technology and so on – may no longer be meaningful' (Turner and Myerson 1998: 13). The office as home is an environment that has many facilities and comforts, some-times exceeding those found at home and mimicking those of hotels or vacation resorts (Hochschild 1997; Zelinsky 1997). It is true that paternalistic employers have always provided recreational opportunities for staff, but in the past these were located outside working spaces and were intended to be enjoyed 'after hours'. Now, increasingly, they are the work-place. Overall, then, the aesthetic of participation blurs the boundaries between work and non-work, creating a more unified lifeworld.

> What I find with this place is that your work person and your home person come much closer together.
>
> > (Vanessa Frank, Consultant, Cool Marketing)

> Work and play are kind of mixed up together.
>
> > (Polly Chan, Account Manager, Cool Marketing)

Learning to Portray the Aesthetic

Workers do not appear fully prepared as performers of a corporate land-scape or workplace aesthetic. Rather they are groomed, or 'made up' (Du Gay 1996), to become competent representatives of the organization. In this process, they may come to incorporate organizational aesthetics into their personal style but they may also subtly reinterpret workplace aesthetics in their own performances. Hence, their performances are not merely mechanical reproductions of fixed scripts. Witz *et al.* (2003) suggest that aesthetic orders are transmitted to workers in various contexts, including: selection processes that focus on acceptability rather than suit-ability criteria, induction programmes concerned with imbuing corporate cultures, and performances that foreground personal skills and aesthetic performances over technical skills.

In Cool Marketing, a rigorous selection process included consideration of personal qualities and acceptability criteria (although in Development Council, the recruitment process placed less emphasis on the tacit skills required for effective functioning in the collective office).

> We have to be really tough about recruitment. We have to be honest about how hard it really is.
>
> > (Declan O'Dea, Planner, Cool Marketing)

A number of respondents commented on how difficult they had initially found it to develop new technologies of the self, associated with planning, managing and defending the spatial and temporal sequencing of work tasks in collective offices.

It's this pain barrier, just getting through this transition phase. It's almost a third discipline of becoming more organized . . . it is something that is time consuming in the early stages but once you get the new habit, then it becomes your new routine. People don't actually want to push themselves through the pain barrier if they don't need to. So there is an element of management really have to encourage that and really have to push that out.

(Rosemary Laithwaite, Project Manager, Development Council)

You sort of gradually become more comfortable with having to run up to grab a piece of information, and moving to another room, and moving several times during the day.

(Vanessa Frank, Consultant, Cool Marketing)

The aesthetics of participation in collective offices – reflected in the intensity of relationships among co-workers – represented a barrier to some newcomers.

It's hard . . . because when you first walk in, it really looks like they're so friendly with each other . . . it feels cliquey, as you're walking in. It feels intimidating . . . because everybody looks like they know each other so well. I think it's hard for people to realize that, actually, the people don't know each other well – that there's different degrees of knowing each other well and those relationships have formed over time.

(Vanessa Frank, Consultant, Cool Marketing)

In Development Council, members of the concierge were an important source of training in making the best of collective office spaces. In Cool Marketing newcomers were more likely to pick up tacit knowledge in interaction with others, although a proactive approach was likely to be required.

You have to be quite fierce. It's quite, it's weird, it's always very friendly, but it's quite opaque when you first arrive. Because it's very, very hard to figure out quite who's friends with who and why. And how particular relationships and groups work. . . . They probably won't approach you unless you, kind of stick your hand up and go, 'please pay me some attention'. . . . Basically you have to just be fearless.

(Declan O'Dea, Planner, Cool Marketing)

Some respondents recalled that an initial failure to master aspects of the aesthetic of the collective office, such as coping with polyoptical visibility, had resulted in specific directions from managers.

When I started working here, I found it very, very hard, to be doing things –
to do something and having people watching you do it. I wanted to go away
and do it on my own, kind of thing. And I was able to do that. But at the same
time I was told, 'You *must* spend more time in the [client room], you know,
"with your team".'

(Polly Chan, Account Manager, Cool Marketing; respondent's emphasis)

In most cases success had involved developing a heightened sense of
self-awareness combined with self-control, vividly described by one of our
respondents.

You know, like when you have a bottle of coke and you open it and all the fizz
rises to the top. . . . And you know that it's going to spill over and you turn the
top to keep it all in – and then you open it slightly, and then you close it again,
you open it slightly and you close it again.

(Polly Chan, Account Manager, Cool Marketing)

Conclusion

This chapter has explored the implications of the absence of personal
space within collective offices for the lived experiences of workers and the
efficacy of managerial strategies of control. It has argued that collective
offices institutionalize movement and flows within the workplace but also
generate forces that prompt workers to stall. Stalling represents an on-
going site of contention between management and workers within
collective offices. We have further argued that, whilst collective offices
undermine some of the central elements of long-established strategies of
managerial supervision, they also introduce new forms of social engagement that facilitate innovative ways of regulating the workforce, through
the construction of embodied experiences incorporated in the aesthetic of
the workplace environment.

Gabriel (2002) has suggested that the 'iron cages' of Weber's legal-
rational modernity are being replaced by the 'glass cages' of post-
bureaucratic organizations, mobilized around flexible consumption of
image and spectacle by customers and workers alike. Collective offices are
part of this landscape. Although they are places of work, many collective
offices acquire the characteristic features of palaces of consumption and
theme parks, replete with 'disneyization', branding and emotional labour
(Sorokin 1992; Bryman 1995, 1999, 2004; Davis 1996; Gottdiener 2001b).
Their appeal to staff is comparable to that of shopping malls and urban
spectacles to consumers – locations in which workers frequently find
themselves and in which they forge powerful social identities (Hannigan

1998; D. Miller *et al.* 1998). The rise of social interactions of these kinds appear to eclipse the harsher worlds of capitalist exploitation and bureaucratic regulation; they re-enchant a disenchanted world (Ritzer 1999). However, their ultimate purpose remains that of profitability and control, achieved by manipulation of the desires and fantasies of consumers and workers who seek to participate in the parade of signs and symbols that acquire increasing salience within much twenty-first-century capitalism (Lash and Urry 1994).

The collective office thus transmutes workers into actors on a very visible stage. They are required proactively to perform the organization, their jobs, their careers and their selves. At the same time, they consume and evaluate the performances of colleagues and peers. This kind of work situation puts a premium on the capacity of individuals to project a convincing display, evoke appropriate cultural symbols and show an easy familiarity with current styles and signs. Sullen acquiescence will not do; charm is the order of the day. These features of social interaction are intended to obscure and mystify the underlying inequalities and insecurities of wage labour within flexible organizations competing in globalized capitalist economies. Thus, collective offices foreground aesthetic labour within the organization itself, not just to customers and clients outside (Nickson *et al.* 2001; Nickson *et al.* 2003; Witz *et al.* 2003). As a result, what our respondents referred to as 'character' becomes of crucial significance to the performance of work. In this context, character comprises the skills of outward display, attractive performance and perceived acceptability, rather than those of inner direction (Knights and Morgan 1991; Sennett 1998). These are what it takes to participate in the workplace carnival, such as making an impression while 'bumping into' potentially useful others. Self and identity become stock in trade. Emotional intelligence becomes as valuable an asset as rational intelligence (Goleman 1998). As Gabriel remarks: 'Salesmanship, showmanship and acting are the essential virtues of the flexible individual' (2002: 8).

It should not be thought, however, that the denizens of such workplaces are incapable of resisting the forces that seek to control them. In the wider world, it is apparent that, from time to time, groups of consumers reappropriate or reinvent the styles of popular culture, translating them into narratives of rebellion, fantasy or escapism. Similarly, under some circumstances, it is possible for workers in collective offices to recapture elements of the informal buddy group culture that management seeks to manipulate and, thereby, shift the balance of power. This is made possible, in part, by changes in the currency of regulation within the collective office. Senior staff are subject to polyoptical visibility as well as junior. Managers are required to become part of the bonhomie of compulsory fun, potentially exposing them to the sanctions of satire and banter. Such countervailing pressures may not be capable of reversing power differentials but they can sometimes amend them (see, for example, the ways in which female shop floor workers deploy ribald banter against male managers: Pollert 1981, Westwood 1984). The collective office may, then, be a contested aesthetic.

The space/time disciplines of personal offices called for reliable attendance at designated places and sustained diligence through specified periods of time. This office worker was a *keeper* of times and spaces imposed from above. In contrast, the challenge of the collective office entails the construction of times and spaces of work from a range of different options in the face of a variety of competing demands – and making those times and spaces productive despite the likelihood of disruptions and interruptions. Collective office workers are *makers* of times and spaces. It may be that these proactive skills and aptitudes stand them in good stead in creating their lives inside and outside their workscapes. It is important to remember, however, that resistance is frequently a complex and double-edged form of behaviour (Gabriel 1999; Fleming and Sewell 2002). Indeed, the actions of workers are rarely entirely compliant or entirely rebellious. They are more commonly rooted in a shifting amalgam of attitudes, beliefs and identities that weave together complex and ambiguous threads of confrontation and conformity. Stalling in the collective office is a case in point. In some instances, stalling can be a form of direct opposition to, and defiance of, the socio-spatial organization of the collective office. However, in many cases, stalling is derived from the impulse to achieve objectives and pursue relationships that the collective office is specifically intended to promote. A crucial issue for future research, therefore, is to determine under what conditions collective offices are effective in colonizing the lifeworlds of workers; and under what conditions workers in collective offices succeed in creating spaces and times of irony, detachment and misdemeanour.

5

Working at Home

I'm aware that some people can't concentrate at home. They get distracted because there are so many other things they could be doing . . . Some people find it really quite difficult, actually, the discipline of working in an unstructured environment.

(Adele Dickens, Consultant)

Introduction

The lived experience of those who work at home is shaped, on the one hand, by spatial proximity to the domestic life of the household and, on the other, by geographical distance from co-workers in the organization. These twin characteristics, intrinsic to the social relations of home-located work, pose distinctive dilemmas and challenges. Responses to them generate a range of different ways in which people construct their lives.

The close proximity of domestic relationships and environments draws home-located workers into negotiations with other household members over the use of time and space. Our research suggests that most professional and managerial home-located workers and their families respond by devising workstations in their homes that closely resemble what we have called personal offices; that is, insulated cubes of space, dedicated to work purposes, that sharply delineate between paid employment and the domestic sphere. Thus, although plural workscapes are associated with the emergence of collective offices elsewhere, they tend to generate personal offices in the home. Nevertheless, a minority of home-located workers in our sample did experiment with other ways of combining home and work. For all, however, arriving at acceptable solutions to these challenges called for self-discipline and a range of 'technologies of the self' (see Felstead and Jewson 2000: 120–42).

The geographical distance between home-located workers and their colleagues, particularly managers, is responsible for another set of uncertainties and ambiguities. As we have argued above, managerial strategies of control have long rested on the visibility and presence of workers within employers' premises. The absence of continual surveillance associated with working at home is a mixed blessing for many employees. It creates opportunities for enhanced autonomy and, even, for evasion or avoidance of managerial supervision. However, the corollary can be feelings of isolation. Access to information, guidance, advice, support, instruction, tacit knowledge, learning contexts and promotion prospects can become difficult. The supervisory relationship can become problematic. Our research suggests that workers and managers adopt a range of responses, with varying degrees of success.

This chapter draws on interviews with 60 professional and managerial employees who worked at home and their partners (120 respondents in total). In 37 households, the home-located workers were male and in 23 they were female; all worked at home for at least 40 per cent of their working hours, most for longer. In ten cases it transpired that the partner/spouse also worked at home. Interviews were conducted in employees' homes. Wherever possible, partners were interviewed separately. All respondents were married or cohabiting; 12 households contained children of pre-school and/or primary school age. Respondents were asked about the distribution and use of household spaces, the timetables of household members, the division of domestic labour, and the impact of home-located working on their lives. With their permission, we also took over 300 photographs of respondents' workstations and surrounding areas. In addition, we interviewed 82 line managers, directors and policy-makers in 13 case study companies that had established programmes of home-located working. They were asked about their experiences of managing home-located workers, the drivers of this type of working and support for home-located working within the organization – as well as more general questions concerning organizational structure, the labour process, managerial strategies and the history of the enterprise.

The next section briefly explores the underlying institutional context within which working at home takes place. The chapter then goes on to consider the issues raised by carrying out work tasks in the home, with particular reference to boundaries of time and space. This is followed by an analysis of managerial strategies of control and the potentiality for resistance they entail.

Workscape Meets Homescape

Media stories frequently portray working at home as conducive to uninterrupted productivity and family harmony (see, for example, *Financial Times* 2002; *Independent on Sunday* 2003). However, people whose lives bring workscape and homescape into close proximity face the challenge of reconciling competing demands of two contrasting worlds, based on different principles and practices. As with our discussions of the collective office and working on the move, then, we will be concerned in this chapter with the management of ambiguity and uncertainty. To appreciate the sources of these challenges, we need to recall the features of household relations that mark them out from relations of employment.

The separation of home and work during the course of industrialization had huge implications for identities and selfhood. It was crucial to the social construction of age, gender, marriage, sexuality, parenting, leisure, labour, time, place, discipline and personality (Allan and Crow 1989; Mack 1993; Benjamin and Stea 1995; Chapman and Hockey 1999; Moore 2000). It has been fundamental to the emergence of the separate spheres of public and private life (Humphries 1982). It has shaped the organization of cities. It has delineated leisure and non-leisure. Social security payments and welfare policies are grounded in this institutional separation. Basic feelings of self-confidence, generalized trust and being in the world – 'ontological security' – are achieved by situating ourselves within and between home and work (Giddens 1991; Dupuis and Thorns 1996, 1998).

Notions of 'house' and 'home', then, carry personal symbolism, cultural meaning and ideological significance (Davidoff *et al.* 1979; Saunders 1990; Silverstone and Hirsch 1992; Madigan and Munro 1996; Valentine 1999; Bhatti and Church 2001; D. Miller 2001; Bennett 2002). Although reality often differs from the ideal, home is represented in numerous contexts as a place of escape, sanctuary, privacy, individuality and security; 'a haven in a heartless world' (Lasch 1977; Madigan *et al.* 1990). The relationships of home are organized around bonds of gift exchange rather than market-based ties. The look of the home is often regarded as an indicator of personal status and values. The feelings of home are embedded in relationships between family and friends. It is, of course, also true that the strength of such ties can make home a site of physical violence, emotional cruelty and personal oppression, much of which may be hidden from view. However, for *all* these reasons, home has become a crucible in which unequal but highly personalized power relationships are forged between men and women, adults and children.

This, then, is the site in which home-located workers seek to conduct paid work. The principles and practices of employment relations are quite different from those of home. There is a far greater requirement for public scrutiny, instrumental calculation, formal regulation and market-based exchange. Two very different ways of life are brought into close physical proximity, each with their distinctive timetables, rituals, rules, etiquettes, practices, values and ceremonies. The extent to which this poses serious issues for any individual depends on a variety of factors, including family circumstances, financial resources and emotional disposition. There are a range of processes through which these tensions may be resolved, largely depending on the character of relationships among household members and those between workers and managers. Furthermore, the spatial and temporal responses to these dilemmas can take a variety of different forms. This chapter seeks to map and analyse some of this diversity.

The current growth in home-located working has occurred at a time when the home itself is becoming far more technologically sophisticated and 'informated' with ICT (Zuboff 1988; Darrah *et al.* 1997; Gurstein 2001; Avery and Baker 2002). Indeed, in some respects, it is the general presence and acceptability of communication technologies within the home that makes home-located work possible. Contemporary houses are places of considerable investment in electronic devices devoted to consumption, leisure, friendship and family. This generates both a cultural familiarity with ICT and the possibility of interweaving the electronic envelope of home with that of production and work. Furthermore, the blurring of work and non-work relationships in the home is mirrored in business organizations. The collective office, described in Chapter 4, is a particularly intense example, but other workplaces, that retain some degree of personal space, are also experiencing this trend. Hochschild (1997), for example, detects a tendency for offices in the USA to become campus-based, offering a wide variety of social and leisure facilities and activities, either directly or indirectly. With long hours spent at work – combined with 'pure relationships' (Giddens 1991) at home that may heighten stress, frustration and disappointment – the workplace may increasingly be seen as more 'homely' than home. Our analysis of the totalizing aesthetic and culture of the collective office illustrates one way in which workplaces can become a primary focus of relationships, commitments and sense of self.

In the language of sociological theory, these are system changes rather than social changes. Our interviews are concerned with the social responses of workers and managers to these systemic developments. As we shall see, the responses of some appear to be quite conservative; particularly those who go to great lengths to recreate the separation of space, time and activity of work and non-work within the home. Physically, psychologically and socially, they attempt to insulate workstations from the rest of the home, thereby creating workstations that resemble personal offices. However, although the actions of many may seem conventional, they are nevertheless responding to new challenges with novel solutions. Our interviews reveal on-going processes of negotiation, reflection and experimentation by our respondents, both workers and other household members. Often they have little access to the domestic lifestyles of other employees engaged in the same challenges. Hence, by and large, they had to work out their own solutions with little collective guidance and with few available role models, other than those communicated in simplistic media accounts.

Proximity to Household Relationships

This section of the chapter examines the processes by which those who work at home manage the proximity to other members of the household and the domestic landscape, particularly how they make and sustain boundaries of space and time within the home (Beach 1989; Ahrentzen 1990, 1992; Armstrong 1999; Felstead and Jewson 2000; Steward 2000; Sullivan 2000; Tietze and Musson 2002).

Spatial and temporal boundaries surrounding workstations within the home are often complex. They may shift through time, depending on the domestic activities taking place, or who is present, in the house. Desks and computers that are used for work activities between certain hours may be reclaimed by other household members for non-work purposes; such as homework, playing games or e-mailing friends. The precise delineation of these boundaries may have to be negotiated case by case. Spatial and temporal boundaries that are clear cut in one context may become shaded and problematic in another. Although there may be general understandings of the hours worked by home-located employees, other household members may shift their expectations when domestic crises develop, such as burst water pipes or a sick child. Some working times and places may be permissible, others negotiable and yet others out of the question. Their acceptability is likely to be shaped by their location within the home and their conjunction with domestic timetables. It should also be emphasized that boundary-making within the home has a history; today's arrangements incorporate past negotiations, changing family circumstances and evolving household memberships. Thus, the routines and rhythms of the home as a place of work are a palimpsest of shifting space, time and activity.

Time

For our respondents, managing the temporal boundaries of home-located working primarily entailed: getting started at the beginning of the day, maintaining uninterrupted periods of work activity, controlling the duration and conduct of short breaks, and bringing long periods of work activity to an end. Each of these will be considered in turn.

Getting started called for psychological and social processes of distancing from domestic timetables and engaging with those of employment. For workers who begin their days by commuting to an office, this transition is activated by physically leaving the home and is framed by the interstitial times of travel. However, those who work at home need different cues and signals that indicate to themselves and other household members that this switch is under way. They must disengage from the social relations of home while physically remaining in the house. In our sample, this was easier for childless employees than those with dependent children. One of the former commented:

> I get up and . . . put my jeans on . . . shave and I am ready for the day.
> (Rory Mansfield, Buildings Surveyor)

Home-located workers with children found starting work much more difficult and, unsurprisingly, dependent children created the most disruption. Getting children awake, dressed, breakfasted and off to school could all too easily encroach on the timetables of work. Nevertheless, these tasks could also provide a structure to the beginning of the day that, despite the difficulties, framed the beginning of work.

> I'm pretty strict. About, oh, half past eight, they walk out the door, I walk in the study . . . half past eight I'm in there.
> (Kevin Fenning, Consultant)

Childless respondents deployed other prompts to begin work at the start of the day. One relied on the canine members of her household.

> I get up at six and that's to feed the dogs. It sometimes takes me two hours to get the dogs organized – walks, breakfast and that sort of thing. [Name of partner], I suppose he probably leaves around 7.30, by which time I'm already out with the dogs. I come back, he's gone, the dogs settle down quickly because they've been walked. It's just really easy, you know, just start work.
> (Olivia Wareing, Marketing Manager)

Others drew on familiar rituals that mark the start of the working day.

> A cup of tea first, I think. And recording my message. That's the first thing I do, is record my [voicemail] message. So those are the set things I do.
> (Sarah Hinds, Senior Project Manager)

Our research sample included 12 home-located workers with children of pre- and primary-school age, seven of whom were male. Only one of these men took responsibility for delivering children to and collecting them from nursery school, the remainder depending on female partners to provide this aspect of childcare. These women were either not in paid work or were employed part-time. In two of the remaining five households the home-located worker was female, working part-time, with a partner employed outside the home. One of these employed a nanny, the other undertook the 'school run' herself. In the other three households both partners worked at home. Two employed nannies and one shared the delivery and collection of children. Respondents who employed nannies, or other hired help, arranged starting times so that these helpers could look after children in the mornings and take full responsibility for a range of tasks, including shopping, cooking, washing, ironing and escorting children to clubs and activities. This form of childcare was only used by couples with young children and, although costly, was cited as the ideal form of paid care.

These arrangements appear to reflect complex interactions between the gender, employment status and occupational level of home-located workers and their partners. Of crucial significance was whether the home-located worker and partner were in paid work and, if so, whether they worked full-time or part-time. Where the home-located worker was employed full-time, routine childcare was usually done by someone else, such as a partner not in employment, a partner employed part-time or hired help. Although this pattern appeared to hold for both male and female home-located workers, gender is of course heavily involved in determining the occupational standing of household members. Where the partner of a female home-located worker was employed in a demanding full-time job, childcare was likely to be delegated to a third party, such as a nanny. Female home-located workers were thus more likely to employ nannies. During working hours, none of the female or male home-located workers we interviewed attempted to combine childcare with paid work. However, those responsible, prior to beginning their own work, for preparing and transporting children were likely to be employed part-time.

Once the working day has begun, home-located workers confront the challenges involved in maintaining productive activities in the face of various disruptions. Our respondents said that working at home mini-mized interruptions; it was considered a particularly fruitful venue for tasks that required concentration and thought. Nevertheless, there were interruptions from colleagues, clients and co-workers who wished to discuss business matters. In addition, friends, relatives and neighbours sometimes regarded someone physically located in the house as, by defi-nition, available for social visits or friendly conversation.

It was on my birthday or something and [my father] had got me a present and he wanted me to try it on . . . And I was like conducting a business call and it was really crazy. And I was like, 'No. I'm not here, you know, I'm working here'. And I got quite cross and I think I basically said; 'Go! I'm working and you shouldn't be here'.

(Phil Prince, Project Consultant)

Educating other people that when you're at home you're not available for coffee, to go shopping or for somebody dropping in [is not easy]. I had to be quite firm to start with and say 'I'm working at home'. People now know.

(Margaret Tatler, Social Services Inspector)

Those who work at home usually find that the main source of disruption comes from within the household, principally children and partners. Even though nearly all the parents we interviewed arranged childcare with others (either domestic partners or hired help), working at home when children were in the house could still be problematic. Some worried that noisy children threatened their ability to work in a professional and productive manner. An on-going challenge for parents was that of enforcing strong boundaries around their working times and teaching children not to interrupt. Male and female interviewees spoke of similar approaches to coaxing their children to respect their temporal and spatial working patterns.

The kids know that upstairs there is Mummy's office and she's at work and they do not go and interrupt her. She may come out of the room every now and again and come downstairs, but once she's upstairs they do not interrupt. If they go upstairs they don't make a noise because she could be on a phone call.

(Anthony Ball, partner of home-located worker)

I've told them that if they come into the study they have to be quiet. They haven't to keep coming in asking me things. . . . if Ross [respondent's son] wants something to drink or eat he has to ask Beth [respondent's daughter] to get it for him. And Beth gets their lunch and that kind of thing.

(Roberta Arnold, Adviser)

I just wave at them [children coming in from school] and tap the earpiece. And they know that if I'm on the phone, they've got to wait to come in.

(Amanda Squires, Relationship Manager)

In some households, ensuring that children continued to respect these boundaries shaped the roles of nannies and hired carers.

We have an understanding that with [name of the nanny] the children come first. So she knows that when she's here, she's responsible for the children and if they come to me, then she'll try and remove them from me. When the children are here and she's here and I'm here, it's her that makes the decision for the children. So, they wouldn't come and say, 'Mummy, what are we having for dinner?'

(Adele Dickens, Consultant)

They have to ask her [the nanny] if they want to talk to me. Sounds ridiculous but . . . it's the only way. And they're not allowed to interrupt. And if the door is closed that's it, which most of the time when they're around it is. . . . Since they've been little they've understood that it's out of bounds.

(Louise Blount, Senior Associate Director)

Most parents we interviewed were successful in disciplining their children, but some struggled to create and maintain time boundaries. Even those who had established temporal divisions found it easier when their children were out of the house.

It is easier when they go out and then you can have a bit of peace and quiet. I must admit at the end of the school holidays when they go back to school it's bliss, to actually work in an empty silent house! [Laughs]. Much better.

(Cathleen Ball, Adviser)

A number of respondents suggested that the presence of someone working within the house created tensions and conflicts that affected all the occupants. Several partners of home-located workers spoke of how stressful it was to keep children away from workstations.

I'm always conscious if the children come in [to partner's work room]. They're touching the papers and the work. 'Don't touch that, don't open the drawers'. So there's nothing relaxed about it.

(Claire Tompkins, partner of home-located worker)

Others found it difficult to keep children quiet when managers, co-workers or clients were visiting the home.

The majority of home-located workers that we interviewed who were parents felt it was legitimate for them to expect their children to be quiet during the daytime. Many were frustrated by the distractions in their working lives caused by their children. Furthermore, they were worried about the impression that apparently unruly children might make on superiors, colleagues and customers.

When [name of daughter] is in the dining room and I am, say, in the lounge, if she is playing, screaming, I can hear her. I keep the door shut and my customers can hear her. They know that I am at home and they don't really like to think you are working at home.

(Emma Watling, Bank Manager)

Some had gone to considerable lengths to stifle domestic noises.

We've got locks on the living room door and on this door – but because the toilet's upstairs, the kids are often coming up and down the stairs. And there's a bit of screaming and fighting when the two of them are about. And I'm very conscious that when I'm in here, even with the door shut, that the noise does travel.

(Tony Tompkins, Adviser)

However, at the end of conventional office hours, domestic claims over the times and spaces of the home were increasingly reasserted, even when employees were still engaged in work activities. Thus, our interviewees were less worried about clients and others hearing the noise generated by their children outside traditional 'office hours'.

There was one time Keith [respondent's manager] was speaking to me and it was about six o'clock and Tilly [respondent's daughter] decided . . . she wasn't going to stop. And I had to say: 'I am sorry Keith. I am going to have to get back to you'. And he said: 'That is fine, I understand'.

(Emma Watling, Bank Manager)

I'm conscious that if I can hear it then the person on the other end of the phone can. . . . But if it's in the evening then I don't make any apologies for it at all.

(Tony Tompkins, Adviser)

Although most did not like being disturbed by their children while working at home, some parents had strong views about how much they would allow work to impact on family time. Thus, as well as putting boundaries around the activities of children, they also sought to impose boundaries on their own activities as workers. Most notably, those who had been compelled to work at home by their employers felt uncomfortable about silencing their offspring. They considered, first and foremost, the house to be their children's domain.

We don't want it to be that [name of daughter] doesn't have friends round . . . And, of course, they want to go screaming up the stairs, shouting and whatever else . . . Because, at the end of the day, it is their home as well.

(Emma Watling, Bank Manager)

Similarly, in some situations the role of parent was seen as taking precedence over that of worker.

You do feel responsible if the kids are sort of really playing up and they need a damn good talking to that Dad can do. You do feel obliged to go and do that.

(Tony Tompkins, Adviser)

However, in some households, exactly where these divisions of time and space should be drawn were a source of friction between partners. Temporal and spatial boundaries were contested. For example, one respondent was critical of her husband's inability to create a window of time in his work schedule for his daughters. She was also unhappy that his work prevented the family from enjoying their home in the way she felt was appropriate.

> Even when we were in our other house, when the kids had the music on or something like that, it's 'Sh, sh, sh'. When they come home from school – they get home about 5 o'clock – that's a cut-off point. Because this is their space as well. Because *they've* been to work, so they need to come home and do that. So, [addressing her husband] *you* need to acknowledge them. The kids have come home from their job, so you need to switch off from your job. But then they have to be quiet in order for you to carry on doing your job.
>
> (Jennie Roberts, partner of home-located worker, respondent's emphasis)

Children were not the only source of distraction for employees working at home. Some interviewees regarded creating and maintaining boundaries with their partners as even more testing. Furthermore, the emotional dynamics and power inequalities of relationships with partners were quite different to those with offspring. Some respondents were drawn into delicate negotiations and sensitive interactions, not always with success.

> If Helen from time to time feels a little bit down, or wishes to procrastinate, or wishes to talk to me, she comes into my office. And I have been known to say, 'Look, would you come into Luton to talk to me about this? Do you mind just going away and we'll talk about it later?' Because I don't want unnecessary interruptions. I can't see the point.
>
> (Derek Hoyle, Adviser)

In this case, as in a number of others recorded in our interviews, uncertainty surrounded the different meaning imputed to brief encounters between household members by the parties involved. The home-located worker wished to define the situation as primarily one of business rationality. His partner perceived it as an informal exchange of affection, governed by rules of gift exchange and mutual grooming. She jokingly, but pointedly, responded to his remarks with the observation: 'Do people bring you cups of tea in Luton?!'

Similar misunderstandings characterized another interaction, recorded in our interviews, between a home-located worker and his partner.

I mean Claire will come in sometimes and talk to me sort of about the kids. And I just think, 'Just go away. I'm not interested, I'll talk to you about it later'. I think she does get a few rebuffs that probably hurt her occasionally, but it's not a personal thing. It's just that I'm . . . in work mode. I mean, I'm not so blinkered I can't switch between the two, but sometimes I think, 'I must make these kind of phone calls' and just don't want interruptions.

(Tony Tompkins, Adviser)

This respondent's wife offered a different account. She felt the treatment she received fell below the standards of etiquette that applied between colleagues in offices, let alone spouses in the home.

I'll always knock on the door first to see if he's on a phone call rather than sort of walk in . . . But I can always sense when, you know, he doesn't want to chat. It'll be, 'Oh yes, oh right, OK' and, you know, you can sense when he's in work mode. . . . Sometimes [I am] a little bit irritated and you think, 'Well, you're here'. You know, if it was a work colleague you'd probably stop, put your pen down and talk then, sort of thing.

(Claire Tompkins, partner of home-located worker)

As in other workplaces, home-located workers often take short breaks in their working days, punctuating long stretches of activity with brief periods of relaxation. These might take the form of a short stroll, hot drink, quick lunch or brief conversation. Home-located workers have additional reasons to engage in these practices because they spend long periods of time alone. Hence, controlled breaks may be a way of relieving isolation (Felstead and Jewson 2000: 134–6).

It's funny . . . when I'm at work I don't consciously have a coffee break or a tea break but I do when I'm [working] at home . . . I do consciously make an effort to have a break . . . you're not getting the desk interruptions that you would get in the office. So, if I had desk interruptions, I'd be less inclined to have a break. Because some of the desk interruptions you get are not always work-related, are they? [laughs]

(Sarah Hinds, Senior Project Manager)

A few home-located workers said how important the garden was for allowing them to restore calm.

When I have had enough of phones and aggravation and stuff, I just get myself a cup of tea and stand out in the garden for twenty minutes or so. I'm quite lucky, I live next to a nature reserve, so it's quite peaceful and has lots of birds and things flying about. And it just brings me back, do you know what I mean?

It sort of gets you out of the white heat of the office and the phones, and all the aggravation and the problems, and just sort of allows me to come back to earth a bit. It is sort of probably the most valuable tool I have got in my job, working from home.

(Rob Davies, Sales Manager)

However, there is scope for misunderstanding when such breaks take place in the home. The scripts and etiquettes governing the beginnings and endings of domestic interactions are different from those that routinely apply in workplaces. Abrupt openings, compressed farewells and ritualized dialogue are familiar in many workplaces but may be misconstrued in the kitchen or bedroom. While it is acceptable to close down conversations with colleagues when busy, it can be more difficult to do so with a partner in the home who wishes to strike up a conversation about matters of emotional significance to both parties. Moreover, partners and children may not understand why the home-located worker can take respite breaks when they need them but not interrupt their schedule when other members of the family want to chat.

Laptops and mobiles make extending working hours, or breaking into family time to deal with a work task, ever present options. As a result, some interviewees found it difficult to tear themselves away from their screens and return to the domestic sphere at the end of the working day. When in 'work mode', to use the phrase of a respondent quoted above, they found it difficult to switch off. In these circumstances, work pushed back the boundaries of home and family life.

Sometimes . . . you might nip upstairs and the answer machine's flashing and you think, 'I wonder who that is'. So you have a look, and it's somebody you've been trying to get a hold of all day and their message says they won't be in tomorrow and, before you know where you are, you've phoned them. And then that leads onto another phone call and, before you know where you are, you're working again.

(Cathleen Ball, Adviser)

There's a temptation on Saturday when the post comes to be nosey and have a look – 'Oh well, I'll just do this because I'll be busy on Monday'.

(Jayne Black, Adviser)

This inability to draw a line between work life and home life was the source of tension between several couples. A number of home-located workers were said by their partners to suffer from 'workaholism'. Others complained about the noise which working at home created, claiming that telephones ringing and night-time faxes disturbed family life.

One of the features of working at home that can make switching off problematic is the absence of intermediary or transitional times between paid employment and other activities. There is no journey home at the end of the day, providing a relief valve and an opportunity to refocus. On leaving their workstation, home-located workers are immediately launched into the domestic sphere.

> You walk out here where the kids are noisy and that. And you just haven't had any down-time. . . . Although driving home is stressful, it is that period of switching off from work and switching on to home that you don't get with working at home.
>
> (Tony Tompkins, Adviser)

> He walks out of that door, just across the hallway . . . If he's been out to work on a visit or something, that journey in the car, even if it's only five minutes or thirty-five minutes, to unwind and just, you know, have that break. But now he comes in and there's all the children sort of jumping over him, making a lot of noise. I think he does find that difficult to cope with sometimes.
>
> (Claire Tompkins, partner of home-located worker)

In summary, then, time takes on new dimensions when working at home. In some respects, timing is more within the control of employees, with working schedules more directly open to construction by workers themselves. However, the use and meaning of time may become an issue of debate and contest with other household members. Moreover, in some respects time may become less easy to control, precisely because of the absence of fixed and imposed hours of work.

Space

In this section we turn from the temporal to the spatial boundaries of working in the home: in particular, the characteristics of workstations devised by or for home-located workers and their implications for relationships with other household members.

In a study of industrial and manual workers, Felstead and Jewson (2000:144–5) summarized two approaches to organizing working space in the home (Haddon and Silverstone 1993; Haddon and Lewis 1994; Salmi 1996, 1997; Michelson and Linden 1997). The first approach establishes a clear separation between the spaces designated as domestic and those allocated to employment within the home. In this situation, there are clear spatial boundaries between areas dedicated to different purposes, thereby replicating the conventional divisions of home and work under the roof of the household. The second approach is characterized by integration within the home of sites of domestic and employment activities, thereby blurring the boundaries between work and non-work locations. In extreme cases, the spaces of home and work may even become fused or synthesized into a third entity.

One of the aims of the research reported in this book was to explore how professional and managerial staff organize spaces of work within the home. Our findings suggest a continuum stretching from strict separation through to the wholesale integration of domestic and working spaces (cf. Nippert-Eng 1996). We identified five points along this continuum, each representing a distinctive socio-spatial configuration of home and work (Magee 2000; Felstead *et al.* 2004). We have termed these:

- detachment
- juxtaposition
- assimilation
- collision
- synthesis.

Moreover, our interviews suggest that these spatial arrangements had temporal dimensions. Thus, for example, working spaces that were strictly detached during agreed working hours could be assimilated as general family space at other times.

'Detachment' was the most common way our interviewees organized working space in the home, accounting for three-fifths of the households interviewed. These respondents established clear and precise physical and aesthetic divisions between working spaces and domestic spaces, with sharply contrasting décor and ambience in the two sites. Usually this meant that the workstation was located in a separate room. Entry was often delineated by strong symbolic and physical markers, such as doors, stairways and corridors. In one household a 'do not disturb' sign underlined the point. In some cases rooms had been converted to offices in such a way that nothing indicated they were actually part of a home. Furniture and decorations had been purchased from business catalogues. Separate telephone lines had been installed. Props, such as business-type pen sets and office-type pot plants, further embellished the scene. Outside this space the aesthetic of the home ruled, with nothing to indicate that one of the nearby rooms comprised a workstation.

Detachment, thus, re-creates the spatial categories of work and home under one residential roof. It was perceived by most of our interviewees as the ideal socio-spatial scenario because it minimized interruptions from children and partners, provided employees with an environment that prompted concentration, and compartmentalized work.

> The opportunity arose to give me this private confidential area that I could take the job and keep the job there.
>
> (Derek Hoyle, Adviser)

> I do like to work and be separate . . . I don't sort of spend the days when they're here thinking, 'I'd rather be downstairs playing with them [the children]'.
>
> (Cathleen Ball, Adviser)

Some respondents had gone to great lengths, and expense, to create this arrangement within their homes. Hence, ironically, our research suggests that working at home is a growing aspect of the workscapes of professional and managerial workers but one which is likely to generate a traditional type of personal office that is being eroded elsewhere.

It was noticeable that most of our respondents who had opted for detachment nevertheless, at certain times, also shared these spaces with other household members. It was understood by all concerned that the home-located worker had first claim on this space during agreed hours. However, others sought to reoccupy these locations outside these times or once they had been vacated. Most home-located workers we interviewed were happy to share, as long as they had first call. However, these divisions could become the subject of negotiation.

> The difficulty is in the evenings because they want to use the personal computer. Well, my daughter does. And I sometimes need to look at my laptop, so we do have a conflict. . . . We just agree: 'You have a look at your e-mail and hurry up!' [laughs] and: 'I'll do this when you're finished' . . . it's just a question of agreeing.
>
> (Ian Fisher, Project Manager)

Several commentators have argued there are gender differences in the way space is organized in the home and that this is reflected in the spatial ordering of home-located work (Ahrentzen 1992; Haddon and Silverstone 1993; Salmi 1997; Sullivan 2000). They report that women who work at home are less likely than men to work in a separate room. In this view detachment is a gendered option. However, this was not the case among the professional and managerial employees we interviewed. Male and female home-located workers in equivalent jobs were equally likely to opt for detachment. However, the opportunity to adopt this strategy was shaped by household income (determining the size and numbers of vacant rooms) and stage in the family life course (determining numbers of children and other household members competing for space).

'Juxtaposition' was the second most common way of organizing working space within the home, accounting for a fifth of our households. It refers to a spatial organization in which work activities are clearly demarcated from the rest of the house but in which they are in close proximity to, and visible from, the domestic sphere. Two worlds are maintained but within touch, sight and sound of one another. Hence, the aesthetics of home and work are juxtaposed but do not impinge on one another. A common arrangement here was for a workstation to be located in a room used for other purposes, such as the corner of a bedroom. Sometimes the room was symbolically divided by curtains, furnishings or other objects – leaving the workstation marooned in the middle of a domestic world. In some cases, the appearance of workstations had been made more domestic by choosing furniture and fittings perceived to have a 'homely' look or ambience, softening the visual contrast. As a result, furnishings in work areas were more liable than in the detached scenario to have cosy overtones, rather than being sparse and strictly business-like.

Juxtaposition was common among employees with smaller houses and those with resident children who occupied all the bedrooms. However, some home-located workers found that this spatial organization problematized their capacity to manage working times, such as the ability to 'switch off'.

> I now have a workstation in our bedroom, which isn't ideal. Not because of the space issue, because the bedroom's fairly large. It's not that we don't have enough space. But it's not good to have your work facing you when you're going to bed [laughs] . . . I'm sure that I don't relax and sleep as well as I used to [when I had a separate home office].
>
> (Cathleen Ball, Adviser)

'Assimilation' was a socio-spatial configuration adopted by approximately one in ten of our respondents. It refers to a spatial form in which the aesthetic and ambience of the home swallows up or obscures that of work. As a result, work activities are invisible to both outsiders and household members for all or part of the time. Typically this is achieved in one of two ways. In some cases the workstation is temporary; all signs of it are cleared away at the end of each work session. Thus, for example, the home-located worker may operate on the dining room table between meal times. Alternatively, where workstations are permanent, they are heavily overlaid with domestic decoration or décor that camouflages their real purpose. This configuration represents the triumph of one spatial and temporal form (home) over another (work). By these means, the aesthetic of the home is preserved and the presence of work disguised or obscured.

Several of our interviewees adopted this way of working during the daytime, with the dining room being the most common location. Work was cleared away every evening, either to make way for the evening meal or to act as a signal that the working day was over.

> I don't have a spare room I can hide myself in. For those with older children or a larger house it's perfect, because you can actually shut yourself away and call that your workplace. With me, I tend to sort of set up and I'll close down again and put it all back in the bag, sling it in the back of the car for the next morning.
>
> Everything's on the laptop. I don't print anything off. I've got no files, nothing like that. I wouldn't want the house to be cluttered up like that, really. That's why I don't even have a printer at home. I think they're ugly, big horrible things . . . I just don't like office equipment in the house. But if I had a spare room, I probably would have it more decked-out and available.
>
> (Stephen Drury, Middle Manager)

Assimilation was more likely to be regarded as a viable option by those who worked at home for relatively short periods of time or only when the house was empty. Some respondents reported that they had started working at home in this way but found it ineffective.

> When I first started, I used to just sit in the kitchen and work. And then that got a bit . . . fraught really, because you had to clear everything away.
>
> (Jayne Black, Adviser)

A small number of households adopted the socio-spatial configuration we have called 'collision', accounting for about one in ten of the sample. Collision is a spatial ordering in which the activities of both domesticity and employment compete for the same space. Elements of work and non-work occupy the same locations, overlapping or colliding with one another in more or less harmonious fashion. This pattern might be confined to a part of the house or spread throughout the home. Thus, for example, one of our respondents worked in a room that functioned as his office but also contained non-work artefacts, such as family games, personal trophies, compact discs, a piano, and so on. This room was used by and accessible to the whole family. Home and work mingled.

> The family computer's in there and a few books and things like that are in there as well. And one of the things that the children do like to do from time to time is go on the internet or play on the computer games. And computer games tend to be quite noisy, so that can be a bit of a problem sometimes in the school

holidays. But basically they just have to understand that if I'm working they can't have it at 50 decibels and it has to be turned down to 5 decibels [laughs] . . . if they disturb me then they know they have to go.

(Roberta Arnold, Adviser)

Collision, therefore, represents a significant move along the continuum from separation to integration. Internal boundaries and barriers between different kinds of activities within the household are less obvious and more attenuated than in any of the three socio-spatial models considered thus far. However, this spatial type does not truly blend the two worlds of home and work into a new synthesis or third type of space. Rather, the aesthetics of home and work remain recognizably distinct, even though they are mixed up together.

'Synthesis' was empirically the least common and least developed of our socio-spatial models among our respondents. Only one or two households could be said to have taken this approach. Synthesis represents a genuine combining and blending of two elements to make a new third entity. Boundaries and divisions between home and work are not just disguised (as in assimilation), or eroded (as in collision), but rather are superseded and replaced by a seamless unity. A new aesthetic, that transcends the divisions of home and work, comes into being.

A female executive we interviewed, working for a high tech company, had achieved a high degree of synthesis in the room where she worked. She had brought together antique furniture, chintz patterns and standard office equipment to form a seamless web. A nest of antique tables supported her printer and her in-tray stood on a nineteenth century blanket box. No attempt was made to hide or separate office equipment, which formed an integral element of the décor. She had deliberately chosen unobtrusive items of equipment that would fit into the scene, as well as commissioning a craft worker to produce custom-made wooden filing cabinets. Office facilities were permanent and visible items that were incorporated into a multi-functional space that also served as sitting room and guest room. Furthermore, the door of this room was never closed because our respondent enjoyed looking in when passing and did not want to isolate part of her house as a workstation.

[Respondent's employing organization] have supplied us with the sweetest little printer, fax and scanner. They're tiny, it's marvellous. I use a laptop rather than a PC because it's smaller. When I first thought of the idea of working from home . . . I just imagined this room full of ginormous filing cabinets, great big sorts of desks and I just thought, 'Oh no, I couldn't do that from home'. Now in fact the equipment is so small, it's so easy, it just fits in. I've got an old antique desk – my grandmother's – so the laptop sits on that, whereas a great big PC just wouldn't. The filing cabinets, I bumped into somebody at a trade fair who did woodwork and they made me the filing cabinets. . . . It's just across the corridor from my bedroom and I just feel that I quite like to be able to sit there. I quite like to feel it's integrated. I don't want to feel that part of my home has become a no-go area and should be shut off.

(Olivia Wareing, Marketing Manager)

In a few households, elements of synthesis emerged at certain times of the day. In the evenings, several parents worked in the same location as children doing homework. Notably, though, this only occurred outside normal working hours, when detachment was the preferred option. Other interviewees were less happy about space sharing and, in truth, reluctantly accommodated their children's presence.

The five-year-old has started to use the computer, so he comes in, plays the computer games, and that sort of thing. But generally, I call it 'Daddy's Room' as far as the kids are concerned. And they know it's not a room where they come and bring their toys in. But they'll come in to do things and so on.

(Tony Tompkins, Adviser)

Although the majority of our interviewees had created only one dedicated workstation in their home, a number said that, on occasion, they roamed around working in a variety of locations. Some worked in various parts of the house, in addition to the detached areas that had been designated as their workstations, in order to add variety to their working lives.

Sometimes I work in [detached office] because that's where my main computer is. Occasionally, or quite a lot of the time, I work out in the conservatory, because it's nice and light in there and a lot of the documents I can just read. I have worked out here [on the patio]. So I haven't got . . . one fixed working place.

(Don Rice, Consultant)

Thus, some respondents combined several spatial arrangements in their working lives. However, in general, employees with young children were less able to perform work tasks outside the designated spaces they had negotiated for themselves.

In a few instances, disagreements about the distribution and form of space in the home had generated conflicts that culminated in the imposition of spatial divisions by one household member on another.

When we were designing the office, I thought I was getting a lot more space than I did . . . He calls it 'his' office. It's not 'ours', it's 'his'. It really concerned me when I realized he hadn't really designed it for me to work in. He'd designed me a workspace but not one that I could work in.

(Adele Dickens, Consultant)

In most cases, however, the social-spatial order of the home had been agreed between household members through negotiation and discussion (cf. Finch and Mason 1993; Jensen and McKee 2003). Such negotiations were often continuous; they were driven by processes such as families growing older, children leaving home, elderly parents moving in, job demands changing, new properties being purchased, older houses being extended, and so on. Hence, in many instances, the socio-spatial order of the home was not simply the choice of the worker but rather emerged from joint decision-making. Moreover, just as the physical parameters of workstations were often negotiated, so too were their aesthetic appearance. One respondent described how his wife and daughter had redecorated his home-located office as a surprise. Although undoubtedly an act of benevolence, it also ensured that this space acquired a distinctive look.

My daughter had done a 'Changing Rooms' job on it. . . . the colour scheme you would think wouldn't stand a prayer, but it actually works. That's a pale green and that's a yellow and that's a blue and the door is red. . . . And they've put photos up, or pictures up . . . I think it's great, I really, really do. I am very, very proud and pleased with it.

(Peter Boughton, Principal Consultant)

Decisions about changes in the use of domestic space could be poignant. In some cases, cramped spaces occupied by home-located workers were a result of grown-up children, no longer living at home, continuing to store their belongings in the domestic nest. One or both of their parents were reluctant to clear their rooms for sentimental reasons or because they felt it inappropriate to disturb their children's possessions. This scenario highlights the delicate emotional calculations and symbolic significances at play in negotiations over the use of spaces in the home.

Another issue that caused underlying tensions concerned the feeling of some partners of home-located workers that they had come under a new kind of surveillance within their own homes. Of the 31 male home-located workers we interviewed, 17 had partners who were not in work or were employed part-time. Several commented that they had become accustomed to exercising a high degree of personal control in the home during the daytime. They found it disconcerting to have their partner present, particularly when partners made significant claims on household time and space. These women felt they had lost some of their autonomy in the domestic environment and spoke of feeling monitored in ways they had not previously experienced.

> I just feel that I should be doing things. If I want to sit and watch TV all day I feel that he might come in and say 'You should be doing something else'. He can watch what I'm doing! . . . I don't feel I can always necessarily relax.
>
>   (Amelia Ashton, partner of home-located worker)

> I didn't like it at all at first. . . . I didn't feel sort of relaxed about it all, I think. And also, sometimes at lunchtime, he'd come out . . . and lunchtime used to feel a bit . . . that he might be checking up on me to make sure I was doing the jobs. It's better now, but, yeah, I didn't feel quite so relaxed in the home.
>
>   (Claire Tomkins, partner of home-located worker)

Some of these women felt guilty if they relaxed while their partners were working elsewhere in the house.

> I was used to having the house to myself and feeling that I could come and go as I please . . . I guess I would feel guilty. I don't know why I would feel guilty about sitting out in the garden and Rory was upstairs working away. Which is what I would do if I was at home in previous summers, but I didn't feel necessarily comfortable. I would only really do it if Rory had to go out and I would go and sit in the garden then. I won't feel guilty, because he is not up there working.
>
>   (Alethia Mansfield, partner of home-located worker)

Others commented on restrictions to their social lives.

> I always feel reluctant to invite, say, other mums and people round when Tony is working at home. You've got to be quiet because he's on the telephone a lot and that sort of thing. I am always reluctant to ask people round unless I know Tony is going to be out, you know, visiting someone with his work. Then, you can invite people round with their children.
>
>   (Claire Tompkins, partner of home-located worker)

More generally, it was apparent that the routines of home-located workers' paid work took precedence over the rhythms of unpaid domestic labour.

> We have this system that if she's going to Hoover upstairs she'll say 'I'm going to Hoover upstairs, is that all right?'. And I'll say 'Yes, of course it's all right.' But if there was an important phone call, and she was right next door to me, I'd sort of say, 'Look . . .', or knock on the wall or something. We have this system and she just stops.
>
>   (Derek Hoyle, Adviser)

These comments suggest that working at home opened up new areas of unease and negotiation within the relationships between home-located workers and their partners. This could affect issues such as the domestic division of labour. In most instances, any increase in contribution to household chores by men working at home was welcomed by their female partners. However for some women, particularly those who worked part-time or were not in paid work, greater involvement in domestic work by the male home-located worker could be experienced as an intrusion.

> When I first became a homeworker I used to sort of do things like washing up and that sort of thing. And it was a bit of a conflict because she'd been used to that being *her* territory. And here was me starting to try and organize things and, you know, she'd be, 'Oh, leave that, I'm doing that'. But we've got it sorted out, I think.
> (Tony Tompkins, Adviser; respondent's emphasis)

Just as partners could feel subject to the surveillance of home-located workers, so too those working at home could feel a sense that their professional activities were open to scrutiny by household members in new ways. In both cases, the close spatial proximity of paid work and domestic life made possible comparisons that had not occurred before.

> I suppose, though Diane's never actually said it . . . if she is working round the house or whatever and I am sitting upstairs listening to a CD or something while I am doing some work, you know, there might well be perceptions, 'That is not a bad life, is it? I am here working and, you know, cleaning the house and Patrick is upstairs just listening to a CD!' So I think there can be tensions like that.
> (Patrick Blount, Adviser)

In summary, as with temporal organization, the spatial ordering of the residences of home-located professional and managerial workers in our sample were a product of negotiation and conflicting pressures. Detachment, the most popular spatial scenario, was attractive to home-located workers because it offered a way of resolving many of the tensions surrounding the distribution of time between different activities and individuals. Thus, many home-located workers responded to the structural blurring of boundaries between home and work by creating a traditional personal office in the midst of their own homes. Only a few experimented with the spatial and temporal integration of home and work.

Managing at a Distance

Managerial regulation has long rested on allocating employees to specific workstations within specialized workplaces, restricting their movements and observing the diligence of their behaviour at appointed sites. Although many different managerial strategies of control have been advocated and implemented during capitalist industrialization, presence and visibility have remained at their heart. Working at home problematizes these approaches because workers are no longer present in fixed sites and can no longer be subject to panoptical surveillance. This creates uncertainty, ambiguity and unpredictability for managers, as well as co-workers and subordinates. Relatively little empirical research has been conducted on the management of home-located workers (Huws 1984, 1993; Hendry 1994; Standen 1997). The limited available evidence suggests that traditional bureaucratic and rule-based forms of supervision are particularly problematic, since physical visibility is crucial to such forms of control. As a corollary, it has been argued, flat and devolved forms of management that maximize worker empowerment encounter fewer problems with home-located working. Under these regimes, it is suggested, control focuses more on achievements – such as direct contributions to the 'bottom line' – than on standardizing behaviour. Hence, variations in local working practices, that may result from the lack of visibility of the workforce, are not regarded as problematic, provided that organizational performance does not suffer. The management of output supersedes the management of input.

In this section, we focus on the texts, devices and disciplines employed by management to cope with these issues. Notwithstanding their attempts to reconstitute visibility and refashion presence, there remain gaps and cracks in the networks of controls that managers of home-located workers are able to put in place. We shall, therefore, also examine opportunities for workers to evade and resist regulation (Felstead *et al.* 2003a).

Reconstituting Visibility

Of all the senses, sight is regarded as the most powerful and revealing. The 'hegemony of vision' is reflected in everyday speech (Rorty 1980; Westwood 2002: 115–32). We claim to 'see' something that is understood; those who do not 'see the point' are said to have 'blind spots'; long-term thinkers are regarded as 'visionaries'; and academics aim to 'illuminate' or 'shed new light' on their chosen topic (Urry 2000a, 2000b: ch. 4). Eye contact signals a degree of intimacy and trust, strengthening bonds between individuals. The eyes are popularly regarded as the 'windows on the soul' (Goffman 1963; Boden and Molotch 1994). It is not surprising, therefore, that having workers in view remains at the heart of managers' reluctance to allow staff to work at home.

I think it is fairly well known that the perception is that managers lose control of people if they can't physically see them working . . . How do I know they are doing the job? How am I going to manage them if I can't see them? If I ring them in the afternoon, and they don't answer the phone, where are they? And how do I know what they are doing?

(Shirley Phillips, Manager)

Many of our managerial respondents found it disconcerting to supervise staff who worked at home for long periods of time. They feared that lack of visibility would result in a decline in the quality and regularity of interaction with their subordinates.

What you can lose, from a manager's point of view, is just seeing people around from day to day, seeing their body language and seeing what they're like. How they're coping . . . you miss a lot of the signs whether people are stressed or whether they're not coping . . . so you've got to find other ways of dealing with that. And that's a bit of a challenge.

(Minesh Chatterji, Middle Manager)

If I'm used to seeing people in the office every day, I can tell if they're under pressure. Sit down have a chat if they've got too much. Whereas if I don't see them it's very difficult to tell if they're under pressure or not.

(Christopher Robinson, Head of Service)

Home-located workers themselves also found their relative invisibility to be disturbing, making it difficult for them to demonstrate their honesty, reliability and productivity. Virtually all were subject to banter and joking relationships with in-house co-workers, who portrayed working at home as an opportunity to watch television, sunbathe, paint the house or 'skive' in other ways. Although much of this was said to be 'good natured', it also constituted a source of unease for many respondents. Since most had been selected to work at home precisely because they had a reputation for trustworthiness, few had previously experienced such a depiction of themselves.

It's weird actually because I can get quite defensive about the whole thing . . . You know I don't sit and watch 'Richard and Judy', I do get down to my work. And it always used to be a joke – but after a while there's some people who always used to go on about it. And it actually did really annoy me. But they thought that all I did at home was sit and watch TV.

(Trudy Moss, Senior Business Analyst)

I've had the odd smile. Oh yeah, 'Going home are you? Have a nice time'. And on a sunny day they'll add, 'Mind your tan, make sure you put plenty of cream on!' Those sort of jokes – which sometimes are jokes and sometimes, I think, they're quite angry that I'm going home to work.

(Paul Lefy, Head of Service)

Those who worked on the move (see Chapter 6) experienced similar stereotyping. However, they were subject to less suspicion and fewer jokes when they were 'on the road' than when working at home. The former was regarded as a more legitimate and less distracting place of work. Distrust of home-located workers was particularly aroused when they could not be contacted by phone.

There is still very much a perception that if you are down in weekly movement sheets as working at home that if you don't answer your phone you are watching TV or in the shops or in the garden or something like that . . . There is more scepticism when the phone isn't answered.

(Dave Lee, Project Manager)

Our interviews indicated that attempts to make home-located workers more visible entailed the use of documentary records, technological devices and disciplinary practices. One tactic was to require staff to complete time sheets, documenting the numbers of hours worked at home. However, both workers and managers were aware that these were open to distortion and misrepresentation. Interviewees consciously manipulated timesheets in order to disguise their pattern of working and to give the impression that their activities were evenly spread throughout the week. In reality, as with most jobs, their work at home was subject to peaks and troughs, but respondents believed a truthful account could spark resentment and distrust.

Everybody does time sheets . . . If you're going to have a short day, don't let on [laughs] – or have a week of short days. Don't make it too obvious!

(Ken Douglas, Consultant)

Documentary evidence of performance was also used to trace the activities of home-located workers in other ways. Many respondents were aware that a widely recommended approach to managing home-located workers is that of monitoring their outputs rather than their inputs (Department of Trade and Industry 2000; Dwelly 2000). This often involves setting a series of targets, representing a rolling picture of employee productivity. Although this strategy was deployed in several of our case study organizations, our interviews revealed some of its limitations. For example, service-oriented organizations had problems defining relevant output targets that could be readily monitored.

We just can't measure what we do. We *do* measure it, but they are *crude* measures ... We don't have a job that comes in and we do it and it goes out. So, I can't say, 'He's done ten jobs and you've done fifteen', because every job is different.

(Oliver Wilson, Middle Manager; respondent's emphasis)

Targets sometimes diverted home-located workers into secondary goals, eclipsing their primary purpose. Target-chasing could provide a welcome opportunity for home-located workers to prove their mettle, leading them to embrace output measurement in a way that was seen as short-sighted or unhelpful.

It encourages people to identify with their project rather than with the underlying themes of their work.

(Gary Westbury, Unit Manager)

In addition, output management was said by some managers to entail a high cost in terms of alienated customers, lost orders and tarnished reputations. Early warning of problems was preferable to late evidence of under-performance.

You can manage it through the higher-level indicators around income, utilization, customer satisfaction, all those sort of things. But they're all 'too late the horse has bolted' measures. So, yes, you can see if someone is detached and go and solve it, but you'd never *prevent* it happening.

(Gary Westbury, Unit Manager; respondent's emphasis)

In the *long term* you'll spot it. In the old system [before home-located working], *short-term* skiving you could spot.

(Edward Sutcliffe, Unit Manager; respondent's emphasis)

Another way of reconstituting visibility is to introduce new surveillance devices or to activate the surveillance capabilities of existing technologies (Lyon 1994, 2001). Computers may be adapted to count individual keystrokes, monitor time spent at the keyboard, check the completion of tasks, and measure activity speeds (Huws 1984; Ford 1999; Lankshear *et al.* 2001). Some companies even establish visibility by placing cameras on computers. More insidiously, seemingly innocuous features of ICT can be used by managers to snoop on those in their charge. E-mail, for example, is equipped with the facility to check the date and time that messages are sent, opened and returned. A survey of 212 legal companies found that a fifth monitored employee e-mail use on a daily basis (*Financial Times* 2003b). Awareness of potential or actual monitoring of this kind may, knowingly or unknowingly, alter employee behaviour (Brigham and

Corbett 1997). Such strategies of control were rarely experienced by our sample of professional and managerial workers, who were, for the most part, trusted to act in the interests of the organization. Nevertheless, respondents were conscious that date and time stamps of e-mails could be formally or informally monitored by co-workers. Moreover, home-located workers were also aware that this presented an opportunity for them to manipulate perceptions and feign commitment. As a deliberate ploy, some chose to send messages at times calculated to impress recipients with their dedication to the job, their long hours of work or the difficulty of their tasks. This was the equivalent to leaving the car in the company car park late at night, or arriving early in the morning, regardless of the amount of work produced – a phenomenon known as 'presentism'.

> I do like to send an e-mail early and I do like to send an e-mail late . . . Because, for those people who do worry about those kinds of things, it's a little symbol that you are engaged in some auditable activity at that time . . . It's a total non-sense because you could be doing nothing between half past 6 am and 5 pm. But if the difference between keeping somebody happy and not keeping some-body happy is logging on at 5 o'clock and sending an e-mail, then frankly it's a price worth paying. So I do . . . I'm a bit kind of manipulative in that way.
>
> (Stephen Drury, Middle Manager)

However, our interviews also suggest that managers of home-located workers do not always judge 'out of office hours' working favourably. Some saw it as a sign of commitment, others read it as indicative of incompetence or inefficiency. One of our managerial respondents discussed ways in which existing technology allowed him to detect problems in his team by identifying who was working late. Some members were located at home and some in personal offices, but all worked beyond his immediate field of vision.

> When they fire them up [computers] the system effectively logs them on and they're shown as logged on. And if they go for lunch, most of them log off and it shows me that they're out the office . . . It gives me an indication that if I want to ring them they're not actually there. It's a sort of a basic supervision thing. I do use it . . . if they're still logged on at 6 o'clock at night, when I know they should have gone, I've got some indication there's perhaps a problem there . . . the only person left at the end of the day should be me because I'm usually last to go 'home' [although, in fact, the respondent worked at home].
>
> (Oliver Wilson, Middle Manager)

Those working at home are often expected, by managers and colleagues alike, to be on call at any time of the day. Equipping them with additional phones – whether a fixed business line in the home or a company-provided mobile – serves to underline this point.

> When you work from home you're expected to be on call all the time. Even if you write on your planner that you're taking a day out, or you've worked all night the night before, people will still expect you to be at the end of the phone. I've got a business line at home, so I can choose *not* to answer it, in which case they then ring me on my mobile [laughs] . . . You have all three phones going here at once. If they can't reach you on one, they think you can talk to them on another one.
>
> (Sara Kimball, Regional Manager)

However, as we have seen earlier in the chapter, home-located workers and their families often have their own ideas about when it is legitimate for business calls to be made at home and how they should be conducted at different times of the day.

Managers of home-located workers also imbue taken-for-granted communications systems with new functions in order to elicit information about the whereabouts, activities and effectiveness of home-located workers. Telephone calls, for example, may take on new roles and significance. In collective and personal offices, where people frequently converse face-to-face, many telephone calls between managers and staff were said by our respondents to be brief and business-like. Where there were no such contacts, calls changed in length, content, tone and purpose. Managers remarked that they consciously introduced additional gossip, jokes and chat on the phone, with the aim of detecting early signs of work problems. Research suggests that about two-thirds of all talk is 'vocal grooming' (Dunbar 1996; Fox 2001). The absence of regular face-to-face encounters inherent in working at home puts more emphasis on the exploratory, expressive and even therapeutic aspects of telephone talk.

> The voice and e-mail communication is becoming more important. And I do now just pick up the phone and call and leave long, jabbering messages to them. Whereas, you know, I wouldn't do that with people [in-house].
>
> (Peter Banham, Department Manager)

> In an office, you've got them under your eye and you can tell whether they are gossiping too much or taking too many breaks or what have you. You can't with homeworking. So, I think you need to perhaps talk casually to people more often. In fact, I'm a great believer in management by walking about as one of *the* most effective methods of managing in any given situation. So, there needs to be more management by 'walking about' as regards homeworking . . . it just means the casual phone calls, the conversations.
>
> (Ralph Sisson, Adviser; respondent's emphasis)

There were said to be skills involved in this use of the telephone that both managers and workers had to learn.

> The others are just learning that process. And, because it's communicating virtually all the time by telephone, it's something they're not used to ... After three years of practice you know when they're happy, sad, stressed, because you've been doing it for a longer time. With the ones who have recently gone flexible working, that is the hardest area. They phone you up and deliver something they want to say, they pass the message on, and then off. Whereas [names two colleagues] will phone up and have, in effect, a social chat on the phone – the same that you would have with somebody if you bumped into them in the office. So they're farther down the communication line than the others.
>
> (Bob Richards, Manager)

The functions of meetings also changed. A simple way of increasing the visibility of home-located workers was to set and monitor attendance at meetings. These became proxy measures for work effort. More subtly, the agendas of some meetings were shifted so as to require individuals to account for their plans, practices and activities. In these circumstances, talk in meetings acquired similar functions to chat on the telephone.

However, in our case study organizations the activation of surveillance-capable practices and devices was only partially successful. The limitations were partly practical. Large numbers of daily calls to employees at home could be too time-consuming. The devices used to connect home-located workers to the organization were fallible and fragile. Logging on to remote servers from home, even if using a broadband connection, was not always possible and so messages might be missed, intentionally or otherwise. More generally, these practices often entailed indirect or subjective measures of employee productivity that ultimately proved unhelpful. Thus, diligent attendance at meetings and skilful presentation of self in informal telephone calls might have little bearing on worker output.

A different response to the lack of visibility of home-located workers was that of schooling or coaching their behaviour in various ways. Managers in six of our 13 case study organizations made home visits. These had a variety of ostensible purposes, including health and safety assessments, appraisals, training, sickness monitoring, feedback, socializing and informal chatting. However, managers routinely noted that these occasions also facilitated closer inspection of the demeanour, attitude and circumstances of the worker. Some respondents – both managers and home-located workers – described home visits as unproblematic. Others, however, encountered several problems in using them as a disciplinary method of control. The geographical dispersal of home-located workers was a practical limitation. Furthermore, while some home-located workers and their partners were comfortable with work tasks coming into the home, they did object to managers and co-workers entering the house.

> The husband thought that it was a bit of an intrusion. When the team manager went, he was greeting him with sort of like, 'What do you want, *again*?' . . . It wasn't necessarily the person *working at home* . . . It was just the intrusion of people coming *into* the house.
>
> (Mary Fell, Manager; respondent's emphasis)

> I don't encourage people to come here because I very much see this is my home and . . . I like to keep home and work separate in a sense. . . . I mean the house needs decorating in places and things like that, I think there's an element of pride there . . . It's also parking and things like that, neighbours, . . . but the main thing is . . . I prefer to keep my work away from home. It's a strange thing really because working from home is, hmm, weird. It's just having people here.
>
> (Kevin Fenning, Consultant)

Even when visits were acceptable, the private and personal character of home shaped the worker–manager encounter. Managers were now guests in the homes of their subordinates. Both sides reported experiencing ambiguities and uncertainties of power, authority and status in these interactions.

> I think at first you feel strange. Until you get a rapport. . . . it's going *through* the house . . . Once you get into the room then you're in their *work* area.
>
> (Elaine Dewsbury, Manager; respondent's emphasis)

> I didn't really like it to begin with. I felt it was . . . a bit of an invasion in a way. I'm very much a lady! Should the house be tidy because they're coming?
>
> (Claire Tompkins, partner of home-located worker)

Problems with home visits became acute when bodily functions were involved. One manager reported feeling embarrassed about asking to use the toilet, particularly when employees were members of the opposite sex. Another reported discomfort in encountering other family members eating meals. A female manager carried a small folding chair, so that she would not have to sit on the marital bed next to a male colleague's desk located in a corner of the main bedroom (cf. 'juxtaposition' above). For these reasons, some managers frowned on home visits as potentially leading to embarrassment and misunderstandings. However, the form of socio-spatial arrangements adopted in the home, discussed earlier in this chapter, could clearly be of relevance. Detachment was likely to afford managers visiting home-located workers the highest levels of

insulation from potentially embarrassing interactions with other household members and domestic landscapes. Other arrangements, in which
home and work were more integrated, posed greater risks of uncomfortable social encounters.

The advice given, and furniture supplied, by organizations to home-
located workers also serves to set the boundaries of acceptable employee
behaviour and to communicate required disciplines. Managers expressed
a strong preference for spatial arrangements that divided work and non-
work activities within the home – detachment – at least between the hours
of 9 and 5.

> The way that it works best is for there to be an area that can be dedicated to
> work within working hours, but probably performs another function . . . It
> could be the corner in the lounge, if during working hours it isn't utilized by
> the rest of the family. If you've got a partner at home, and young children, and
> the telly is in one corner and your workstation is in the other, then obviously
> that is not going to work. Because we need to maintain professionalism when
> talking to customers.
>
> (Shirley Phillips, Manager)

> Homeworking will not work . . . stuck in the front room or on the dining room
> table . . . As far as I'm concerned, you've got to have a dedicated room where
> you can shut the door and say, 'I'm at work'. One of my guys works in his
> dining room, but it's a dining room with one door and it's not a thoroughfare
> . . . He pushes the table to one side and he has his desk. At weekends he puts
> a sheet over his computer and stuff and it's a dining room again. That's fine,
> but it's no good trying to sit on the lounge table or the dining room table if it's
> a thoroughfare or you've got kids at home.
>
> (Oliver Wilson, Middle Manager)

The furniture supplied to home-located workers reflected this preference.
Desks, chairs and storage cupboards reflected standard office specifications, both technically and aesthetically. The only notable difference was
that they were smaller, so they could fit into the average spare bedroom,
loft or converted garage. Some of the organizations in our study gave
home-located workers the additional option of choosing furniture that,
when disassembled, looked like part of the home; for example, workstations that folded away to appear as drinks cabinets or wardrobes.

Managers, then, regarded the socio-spatial organization and aesthetic
form of workstations in the home as an important element of control. In
particular, they regarded detachment both as an aid to employees conducting occupational tasks in a professional manner and as reassurance
that home-located workers had adopted a sober and dedicated attitude to
their job. Provision of a traditional, detached, personal office in the home

was taken as a symbol that the home-located worker could be trusted. Many home-located workers, who were keen to present themselves as business-like and serious, readily complied with these socio-spatial disciplinary practices. A detached personal office in the home connoted their professionalism and served as counterpoint to the disparaging banter of in-house co-workers. Indeed, one respondent regularly emphasized the spatial separation of her two worlds in formal presentations to colleagues.

> Whenever I do presentations in our team meeting, I would always put at the end of my slides the picture of the [home-located] office . . . because people have no concept of what my office looks like. They have no idea . . . It looks, it could be anywhere, you know. It doesn't look like the corner of someone's bedroom. It's a proper office!
>
> (Trudy Moss, Senior Business Analyst)

Refashioning Presence

Those who work at home have reduced opportunity to be in the physical presence of others in the organization, business unit or team. This poses a problem for cultural engineering exercises, fashionable in contemporary management, that are rooted in time spent in the 'corporate family' (Casey 1995, 1999; Gabriel 1999; Strangleman and Roberts 1999; Grugulis *et al.* 2000; Ezzy 2001). Differential levels of presence may be seen as indicative of differential levels of commitment. Both the managers and home-located workers interviewed were acutely aware of the difficulties this posed for team bonding and 'keeping in the know'.

> We don't like the vision of all the staff working from home . . . It's a cultural thing. We want people to rub shoulders together in the course of their normal work, not on an hourly basis, but we want to do that . . . That culture has to be part of the daily miasma.
>
> (Ray Tomlyn, Board Director)

> That's one of the things about working at home, you don't know all the undercurrent, gossip, or whatever. It's [the employer's office] like coming into a hotel. I'm here today and I'm off. . . . You drop in and out.
>
> (Ken Douglas, Consultant)

To counteract these tendencies, managers in our case study organizations had developed a variety of responses. These focused on: induction to home-located working, use of devices and equipment, and the nature and location of the meetings.

In the majority of case study organizations, employees were required to spend time on-site prior to working at home; in one, a period of six months was stipulated, although this was open to negotiation. This practice was intended to inculcate a strong sense of organizational culture in new recruits.

> You need people to assimilate this culture before they do the job. If you just train them for three weeks and then bung them out into the wide world at home, and they never see anybody after that, you could lose it. But I think if you manage it properly it shouldn't be a problem. I think homeworking's much more of a challenge for managers than it is for individuals really.
>
> (Steve Hodgson, Manager)

Failure to put new employees through an on-site induction was regarded as a serious mistake.

> It's unfair to the people. They don't get a chance to soak-up the culture of the organization, they don't get to know how to do things, they feel, 'How am I going to go about getting whatever?' This is a new cultural issue here. 'What about promotion? How do I progress? How do I get contacts? How do I get work? Who's looking after me?' And it's unfair to do that to people.
>
> (Rupert Dodd, Manager)

While this practice was felt to be useful, there were limits to its effectiveness. Managers suggested that initial on-site induction into corporate culture could not solve all the problems generated by the reduced presence of home-located staff. The impact and relevance of attitudes and information transmitted in the early stages of employment gradually diminished. Furthermore, to be effective, a substantial proportion of the workforce – those who socialize the rookies – cannot themselves be working at home. This was a difficulty for organizations with extensive programmes of home-located working. In addition, a requirement that new staff report on-site for several months at the start of their employment was not helpful in wooing potential recruits who had been attracted precisely because they hoped that working at home would enable them to avoid relocating their families and households. In four case study organizations, attracting highly skilled and sought after personnel in tight labour markets was said to be one of the major reasons for adopting home working.

Another way of addressing loss of presence was to make use of new and/or existing communication channels in an attempt to engender a sense of team involvement and corporate belonging among home-located employees. On occasion, this overlapped with the activation of surveillance-capable devices, referred to above. Indeed, one of the problems with this approach was that sometimes enquiries with respect to visibility (such as pointed questions about hours worked or targets achieved) cut across other messages intended to create a sense of presence (such as invitations to social events or enquiries about personal welfare). The main devices deployed in this way were one-to-one telephone calls, e-mails, conference calls, virtual meetings and face-to-face encounters. Workers themselves also consciously used these channels to keep up to date with corporate developments.

> If I haven't spoken to anybody for three or four days, I think, 'Oh I wonder, I'll ring so and so for a quick word'. It might be on some, if you like, pretext . . . we just chat. I'll say, 'What's the latest? What have you heard?'. . . . It's very casual. So, I don't feel out of touch.
>
> (Ralph Sisson, Adviser)

> We created, like, a virtual network of friends, whereby when we're going into the office in London we e-mail each other and say, 'We're going in on such a day and such a time' . . . We can get together . . . Have lunch or dinner together, and . . . stay in the same hotel.
>
> (Matt Roberts, Consultant)

Mandatory meetings and required visits to employer's premises were used by some managers as a way of bonding home-located staff into the social and cultural orbit of the organization. Some were purely social gatherings (such as dinners or pub visits), others were task focused (such as training sessions and seminars), and yet others were a mixture of both (such as team meetings that were extended to include 'get together' activities and collective problem solving).

> What you have to accept is you can build in things to overcome these problems. So where . . . our team meetings . . . used to take about an hour . . . they're normally about two hours, two and a quarter hours, because I've built in more social time. And I've also built in more discussion time about who's doing what and so on. So people do feel part of a team.
>
> (Carl Rawlings, Manager)

> We have very regular team meetings. In fact [manager's name] used to have them every two or three weeks . . . In a lot of those team meetings, the first hour might just be spent chatting . . . He thinks that's important.
>
> (Tony Tompkins, Adviser)

Our interviews suggest, however, that meetings were not a reliable way of binding home-located workers into the organization. Brief contacts with on-site co-workers were by no means certain to create close-knit ties. Many home-located workers interviewed commented on the need to be very task-oriented when they came back into the workplace. They suggested that co-workers could swamp them with stored-up queries. Indeed, one respondent entered his employer's premises via the back door in order to avoid 'wasting time' interacting with colleagues. Home-located workers came with lists of tasks to complete and people to see during their brief time on-site, often including routine depositing of information and collecting consumables. There was little time for sociability.

Some home-located workers held team meetings in each other's houses in rotation. This appeared to heighten the sense of intimacy and sociability of these occasions.

> One of my managers always holds his team meetings in his house . . . He's quite happy about doing that . . . and the team prefer it. They all sit around a table, like this, in his dining room to get peace and quiet and get away from it.
>
> (Paul Lefy, Head of Service)

Others, who had been provided with electronic equipment at home, were able to form virtual contacts and meetings.

These arrangements boosted the morale of home-located workers but, ironically, could weaken the overall social integration of the organization. In one case study organization (the consultancy company), home-located workers had formed close-knit groups, utilizing company resources to hold meetings among themselves in agreeable off-site locations. Their sociability had increasingly drawn them away from office-based colleagues, generating resentment elsewhere in the organization. As a result, these meetings were curtailed by management. In another case study (the telecommunications company), home-located workers had been provided with excellent electronic communication devices, enabling them to establish strong communications networks with each other independently of management. In both these scenarios, home-located workers generated group cultures that could, from the perspective of management, become misaligned with the organization as a whole.

> They got up to all the dodges . . . They'd speak in code. Some of them used to amaze me. They had pet names for various team managers, zoological names, 'The jackal's coming', 'Have you seen the jackal today?'
>
> (Bill Rocher, Trade Union Representative)

Another way in which home-located workers can be perceived by managers as too detached from the culture of the organization is by getting closer to clients. A shift towards sociability with clients, rather than conforming to the norms of the office, was a major reason for the introduction, by senior management, of a working-at-home scheme in one of our case study enterprises (one of the financial institutions). However, in another, which marketed consultancy services on clients' premises, it was suggested that home-located workers could over-compensate for their social isolation by identifying too closely with clients, rather than fellow team members.

Conclusion

Popular media accounts generally represent working at home as unproblematic, particularly for managerial and professional staff . However, we have argued that working at home generates uncertainty, ambiguities and unpredictability in relationships between, on the one hand, workers and other household members and, on the other hand, employees and their managers. As a result, many of our respondents were developing new ways of behaving and relating to others, both in their 'homescape' and 'workscape'.

Relationships between home-located workers and other household members are shaped by the conjunction of two worlds of meaning, value, belief, practice and action. Both these social orders have long been represented by, and embedded in, specific types of buildings, incorporating distinctive spaces and places. The separate spheres of home and work are not new in themselves, emerging during early industrialization. Nor is it exceptional for workers, male and female, and their partners, male and female, to occupy both these worlds and make routine transitions between. The novelty of the situation faced by our respondents was in bringing the paid work into a territory that is deeply ingrained with the ideals and ethos of home. Workers and partners, parents and children, are fully aware that there are contexts outside the home in which they, and their loved ones, relate to others in ways which are far more emotionally detached and instrumental than those regarded as permissible at home. They know there is 'another side' to themselves and others. When work comes into the home, however, both 'sides' of identities come into close proximity. As home-located workers become less visible to their managers, they become far more visible to other household members. Other household members are confronted with the necessity of relating to the home-located worker in a more complex way, acknowledging them in what our respondents called 'work mode' as well as 'home mode'.

Uncertainties and unease about how to behave in this situation were reflected in the interchanges, captured in our interviews, between home-located workers and their partners. To a greater or lesser extent, our interviewees were conscious of experimenting with new codes of behaviour and re-evaluating the relevance of older mores. Some sought to deal with the situation by reinvoking an older clear-cut division between work and non-work. Thus, several respondents repeated the refrain that during the time they were in 'work mode' they were not at home. The socio-spatial form of 'detachment' was the most explicit territorial expression of this position. Despite the palpable fact that they were under the domestic roof, these respondents wanted to retain the inaccessibility to partners and children of those who commute to work. Whilst household members understood this claim, many found it difficult to incorporate and perform it in the everyday routines of their lives. As the partner of a home-located worker indicated above, it had become uncertain under what circumstances she should make her husband a cup of tea and what remarks were appropriate for her to make when she handed it to him. Other household members found it hard to display emotional distance from home-located workers during their working hours – which were often variable, unpredictable and elastic – only to resume emotional involvement for the rest of the time. They also found it disconcerting when home-located workers themselves managed this division of demeanour.

Uncertainties characterizing relationships between home-located workers and their managers were derived from the difficulties experienced by the latter in observing the behaviour and monitoring the diligence of the former. Working at home diminishes the visibility and presence of workers in workplaces, thereby challenging fundamental aspects of the social relations of control that have characterized capitalist organizations since their inception. Managers responded with a range of texts, devices and disciplines aimed at reconstituting the visibility, and re-establishing the presence, of home-located workers. These required new types of records, conversations and interactions. Each offered managers some purchase on the behaviour of workers, but none constituted a complete solution. Furthermore, managerial strategies pursued in one context could contradict those deployed in others. Most managers deployed a range of more or less compatible strategies in *ad hoc* fashion, depending on the issues under immediate consideration. Many fell back on only allowing employees whom they intuitively felt to be trustworthy to work at home (Felstead *et al.* 2002b). As a result, management of home-located workers itself tended to be characterized by uncertainty, shifting between different approaches towards different individuals at different times.

Gaps and fissures in the network of managerial controls made it possible, to some extent, for home-located workers to evade or avoid supervision. In our interviews, workers expressed their awareness of these opportunities, and hinted at some of the ways they could be exploited, usually by recounting anecdotes about other people or telling innocuous one-off stories about their own behaviour. They also referred to the banter and joking relationships they encountered with colleagues and co-workers. Their professionalism, industriousness and integrity were the butt of these comments and, given their reputation for trustworthiness, few lost opportunities to counter these impressions. Ironically, this could lead home-located workers into explicitly manipulative behaviour, such as deliberately sending e-mails late at night in order to create the impression that they were still at their desks. However, this was intended to demonstrate a wider compliance; it was deception in the cause of conformity (Gabriel 1999; Fleming and Sewell 2002). For home-located workers, it was important that work was not only done but also seen to be done. Furthermore, because of their absence from workplaces, home-located workers often missed the support of co-workers and managers, provided in the form of advice, information and help with problem-solving. Any impulses they might have to disappear from management's view, therefore, were tempered by the need to create at least some degree of presence in order to tap into these valued material and symbolic rewards and resources.

In summary, the picture that emerges from this chapter portrays home-located workers as pulled in different directions by contradictory forces. They value the perceived peace and freedom of working at home but also experience interruptions from other household members and confusion surrounding appropriate demeanour with loved ones. They recognize their invisibility from the managerial gaze but, at the same time, want to be regarded by co-workers and supervisors as worthy members of the organization. Other studies suggest that ambiguities in employment relations tend to generate a state of dependency on figures of authority (Casey 1995, 1999; Parker 1995; Gabriel 1999; Bauman 2001). While we would not describe our respondents as dependent, their experience of marginality – one foot in home, another in work – had the overall effect of drawing them back into ties with their employing organizations. It also required them to give an account of themselves – their motives, abilities and activities – that office-based employees did not need to generate. This chapter has sought to reflect some of these narratives of self and identity generated by home-located workers and their partners.

6

Working on the Move

I am the only constant.

(Emma Reading, Psychotherapy Consultant)

Introduction

The experience of working on the move is shaped by the sharing of public places with strangers – who may be working, talking, socializing or 'chilling out' – and the geographical remoteness of management. The aim of this chapter is to illuminate the everyday lives of people who work in this way. Their places of work comprise vehicles in motion (such as cars, trains and planes) as well as stationary points in the physical networks that comprise transportation systems (such as points of departure/arrival, stopover locations and places in between).

The image of a worker travelling in a predictable pattern from place to place – equipped with light and portable communication devices, such as mobile phone and laptop, which facilitate working whenever and wherever – is commonly conjured up in print, radio and TV advertising campaigns. Workers are encouraged to 'take your office with you' (mobile phone poster advert) and to feel that 'any space is your office space' (mobile operator radio and poster advert). Several adverts suggest that nowhere is sacrosanct – one depicts a worker taking a telephone call while in a public toilet! However, only recently have researchers begun to explore the lives and experiences of those who work nomadically (for example, Doyle and Nathan 2001; Laurier 2001b; Perry *et al.* 2001; Wiberg and Ljungberg 2001). This chapter takes issue with the simplistic message peddled by advertising campaigns that technological artefacts – and in particular, the laptop and mobile phone – are all that is needed to work anywhere/anytime. Rather, those working on the move have to take corrective action to cope with the deficiencies of public environments as places of work and mould their work activities around what is possible and acceptable behaviour in different venues. This chapter explores how they order their lives in order to cope with the heterogeneity, public exposure and multi-functional nature of the places they pass through or occupy and the variety of tasks they are called upon to undertake. It argues that they give structure to this uncertain and fluid environment by developing distinctive modes of self-governance or 'technologies of the self' (cf. Felstead and Jewson 2000: 120–42).

Our analysis is informed and illustrated by a range of original empirical research studies conducted by the authors. We interviewed 46 people who were engaged in working on the move. They included 21 business travellers on an inter-city rail line into London in September 2002 and 25 people who used work facilities provided by a service station operator on a motorway in southern England in April–May 2002. Ten of these respondents were subsequently shadowed for a full day and a further twelve agreed to take photographs of where they worked and the artefacts they used. This qualitative material is complemented by two surveys: an on-board survey of 60 first-class rail travellers who used trains as a place of work; and an on-site survey of 57 users of work facilities in three motorway service stations dotted along a motorway in the South West of England.

The chapter proceeds as follows. The following section considers how, in general, people learn to cope with what we have called 'transitional spaces': that is, spaces that are occupied temporarily whilst travelling, that are often shared with others and may be used by travellers in a variety of ways. Public transport and stop-over points along the way – such as motorway service stations, hotel lobbies and airport lounges – are compared with the privacy afforded by the car. Subsequent sections present our empirical findings on how work is done and managed in these contexts. We explore how different places are made to work, what work is done where, and the mechanisms through which visibility and presence are re-established and resisted. The chapter concludes by reflecting on the words of one of our respondents who pithily commented that 'I am the only constant'. This aptly identifies the constantly changing world in which workers on the move make their living.

Transitional Spaces

This chapter focuses on times, places and spaces that connect with, but extend beyond, employers' premises and employees' homes. We have designated these 'transitional spaces'. The advent of information and communication technology, which permits staying in touch with others while being elsewhere, transforms travel from simply a means of getting from A to B into another potential place of work with an enlarged range of occupational possibilities. Transitional places can become, at least potentially, workplaces. However, this often means that work is carried out in the presence of strangers, if travelling by public transport, or while driving, if travelling by car. The existing literature on travel, transport and mobility suggests ways in which workers on the move may experience these processes (de Boer 1986; Becker *et al.* 1995; Thrift 1996; Wolf 1996; Urry 2000a, 2000b, 2002; Brown *et al.* 2001).

Working while travelling by public transport inevitably requires temporary sharing of space with strangers. Public transport throws large numbers of strangers together in enclosed spaces, often forcing them to sit opposite one another in an arrangement that maximizes concerns about the invasion of privacy. In this context, individuals frequently strive to lay claim to and defend their 'territories of the self' (Goffman 1971: ch. 2). One of these is the personal space surrounding an individual which, if encroached upon by others, may cause displeasure or even prompt relocation. Although personal space contours the shape of the body, the face demands the greatest straight-line distances. Avoiding the stare of the person sitting opposite by looking out of the window, fixing one's eyes on a book or newspaper or closing them entirely were the customary responses used by early railway travellers, and are among those still commonly used. However, today's technologies have added other ways of practising 'civil inattention' towards fellow passengers (Goffman 1959: 222–30). These include looking at the screen of a laptop, talking on a mobile phone without gazing at anyone or anything in particular, listening to music on portable personal stereo systems or playing games on computers of various sorts. All of these tactics aim both to distance travellers from their companions and to connect them to other worlds, whether imaginary or real, work-related or leisure-oriented.

Seating arrangements inside railway carriages also often prompt 'stalling' (that is, laying temporary claim to the use of a particular space). The most common multi-person seating comprises a table between facing seats which accommodate two passengers side-by-side but divided by a shared armrest. First arrivals may attempt to extend their stalls by adopting a number of tactics. Possessions may be left intentionally on empty seats or spread across the communal table, thereby marking it as 'in use' and obliging others to sit elsewhere or ask to have the obstacles removed. Those defending extended stalls may avoid eye contact with those seeking a seat, and hence fail to give permission to new arrivals, who may therefore decide to look elsewhere. Other ruses include spreading out across several seats and/or the table, signalling an unwillingness to give elbow room to those who wish to sit nearby, or sitting in the aisle seat in order to block easy access to a vacant spot.

Whereas public transport prompts 'civil inattention' and 'stalling', the car allows drivers more choice over the type of social encounter to which they are exposed and, hence, makes such tactics redundant. The private space of the car can be used in different ways. First, lone drivers can use it to extend private time; that is, time outside the view of others where the driver does not have to consider their appearance and sustain a 'front' to others. Time in the car can be used to think, to reflect, to talk aloud or to express emotions (anger, frustration or grief), out of sight and earshot of others (although such 'off stage' behaviour may be inadvertently revealed to others on the road). Nevertheless, as Dant and Martin (2001: 151) remark, unlike public transport, the car 'provides an outer clothing or mini-environment for "downtime" from the flow of sociality in people contexts'.

Second, the private space of the car can be used to promote varying levels of intimacy between lovers, friends or colleagues, the close proximity of passengers and driver facilitating such exchanges. While drivers must focus on the road, 'surplus attention' can be given to social interaction with fellow occupants. Although those engaged in driving cannot engage in some activities nor maintain prolonged eye contact, close physical proximity allows body movements and gestures to cue conversations and vocal variation to be detected above engine noise. Furthermore, however discomforting the situation may become, there is no escape from the other occupants until the car comes to a halt. Nevertheless, unlike public transport, drivers and passengers in private cars can exercise a degree of choice over with whom to share space while travelling. As a result, conversation between occupants becomes almost compulsory, as can be seen most vividly in the case of hitchhiking or volunteering to give someone a lift. Car journeys can, thus, accelerate the process of making acquaintances or deepen existing bonds between colleagues or peers (Carrabine and Longhurst 2002).

A third and final use of car space is by connecting it to the outside world via communication devices that allow imaginary and virtual travel. These devices stretch social relations over longer spans of time and space, allowing physical absence to be combined with virtual presence (cf. 'time-space distanciation': Lash and Urry 1994). Many of the functions built into contemporary mobile phone handsets reduce the need for hand–eye co-ordination (*Financial Times* 2003c), thereby increasing the potentiality for combining driving (physical travel) and social interaction without physical co-presence (virtual travel). Unlike the conventional telephone, the mobile phone supplies call recipients with information before the call is answered. Important callers – a client or superior, for example – may be answered immediately, whereas others may be diverted to voicemail and dealt with later. Call recipients can also tailor their vocal demeanour according to their relationship with the caller (Brown 2001). Ethnographic research suggests that the car is one of the best public or semi-public places

to make mobile phone calls, especially when travelling alone, since it provides 'a safety bubble amidst the public' (Mäenpää 2001: 117). In other
forms of travel, such as trains and planes, calls are received and made in
a public setting, and constrained accordingly.

While empirical research on the lived experience of workers on the
move has only recently begun to emerge, an in-depth ethnographic study
of six car-based workers, who were accompanied ('shadowed') by a
researcher for a week, stands out in terms of its substantive contribution
to the field (Laurier and Philo 1999; Laurier 2001b). It revealed the socio-
material practices that make working on the move possible, repairable and
bounded. This study highlights the importance of the ordinary, everyday
materials and devices which permit working on the move (cf Gronow
and Warde 2001). These include mobile phones, laptops, post-it notes,
roadmaps and other paraphernalia that have to be carried around in order
to connect with others – whether physically or virtually – and create,
amend or read documents regardless of location. Pre-assembled materials
and devices may be adapted for working in the car: for example, post-it
notes may be strategically placed within easy reach for note-taking and
stuck on the steering wheel column to prevent forgetfulness, and the
parcel shelf in the boot may be removed to make way for a makeshift
filing cabinet. Assembly practices, too, may be used to prepare for the
day's work (such as charging the mobile phone), initiate the day (such as
loading the car in a particular way), and plan and amend travel plans in
the light of traffic conditions (such as tuning in to local traffic updates
or regular news bulletins). These ethnographic data vividly illustrate the
point, made in Chapter 2, that objects and artefacts acquire their significance and meaning from their context in a network of socio-spatial work
relationships – a workscape – rather than from their essential qualities.

Laurier and Philo (1999) also highlight ways in which the workplace is
repaired when things go wrong: that is, repair work. Unlike the personal
or collective office, the assembly and re-assembly of the car as a work environment makes working on the move fragile and more susceptible to
breakdowns. Strategies and tactics are devised to cope with disruptions
and interruptions as they arise. For example, the short life of built-in
laptop batteries may necessitate periodic and planned stops to known
power sockets for recharging. Appointment schedules may have to be
revised due to unforeseen traffic and weather conditions. The frequent
loss of mobile phone connections, due to interference or poor signals, is
managed via unwritten and unspoken rules of etiquette about how to
re-establish contact.

Another feature of car-based work is the establishment of boundaries
around the working day and the different activities work entails. In office
buildings these can often be marked spatially: entering the doors of an

organization, for example, typically constitutes being 'at work', and on display to the scrutiny of colleagues and/or clients. Certain behaviours and performances are, therefore, expected once on the premises (Crang 1994). In the building itself, a jacket on the back of a chair signals to others that the occupant is 'in', but is temporarily unavailable. Signs such as 'do not disturb' and 'meeting in progress' can also be used to signal visually boundaries which others should not cross, unless invited. Working on the move, on the other hand, requires boundaries to be set differently. Greater reliance is placed on temporal rather than spatial organization of activities, so that accessibility is determined by when, rather than where, someone is available (Green 2002).

The tactics of car-based workers in assembling, repairing and maintaining boundaries around their workscapes provide a useful starting point from which to examine our empirical findings. The existing literature on travel, transport and mobility focuses on ways in which different forms of transport are mobilized by workers on the move, and the use they make of 'non-places' such as motorway service station areas, hotel lobbies and station platforms. In addition, our research explores what workers do before they set off and when they arrive at their destination, and how their movements and work activities are managed and monitored by those to whom they report. We attempt to track respondents through workscapes that incorporate various states of mobility, including periods of movement and semi-mobility (for example, stuck in traffic) and moments of stasis (for example, in motorway service stations, hotel lobbies, at home and on their employers' premises). In doing so, it is also our intention to reflect on: how each of these different settings is assembled, repaired and maintained for the purposes of work, how work activities are selected to fit particular places, and how workers on the move are managed by others despite carrying out tasks in a variety of places.

Making Places Work

The promotion and production of increasing numbers of devices designed to facilitate wireless communication – such as 'third generation' and 'Wi-FI' connections – is one of the most notable features of the twenty-first century. These devices in themselves cannot promote new working practices. However, scrutiny of advertising hoardings at train stations, airports and roadsides suggest that people whose working lives involve movement between different places have been singled out as the most obvious purchasers of wireless communication devices. The implication is that these devices enable workers on the move to remain in touch with colleagues, collaborators and clients around the clock, while sustaining non-work social relationships with family and friends. This is commercially represented as allowing users to 'work here, work there, work everywhere' (mobile phone operator poster advert) in order to make 'any space your office space' – including public parks, trains and taxis (mobile phone operator poster and radio advert).

Transportation venues are being marketed – albeit less vigorously – as conducive to work and, in some cases, altered accordingly. Several train-operating companies, for example, are promoting themselves to business travellers as 'the mobile office'. They emphasize the wider range of activities that can be carried out while travelling by train rather than car; for example, reading, writing, using a mobile telephone and consulting documents. New carriages have in-built features intended to make them even better places to work, such as power sockets for recharging laptops and mobile phones. This will come as welcome news to the business rail users we surveyed on inter-city trains bound for London, nearly half (43.3%) of whom complained about the lack of such facilities.

Other places have also been reconfigured to accommodate working on the move. Some motorway service station areas and motels, for example, have areas set aside for working in an office-style environment. Similar areas are appearing on railway station platforms and have been a common feature of airport departure lounges for many years (Eriksen and Døving 1992). Even pub operators (such as Mitchells and Butler, the UK's largest chain) are experimenting with the installation of wireless web connections ('Wi-Fi') in selected licensed premises in the hope of attracting workers on the move who wish to check their e-mails or surf the web, particularly during quieter mid-afternoon periods (*Financial Times* 2003a). Other retailers have piloted and are now rolling out national Wi-Fi programmes; for example, Starbucks is installing Wi-Fi across its entire estate. In the United States, approaching 3000 of their outlets are already equipped. The aim is to provide those working on the move with a chain of familiar environments so that they 'can really make Starbucks their own' (T-Mobile 2003).

This marketing/advertising discourse assumes that these places and devices make working in a variety of places unproblematic. However, such a view has been challenged by studies which focus on the use of mobile phones for work or leisure in the real world (see, for example, Churchill and Wakeford 2001; O'Hara *et al.* 2001; Perry *et al.* 2001). Despite the rhetoric that mobile technologies allow 'access anytime, anywhere', in practice access is variable. Getting connected may not be acceptable or suitable at all times and in all places.

Unlike their desk-bound counterparts, those who work on the move often do not know what type of environment they will be working in and what resources will be available as they move from place to place. People in office buildings can predict where particular devices – such as the photocopier, printer and fax machine – are located and how they operate. Equipment may be set up according to their particular tastes and preferences. They are able to surround themselves with documents and sources of information, and sources of advice and support are close to hand. The environments that workers on the move occupy are unlikely to be as resource-rich and will vary in terms of both their familiarity and conduciveness to work. The ways in which they make different environments workable are the subject of this section. These include:

- carrying around as many work capabilities as possible
- travelling light
- planning for unexpected changes
- executing tasks with the help of others
- using well-trodden routes to frequented workplaces
- constructing a private enclave within which to work.

Carrying Around Work Capabilities

Mobile phones and laptops allow workers on the move greater capacity to reappropriate travel and leisure sites as places of work than their predecessors, who were bound more to paper documents, postal movement of information and fixed-line telephone links. Not surprisingly, the workers we interviewed and shadowed all made use, to varying degrees, of these devices, recognizing them as essential tools of their mobility. Interviewees were keen to carry the apparatus of work with them wherever they went.

> My office is completely portable. So my office is wherever I need it to be, whether it is on a plane, whether it is in a rented hotel room or, for that matter, in the car. I would work how I need to work wherever I may be . . . my physical location is unimportant.
>
> (Joseph Bates, European Sales Manager)

Mobile phones were the most frequently used communication device. E-mail communication and interaction with remote computer servers were said, by our respondents, to be more dependent on the right connections, more liable to breakdown and less predictable. Heavy users of these forms of communication, therefore, tended to visit sites within their organization and rarely went into the less certain world beyond.

As long as you can get onto e-mail and see the intranet, then there's no difference really. You could be working in Aberdeen or Devon, Exeter, for example,
it wouldn't make any difference . . . I call myself a *'touchdown prostitute' . . . just
using the company's facilities and going off.*

(Stephen Drury, Middle Manager; our emphasis)

Travelling Light

Balanced against the need to remain connected while distant from others
is the need to travel light and remain fleet of foot. Workers travelling by
train and plane – less so by car – were aware of practical limitations on
the extent of their luggage, and hence the number of work-related devices
and texts they can carry in transit. Air passengers, in particular, face
restrictions on the size and weight of hand luggage. People who regularly
work on the move, therefore, seek to travel light, sometimes prompted by
their own safety but more often by the need to maximize nimbleness and
mobility.

I'm manic about weight, about the weight of things that you carry around. I
can't bear being stuck in a city like Manchester or whatever and carting around
a great big bag. And so everything is thought through as to what goes in the
bag. I know it sounds crazy. But actually when you put the whole lot together,
it can be quite heavy.

(Philip Rowling, Legal Director)

Some interviewees went further by segmenting their work materials
according to their clients and tasks in hand, picking up the appropriate
bag each day.

I have three bags. If I'm working on writing up a report for [company A] I take
that bag out and work on it, and if I'm doing [company B] or [company C] I'll
pick up a briefcase or whichever bag is appropriate. It's called a piling system.

(Peter Boughton, Consultant)

Planning for the Unexpected

One of the characteristics of working on the move is the unpredictability
and variability of the environments encountered, particularly when
accessing information held elsewhere. To avoid such difficulties, workers
on the move plan and navigate their way through their workscapes, ensuring they can readily access information when and where required. They

engage in 'planful opportunism' (Perry *et al.* 2001): that is, although not fully aware of what may be required, they can plan to have sufficient resources available to work around changes in the environment. Opportunistic plans are made 'on the hoof', in response to the unexpected, and respondents expended considerable thought on anticipating what might be needed. This planning activity typically centred on making sure that crucial paper documents were carried, such as printed agendas, faxes, e-mails, reference materials and discussion documents.

> If I'm leaving the office for five days and I'm leaving, say at three o'clock in the afternoon, by about lunchtime or even mid-morning, I'm already beginning to sift stuff into plastic folders with labels on for all the component things that I need. So you never leave the office without your phone lists and all the stuff that you need in order to be able to work in another location – the gubbins of a little mini office.
>
> (Philip Rowling, Legal Director)

Paper documents were perceived to be more versatile and reliable than those held digitally. They are portable enough to be taken into meetings for quick reference and referral, can be passed around, provide a useful interactional resource and can be used for *ad hoc* reading when other types of work are not possible (O'Hara *et al.* 2001).

> In theory, I don't keep any paper so . . . any documents I want are on the laptop. However, what would make my life better would be a little portable printer, because sometimes when I'm in a meeting and you're trying to look at a document with someone, you actually do need to print it out.
>
> (Nalita Swift, Regional Manager)

Although, in principle, it may be possible to download electronic documents at any time, paper versions were regarded as quicker and easier to see and use.

Nevertheless, making sure that the correct documents are to hand is a tall order given the uncertainties faced by workers who move from place to place. Even those operating in more certain environments have difficulty in ensuring that they have access to the right document at the right time; a survey of office-based Xerox managers, for example, revealed that 83 per cent of respondents found themselves without the appropriate document at least once a week and nearly a third said this happened more than five times a week (Eldridge *et al.* 2000). In other words, even office-based staff frequently fail to have the texts they require when needed. The efforts workers on the move make to avoid a similar situation were evident in our interviews.

I always think of myself as the bag lady as I depart on whatever day, you know, prepared for the next however many days. Then, you have to trundle it all back. You know, it's just a matter of convenience and a way of being able to work effectively.

(Rebecca Sterling, Regional Development Manager)

You've got to decant everything from the car to the office, to the sales call back to the car, and I find that quite disruptive.

(Rob Davies, Sales Manager)

There are other ways, too, in which workers on the move plan for the unexpected. Among the most obvious uncertainties are those posed by traffic congestion, track repairs, accidents, road and rail closures, flight cancellations and delays, and bad weather conditions. These and other factors make arrival times for meetings and appointments unpredictable. Several tactics are adopted to prepare for delays. Those who work on the move often plan their travel arrangements in order to arrive early. If held up, they phone ahead to apologize to their hosts for the delay. Another tactic to cope with this uncertainty is to give 'arrival windows' rather than precise times to those they intend to meet, although this tends to be reserved for internal meetings with close colleagues. In the expectation of delays, some choose particular modes of transport in order to make the most effective use of any lost time.

I always carry work with me and expect to be late . . . I've always got something to do, so that I feel like I am productively using the time on the train and what have you. And the other thing I would say is, where possible, use the train, don't travel by road. Because that is so tiring and sometimes, you know, when you're sat in traffic, not able to do anything, it's frustrating. When you are sat on the train and the train is stuck, it doesn't matter because you can get your laptop out or you can make phone calls or whatever . . . it just gives you greater flexibility.

(Maria Dearden, National Programme Manager)

Another tactic is to travel the night before to important meetings in order to be punctual and make effective use of the available time.

You do have to organize your day, particularly if you're travelling fair distances as I do. You can forget thinking that you can leave at, sort of, 7.30 'cos it doesn't work – particularly if you're driving, because of the traffic and everything else. So, I tend to organize life such that I travel out of the regular hours – travelling down the night before and staying over.

(Mark Earland, Finance Director)

The uncertainty of travel also has a bearing on planned meal stops. One solution was to eat well before travelling and forgo stopping for meals altogether if travelling by car. This is reflected in a piece of advice offered by one of our interviewees.

> Always have a big breakfast because you never know when you're going to get a chance to stop.
>
> (Rob Davies, Sales Manager)

Another solution is to plan to eat and drink while driving.

> I used to use it [flask] quite a lot . . . If it took me so long to get to somewhere, I didn't then want to sort of hunt around to find a café. So if I was going somewhere where I didn't really know that well, I would take the flask. And think, 'Well, I can just park up outside the call and if I want a cup of tea I can have it' . . . Also . . . this sounds funny thinking about it, I think it makes the car more homely . . . You can just sort of sit there and it's almost like bringing a little bit of home with you into the car, in a funny sort of way.
>
> (Rob Davies, Sales Manager)

Our interviewees were acutely aware of the assembly work they had to undertake in order to navigate from place to place while conducting job-related tasks. They were especially aware of the need to think ahead and plan for the unexpected.

> When you're going from one place to another and doing this kind of working, in two or three different places at any one given time or during any one given day, I think you've got to be quite organized. I find that when we take on new sales guys, there's little things they don't think of. They'll drive into London with no change and then they'll try and park – they're stuffed because they've got no money for the meter . . . You've always got to keep on your toes, I think, a bit more.
>
> (Rob Davies, Sales Manager)

Working by Proxy

Even the well-prepared have to cope with the continuous nature of information flows in the contemporary business worlds, which mean that data rapidly become out of date. Being on the move makes access problematic and uncertain. The mobile phone, however, has hugely enhanced the availability of on-going sources of information – verbal, electronic and written (Churchill and Wakeford 2001). Mobile phones also make it possible to recruit others to act as agents or proxies. For example, one of our respondents would instruct members of his support staff to check a customer's account and process an urgent order on his behalf when he was out on the road. Others were more systematic in their use of proxy working in order to access information and make an appropriate response.

> My main contact is my PA in Cambridge. She is the link. She has to make the decision as to whether something is urgent. If I'm not there, she reads my e-mails and makes a decision as to whether she needs to contact me . . . So obviously she uses the mobile phone and if I'm in a meeting then she'll leave a message. As part of our office protocol I have to ring into the office twice a day, normally mid-morning and mid-afternoon.
>
> (Margaret Tatler, Social Services Inspector)

Proxy working also facilitates collating important information gathered in the field. This can be used to provide a documentary account of developments, serve as a reminder for future encounters or confirm certain arrangements.

> I tend to ring somebody in the office. I tell them what's gone on and I say, 'Send this as an e-mail to me' . . . I can download some information sort of straightaway, while it's still fresh in my mind . . . they can type it up and send it to me. So, you know, it gives me just a few bullet points, so I can remember.
>
> (Roy Simms, Sales Manager)

Well-Trodden Routes to Frequented Workplaces

As we have seen, workplaces and workstations of those who work on the move, and the means to connect them, are complex, variable and uncertain. Navigating around such a network can be daunting (there are interesting parallels with wayfinding by shoppers in malls, see Woodward *et al.* 2000). Our interviews suggest that workers on the move become accustomed to an initially disorientating environment in four ways. First, learning by trial and error: that is, by hands-on experience of maps and other devices, discovering how to get around, what routes to avoid and when, and what hazards may be encountered.

> It's trial and error. The M1 and M25 northern, where we're coming on to, is really horrible in the morning. From Junction 10 it just backs up . . . definitely worth avoiding. You can save yourself an hour basically by doing this.
>
> (Matthew Rogers, Managing Director)

Second, once in possession of local knowledge, adopting well-trodden routes that have, in the past, minimized the uncertainties attached to travel.

> Auto-pilot tends to kick in ... sometimes you are driving along and you suddenly realize you are much further along the motorway because you've essentially gone into auto-pilot.
>
> (Dave Lee, Project Manager)

Third, through practical experience, workers on the move get to know which places are more conducive to work than others.

> When you're travelling and you drop into an office, there are some good ones, there are some better ones. I tend to use the ones I know best ... Somewhere you haven't got to walk half-a-mile from the car park to the building; ... somewhere you know you're going to get a desk and plug-in without a wait or be disappointed; ... somewhere there's a phone line you can use, so you haven't got to rely on your mobile.
>
> (Stephen Drury, Middle Manager)

Our on-site survey of motorway service station users suggests that, once workers on the move become aware of the whereabouts of good places to work, the same sites are visited time and time again. Almost two-thirds (64.9%) of those interviewed were repeat users of the work facilities in the motorway service stations where they were questioned, and two-thirds (68.3%) of them used the site at least once a month. Fourth, workers on the move hone their wayfinding skills by getting to know where the mobile network coverage is at its best and worst, enabling them to anticipate communication breakdowns and minimize embarrassments.

> I'm in an area which will be quite difficult to maintain contact, so how about you phone me again about half an hour [mobile telephone conversation overheard during interview].
>
> (Nalita Swift, Regional Manager)

Constructing Boundaries

The nomadic lifestyle of workers on the move calls for 'camping out' (Philip Rowling, Legal Director), and a willingness to 'perch wherever I can' (Rick Deacon, Trade Union Officer). This, in turn, necessitates coping with a wide range of places, each of which may be subject to competing claims by other users. The strength of such claims varies according to the degree to which the space is public or private (Goffman 1971: ch. 2). Some places are 'fixed' (that is, staked out geographically as belonging to one particular claimant for their permanent and sole use), while others are 'situational' (that is, claimed by patrons for temporary use). This conceptual distinction was evident in our interviews with respondents. They were keenly aware of the relative strength of claims they could exert over particular places of work.

> Certainly it [the car] reflects me more than my desk . . . because it's things that I have in there, that I use all the time . . . I rarely lend my company car to other people, whereas at work, you know, I am quite happy for anybody to sit at my desk when I'm not there. And it's, you know, I use the car at the weekends as well, whereas. . . . I try not to sit at my desk at the weekend [laughs].
>
> (Annie Bennett, Account Manager)

There are also examples of individuals trying to strengthen their claims over situational places through the placement of personalized markers such as photographs on the desk, posters on the walls and screensavers on the desktop.

> I've got my own beer mat, that sort of thing. Just, you know, just bringing small touches into it . . . so it's mine . . . It's like protecting my space as well, so other people think twice about using my desk.
>
> (John Alpine, Senior Commercial Manager)

These tactics are, of course, prohibited in the collective office where all desks are maintained as situational places of work (see Chapter 4).

Length of time in occupation can increase the fixity of situational places of work. Territories available on a 'first come, first served' basis can take on the character of fixed territories, possessed by one individual, after continued and sustained use; for example, a particular desk, chair or hotel room. However, use has to be sustained over a long period in order for proprietary claims to grow.

> If I was staying in a hotel for, you know, two months, [laughs] which I have been known to, . . . then, there is a particular room, probably, I will favour . . . When I was sent down to South Africa to work on the Johannesburg licence application, then, yes, there was a particular room I liked in the hotel. I had my fruit and fresh flowers in there. It was a pleasant place to be because you had to live there.
>
> (Philip Rowling, Legal Director)

The conceptual distinction between situational and fixed places provides useful insights into the ways in which symbolic fences are erected and defended in the presence of others. For example, those who spend some time working in their own homes typically do so by dividing off a part of the house for work purposes and designating it as their space, often a spare room. Rituals of exit and entry serve as 'switching' cues to both worker and other household members. In addition, the home office is often decorated and furnished in ways that mark it out from the rest of the house as a place of work (see Chapter 5). However, working in public places – on trains and planes, in airport lounges and hotel lobbies – poses the challenge of maintaining privacy in the presence of strangers rather than loved ones. Common tactics include extending available personal space by requesting that an adjoining seat be kept vacant, selecting quieter times to travel and intentionally choosing particular seats.

> I try to get an empty seat beside me, so that I can stick all my stuff beside me. Well, I used to. Because I used to fly BA but I have just started flying with Easyjet – and there's no chance! I doubt that I'll be doing much work on the Easyjet flights.
>
> (Emma Reading, Psychotherapy Consultant)

> First class [on the train] is a good place to work, but not at rush hour because you're so hemmed in. You can't spread out. I actually find that if I take a two-seater . . . people are more reluctant to come and sit next to you . . . because it's more intrusive . . . This gives me more private space.
>
> (Rosie Stafford, Managing Director)

In our on-board rail passenger survey, some respondents (16.1%) said that they occupied particular seats in order to seal themselves off from others and maintain privacy, spreading out their possessions in order to claim vacant seats. Moreover, over half (33 out of 60) said that access to personal space was the main motive for first-class travel; in particular, they referred to greater leg room, larger desks, higher levels of seat vacancy and insulation from the noise of non-business passengers (Letherby and Reynolds 2003).

In some places – such as cafés – it may be difficult to make expansive and long-term claims for space. Fast food outlets, for example, operate on quick turnover and a large volume of customers. Tables and chairs are often fixed to prevent customers dividing and redividing the space according to their particular needs. The most common arrangements comprise either two or four seats arranged around a table, a horseshoe-shaped booth with a table in the centre. Another configuration consists of individual breakfast-bar seats dotted along perimeter walls. In these locations, table-sharing and close proximity to strangers is the norm. These formats narrow the size of the geographical space that can be 'stalled' and make long-term claims difficult to defend. For these reasons, interviewees rarely mentioned them as places of work. Those who did only used them as a last resort.

Research on mobile phone use suggests that, even in the absence of formal 'mobile-free' restrictions such as those imposed in railway carriages and restaurants, there are tacit and unstated rules of behaviour expected in certain types of eating establishment, but not in others. In particular, there are 'phone-class' and 'non-phone-class' environments which place limits on the aural boundaries of work. Survey evidence suggests that phones are less likely to be heard and seen in formal restaurants (where table service is provided) than in more informal establishments (Plant 2001). The workers on the move we interviewed were aware of this distinction, especially when they knowingly violated the unwritten rules.

> It looks quite strange, somebody sat there going through paperwork with a laptop on a table in [name of restaurant] . . . I do sort of get distracted pretty easily, certainly in this sort of environment; it's quite difficult to concentrate sometimes . . . I actually had a complaint made against me by a customer in one particular [name of restaurant chain] because I was using my mobile phone. . . . To some people it is obviously a nuisance.
>
> (Ben Dixon, Building Maintenance Manager)

At stop-over points – such as hotels – private enclaves can be constructed by moving to quieter areas; including secluded corners of the lobby, bedrooms, or even outside venues. These moves may be prompted by the need to minimize sound interference, reduce the chances of being overheard and lessen the risk of exposure to prying eyes. This 'space-making' behaviour may also be complemented by certain bodily postures, denoting a desire to carve out a private arena from which all external interference is deliberately and visibly excluded (Plant 2001). These include bowing the head downwards, turning the body away from others nearby, and facing a corner or wall.

> If I am reviewing a report or preparing a report, or if I am required to make a conference call, umm, or catch up with my one-to-ones over the telephone, I can do all that, you know, from the privacy of a hotel room. But I would always try to find a private area with a good phone reception.
>
> (Philip Rowling, Legal Director)

Alternatively, background noise may be sufficiently loud to muffle the detail of face-to-face interaction and therefore prevent eavesdropping.

Workers on the move become adept at finding privacy in the midst of a busy and noisy environments, such as international airports (Eriksen and Døving 1992; Iyer 2000).

> Obviously, hotel lobbies are not as private as a meeting room. But generally, when there's an awful lot of people around, there's so much noise about the place you can talk about anything and no-one will overhear.
>
> (Bob Manning, Consultant)

In moving through their workscapes, interviewees were conscious that some places exposed them to surveillance and interuption more than others.

> At home, I have full control of what I do. I will tend to always keep my mobile on but if I want to switch it off, then I can. I can report into work and say, 'I don't want to be disturbed until after four'. In the office I have no control over it, really, unless I go and lock myself away in an office. But even then, if people need to see you then, you know, I still— you have to go and manage people. In the car, it's limited to whoever rings you down the phone. I suppose you have a bit of control there.
>
> (Liz Perredon, Architect)

Mobile phones allow a range of parallel activities to be undertaken while on the phone, of which the caller may remain unaware. However, the acceptability of such parallel activities is limited by the location of the worker.

> At home, when I take a conference call, I've got a hands-free phone with an earpiece so I can walk around. I make cups of tea whilst I'm on the phone and things like that, 'cause I'm just so bored . . . I may give myself a manicure or something!
>
> (Nalita Swift, Regional Manager)

Mobile phones offer a degree of discretion to workers on the move and may be used to shield them from visibility to others. Rather than answering, recipients may redirect calls to voicemail or even prevent the phone ringing by switching off entirely. Historically, the 'off' button on mobile phone was an essential way of protecting the battery life of the phone, but it is has since 'changed from a power conservation button to a connectivity controller' (Brown and Perry 2000: 627). Our interviews suggest that, in some places and under some circumstances, it is considered polite for workers to unplug themselves momentarily from the network in order to display their undivided attention to others present.

In some of the clients' sites, I would turn my phone off, obviously. Because it is so rude to take phone calls . . . I can sort of, be focused, if you like, on the client.

(Michael Ross, Head of Trading)

However, there are other situations where being disconnected is not an option. Drawing and maintaining the boundaries of telephone conversation can be difficult for workers on the move, especially when work demands spill over and colonize domestic times and spaces such as holidays.

It [mobile] can ring as many times on holiday as today because, obviously, people don't know I'm on holiday . . . It's a lot better for me to deal with things there and then than to wait two weeks and come back to a multitude of problems . . . It wasn't too bad this year, because once in the morning and once at night and once in the afternoon . . . I went back to the room to deal with them. In previous years, I've answered them there and then. That's not fair because we usually go with friends, you see.

(Don Lyndon, Regional Sales Manager)

Placing Work

In the previous section, we saw that advertisers of wireless technology frequently assume that suitably equipped business users can carry out work regardless of their location. In contrast, we argued that places vary in terms of their resources, familiarity, suitability and exposure to public gaze. These same advertising campaigns also pay little attention to the type of work carried out by business users and its appropriateness to various environments. In this section we shall suggest that work activities vary in the demands they make on the places. It argues that tasks carried out on the move vary in a number of ways, making some places more appropriate than others for particular kinds of work. Many of our interviewees divided up their work accordingly.

I do tend to split work up as soon as I get it . . . what I will do is when I start getting work in is to say, 'Right, I can do that on the train, I can do that in the office'.

(Paula Allan, Administration Manager)

This section will consider why our respondents placed their activities in particular locations. The evidence suggests that their decisions reflected the demands of tasks in terms of:

- length of time
- amount of space
- concentration level
- image maintenance
- delicacy of the work
- unpredictability
- communication requirements.

Timing

Some work tasks demand more time than others. Writing a project proposal, for example, takes longer than filling out an expense claim; downloading and reading a document from the internet takes more time than having a quick glance at an agenda; and entertaining a client takes longer than having a quick chat with a colleague in the corridor. The 'granularity' of segments of time (that is, their length and usefulness) also varies from location to location. Airports, for example, are transient locations with fine granules of time associated with their use. After check-in, passengers are shuffled to the departure lounge, then to the boarding gate and eventually to the plane. Notwithstanding delays, the amount of time in each place is quite short. However, once on board, passengers sit in the same seat for longer periods, and so the granules of time here are coarser. Similarly, breaks between meetings or during meetings themselves only offer short windows of time to deal with urgent issues. However, overseas trips with multiple meetings spread over several days – arranged to take advantage of the distance travelled – are likely to have longer gaps between appointments, offering more time to carry out other types of work. Workers on the move, therefore, have to match the time requirements of the tasks to be done with the granularity of the times afforded by the places they are in and the modes of travel they employ.

> If I want to speak to somebody at any great length, or privately for that matter, I'll tend to do that from home – and not where you're going between cells on the mobile network and having it completely broken.
>
> (Bob Manning, Consultant)

Other respondents made ingenious use of the, sometimes lengthy, time spent travelling. One had made a do-it-yourself kit to incorporate a hands-free microphone and speaker into the headrest of his car seat. He also had a Dictaphone in the glove compartment of the driver's door. Unlike other respondents, he looked forward to long car journeys in which he could dictate long documents over the phone or onto tape.

> I find the car a great place to work ... If I wanna do some work on the tape, I find that three or four hours ... in the car is absolutely brilliant ... I also use the phone to dictate reports, letters, team bulletins.
>
> (Gary Atkins, Managing Director)

Another interviewee consciously planned and engineered protracted journeys with significant business associates and senior colleagues, who would be otherwise difficult to pin down for lengthy encounters (co-present travel). He was keenly aware that close proximity between familiar occupants while travelling promotes longer, deeper and more wide-ranging conversations than would be possible in meetings or fleeting encounters.

> I probably use certain trips quite strategically, in that if I need to spend time with someone like the Chief Executive, who is very difficult to see ordinarily for any length of time. Then a trip to [name of a Mediterranean location] or somewhere like that can be very constructive ... Because you are forced together ... and you have his undivided attention ... you've got him for three to four hours or, you know, if there's a delay even longer. ... The most bonding times to work with the managing director of [company name] and one or two other senior individuals was when we were on long tours around North America and South America looking at our operations there ... Lengthy flights, six hour flights ... When you're sitting together travelling, you come back ... with a much closer working relationship than before ... You've seen each other sleep and not feel well and ... you've gone through some quite personal experiences together.
>
> (Philip Rowling, Legal Director)

The same ulterior motive prompted this respondent to give an incoming chief executive a lift to his next appointment, prolonging valued interaction in the close confines of a car where mobile phone connections were known to be poor.

> When [company name] was acquiring [company name] I needed to spend time with the acquiring Chief Executive for him to form a view on me and vice versa. So I went to see him. Afterwards he had to go somewhere else in the City so I ran him, in my car, from [company name] to High Holborn, knowing that that journey would take fifty minutes, and knowing that, you know, a lot of it was under tunnels and things so his phone wouldn't be working ... that was valu-

able time . . . These people, you know, are very, very busy people . . . so you've got to mould yourself around them . . . as I put him in the car I thought, 'Right, I've got you!'

(Philip Rowling, Legal Director)

Other respondents also recognized the usefulness of time spent travelling in close proximity to colleagues and the value of overnight stays, although the benefits of co-present travel were often a by-product rather than a motive for such arrangements.

Spacing

Workers on the move must match the geographical space required for certain types of work with the facilities and characteristics of particular places. For example, the volume of work done when travelling by train is very different when there are plenty of seats and room to open a laptop, compared with standing room only. Even when seated, travellers occupy cubicles or stalls that may be too cramped for certain kinds of work.

[Working on planes] you have to pack everything away. And it's just the impracticalities of trying to fit into a seat with a laptop and stuff that has to be put away during the flight . . . It's just hassle . . . So I tend not to work on the aeroplane [but in the business lounge before short haul flights].

(Rosie Stafford, Managing Director)

The car offers more room but its use is limited while in transit.

Catching up on recorded audio-conferences is quite useful in the car, because it's dead time really . . . Let's say, for example, there's an audio-conference about [name of company] strategy or about our results or about the work group you're in: you can dial into it and listen to the replay of that call, including the questions and answers that people have pitched at the end. You can listen to that anytime – you can listen to it at home, in the car, at the desk. So I tend to find myself listening to the replays of those while I'm in the car because it is dead time. You just hope a phone call doesn't come in where you've got to ditch it and go back in again!

(Stephen Drury, Middle Manager)

Interviewees who travelled by car made sure essentials were within easy reach for quick access but found it none the less difficult to keep everything in order during a day on the road.

I don't like working in the car, really, because it's very difficult to maintain any order or structure when you've got bits of paper flying about the car, and you're whizzing about here-there-and-everywhere.

(Rob Davies, Sales Manager)

Even when stationary, it is difficult to sit comfortably in a car while placing a laptop on a flat surface, a key concern according to Swedish research (Dahlbom and Ljungberg 1998).

I find I can't do much on the laptop [in the car] because you can't really see the screen particularly well. And there's not really enough space to spread yourself out and sort yourself out. It's fine for just sitting there reading a few notes before you go into a meeting, making a few notes after you come out of a meeting, but other than that it's not ideal.

(Tim Winfrey, Company Director)

Concentrating

The interviews that are the source for this chapter, as in Chapters 4 and 5, were with professional and managerial workers engaged in complex problem-solving, decision-making and/or client servicing. Their jobs involved tasks such as writing project proposals and reports, planning future strategies and approaches, making calculations and estimates, liaising with colleagues and clients, and reading internal and external documents. Respondents were well aware of the places that worked best for them when high levels of concentration were required. Home was the most frequently cited.

They can get me by the phone [when working at home] but I can choose not to answer it. People don't drop in, in the way that they do in the office locations . . . If I am doing a piece of work – like I was earlier – I would not pick up the phone. I would just let the answer machine pick up . . . I actually have the phone up in the spare room with the desk, and when I am doing concentrated work I sit down here [in the kitchen], so I can't even hear the phone ringing upstairs.

(Maria Dearden, National Programme Manager)

Other places that provided 'a bit of peace and quiet without distractions' (Jason Wild, Consultant) included early morning in the office and off-site locations such as hotel bedrooms and airport lounges. Offices during nine-to-five hours were not regarded as conducive to concentrated work.

> It can be a lot harder to just go in, sit down, get your head down and do a lot of work [in the office] . . . The last time I went into [name of building], it was an hour before I could plug my laptop in because everyone wanted to have a chat, find out how things were going and what I'd been up to.
>
> (Roger Maw, Project Manager)

However, tasks requiring little concentration could be allocated to places where disturbances were likely. Those who work on the move are adept at taking and making only those tasks that can be effectively dealt with in particular environments: for example, when on the road some resist making telephone calls altogether because of the demands of driving (cf Laurier 2001a).

> It doesn't feel comfortable [using phone in car] . . . I'm a flat-out driver. I need all my attention for the road and . . . you can't hear the phone in my car for the exhaust!
>
> (Jamie Simons, Chartered Surveyor)

Some types of work are characterized by variable levels of concentration: for example, different types of telephone calls. Accordingly, respondents filtered calls depending on the intensity of the conversation and the identity of the caller.

> I have different call tones set up for different groups [of callers] and because I store all my numbers on there, it shows me who's ringing . . . If I'm in the car and I see it's . . . someone who's gonna be tricky to talk to in the car and I need more wits about me, then I'll put it on busy.
>
> (Nalita Swift, Regional Manager)

Presenting an Image

The shift towards services has been an on-going feature of labour markets over the last century (Lindsay 2003). The pace of change has quickened during the last decade and has prompted an interest in the capabilities and attributes that service work entails. Foremost among these is the importance of employees 'looking good and sounding right'. So far, much of this research has focused on service work in distribution, hotels and restaurants (Warhurst and Nickson 2001; Nickson *et al.* 2003). However, many of the same principles can be applied to workers on the move who have to make themselves aesthetically pleasing to clients. This 'labour of aesthetics' is made more difficult when, as commonly happens, workers are located in places which do not belong to the organization they represent (Witz *et al.* 2003). In these circumstances, they are the embodiment of the organization's identity but cannot rely on the corporate landscape, discussed in Chapter 4, to support them. Those working on the move, therefore, typically expend effort on framing their interactions with others in appropriate ways. Maintaining a suitable personal appearance and manner is one way of conveying the status of individuals, the image of the organizations they represent and the roles of each party (Goffman 1959). Workers on the move whom we interviewed attempted to keep up appearances by observing many small disciplines: for example, by carrying deodorant and aftershave, avoiding alcohol and certain foods because of their lingering smells, and carrying a change of clothes to be used at the end of a long journey. Some managers insisted that staff drove cars that were appropriately equipped to guarantee a fresh appearance on arrival.

> We insist that all cars have air conditioning . . . I don't like the idea of somebody going there [name of client's premises] – especially if they're like me and they're carrying a pound or two more than they should – all sweaty!
>
> (Roy Simms, Sales Manager)

The settings in which interactions take place can also be used to frame the nature of the dialogue.

> To make sure that people we are appealing to are aware of the size of the company and the success of the company, then we want to create a certain impression . . . I first discovered, for example, [name of serviced office supplier] about two years ago . . . That was very useful . . . for meeting clients and customers . . . To have somewhere that is of a specific standard that will provide us with certain facilities in any city.
>
> (Joseph Bates, European Sales Manager)

> Because of the nature of the work that I do and sometimes the nature of the conversations . . . it's easier for me to meet off site, especially if somebody wants to give me some information . . . If I am wanting to get particular information out of individuals or I want them to relax and behave in a certain way, a drink in a bar facilitates that . . . or a meal in a restaurant.
>
> (Philip Rowling, Legal Director)

Encounters may communicate messages that are intended or unintended, artful or accidental. In Goffman's terms (1959), information can be 'given' on purpose or 'given off' unintentionally. Thus, for example, mobile phones sometimes convey an unintentional abruptness when signals fail without warning or when speaking in a public place.

There's nothing worse than cutting off a customer when you lose the call 'cause you've driven under a bridge or something . . . If they call me, I'll tell them I'm in the car and if they wanna call back later that's fine. But otherwise I'll just press on and have the conversation with them.

(Mike Sandicliffe, Managing Director)

Most respondents used hands-free mobile phones while driving. However, one of those we shadowed took his telephone calls either by holding the handset next to his ear and mouth or by placing the handset in the hands-free cradle on the dashboard. His approach depended on the nature of the call and the importance of the caller. The mobile was hand-held when the caller was less well-known and the call more important, since 'it makes it a bit more personal' (Matthew Rogers, Managing Director). This courtesy was not extended to others, such as his wife or colleagues, since the consequences of inadvertently sounding distant or remote, as a result of using the hands-free device, were perceived to be less serious.

Dealing with Delicacies

Work tasks also vary according to the level of confidentiality involved and the ways in which confidentiality is protected. Preventing disclosure to colleagues may prompt certain types of work to be undertaken in public places outside the organization's physical boundaries, thereby minimizing the chances of being overlooked or overheard.

It [working in a meeting room at a motorway service station] makes dealing with the confidential documents considerably easier because you're not continually wondering who is walking past you or . . . striking up a conversation about issues that . . . really can't be discussed at the centre.

(Dave Lee, Project Manager)

On the other hand, in some circumstances, public places may be considered one of the most hazardous places to do 'electronic paperwork' since the identity of passers-by is unknown.

I can't do any planning work [in airports] because of the confidentiality that you never know who's looking over your shoulder, looking at your laptop . . . [so I do] just admin, expenses, industry reading, light e-mail.

(Calvin Price, Managing Director)

Similarly, mobile phone users may be overheard, particularly when raising their voices against background noise, such as car engines, carriage wheels or public address systems. Moreover, in the absence of nods and glances, audible phrases (such as 'ah ha') need to be loud enough to convey the listener's continued attention and presence on the line (Ling 1997). Workers on the move are acutely conscious of the dynamics of these interactions and, therefore, limit the types of mobile phone calls they make and where they make them. Another tactic is to make the recipient aware of the caller's whereabouts; for example, with the well-known line 'I'm on the train'. This makes the ensuring conversation contextually sensitive, putting constraints on the topic of discussion and the duration of the call (Cooper 2001; Laurier 2001c). For these reasons, those who work on the move typically regard public places – such as trains and airport terminals – as inappropriate venues to make and take anything but trivial phone calls.

> I use my mobile phone to make calls out rather than receive them because . . . the sort of thing you tend to be talking about doesn't lend itself to discussion in public . . . So, for example, if [a company] is planning to move a lot of jobs to India, and we're going to fight a campaign to try to stop it, I can't really discuss those sorts of things on a train. It's OK to phone home and say, 'I'd like egg and chips', [laughs] but you can't discuss other sorts of things in public.
>
> (Rick Deacon, Trade Union Officer)

Our on-board survey of those travelling by rail on business also suggests that the work carried out on public transport differs from that carried out in the private confines of a car. Whereas 10 out of the 60 train travellers interviewed said they did not make confidential phone calls on the train for fear of eavesdropping, and five kept calls short in order to avoid disturbing others, none said that the car restricted phone calls in either of these ways.

Managing Unpredictability

It is commonplace for professional and managerial jobs to generate unexpected tasks and unforeseen demands, but these pose particular challenges when working on the move. Typically, the office – personal or collective – is better resourced to cope with a wide range of varied and unpredictable uses than most places encountered on the move. Staff working on the move may, therefore, 'save up' certain types of work to carry out when they return to their offices, or make special trips to their employers' premises when the need arises.

> Somehow it seems sort of right to start the week off by trying to reduce my e-mail to a manageable level. And I can best do that in the office.
>
> (Margaret Tatler, Social Services Inspector)

However, returning to the office after working on the move can itself generate unexpected and unforeseen work tasks that disrupt plans and schedules.

> I get quality time on the train where it is quiet and I am able to get on with things and prepare for my day. When I'm in the office I'm just fire fighting and just dealing with so much that's coming in. To be honest, I don't always get a great deal done [when in the office] until I'm on the way home.
>
> (Paula Allan, Administration Manager)

Being on the move may itself offer opportunities to 'bump into' potentially useful clients and colleagues, apparently accidentally but with an ulterior purpose in mind. Thus, some respondents made a point of 'dropping in' on clients when they were 'passing through'. These interactions could generate welcome, if unpredictable, additional tasks.

> I will always find time to have a natter [with senior figures in client organization] and pass the time of day . . . Talking to the director has on more than a few occasions just triggered that extra bit of work . . . This keeps my work stream going . . . I couldn't just call up the director for a chat, just in case something interesting popped out. So that's an important thing that happens on the client's site.
>
> (Thomas Freeman, Consultant)

In other circumstances, timetables and plans may need to be defended by keeping clients and colleagues at arm's length while working on the move. All those interviewed admitted to screening their telephone calls, choosing which to answer immediately and which later.

> You can get ambushed by the mobile. When people ring you up and you answer it, it's suddenly like, 'This is so-and-so, I'm bloody-well this-that-and-the-other and I want this-and-that and I want it now!'
>
> (Rob Davies, Sales Manager)

Unpredictability could be further reduced by taking the initiative to make calls rather than waiting to receive them, although this depended on the seniority and importance of the recipient.

> I prefer to make them [mobile calls] because then I can control the conversation, or I'll choose the ones I want to make.
>
> (John Alpine, Senior Commercial Manager)

Facing Others

Managers spend a great deal of time talking. Furthermore, the higher their
rank, the greater their responsibilities and the more complex their decisions, the more they talk. American research suggests managers spend
up to three-quarters of their time in meetings, on the telephone and in
impromptu discussions, about two-thirds of the time in the physical
presence of others. This has been referred to as the 'compulsion of proximity' (Boden and Molotch 1994). The importance placed on face-to-face
contact reflects the meanings, intentionally and unintentionally, radiated by
those present; while 'it's good to talk', it is also important to see how what
is said is delivered and received. These signals may exaggerate, confirm or
contradict the spoken word, prompting a very different, even opposite,
interpretation of the situation. Such signals include eye contact, hand movements and gestures, facial gestures (such as nodding, smiling or grimacing),
and displays of interaction attentiveness (such as active engagement, civil
attention and blocking outside interference). Our interviewees were well
aware of the value of 'face work' for these reasons.

> To be part of the team, normally you would feel that you have to be there with
> the team. So you rely more on communication on the mobile phone and e-mails
> . . . Which doesn't always get the message across as you'd get across face-to-
> face. An e-mail has got no relation in it whatsoever . . . it can be read in many
> different ways.
>
> (John Alpine, Senior Commercial Manager)

For workers on the move, chance encounters with colleagues was
unlikely, given their spatial movement and temporal schedules. Typically,
therefore, our respondents scheduled regular formal team meetings with
co-workers, often at fixed intervals set well in advance. Our interviewees
used such fixed points in the diary to 'pack in' other meetings on the same
day in the same location. Crowding engagements in this fashion was also
seen as facilitating chance encounters of the kind enjoyed by office
workers. These were referred to by interviewees as 'serendipitous' or
'corridor meetings'.

> I use the office there for meetings, so if I need to connect with people I try and,
> you know, get as many people in the one day . . . And because it's a place that
> a lot of people use in the way that I use it, you get some fairly serendipitous
> meetings take place as well.
>
> (Maria Dearden, National Programme Manager)
>
> So much seems to happen in the office, you know almost like osmosis, things
> just filter through and around . . . If you do too much [working on the move]

you do miss what's going on in the office . . . You're meeting people in the corridor and canteen . . . information's just flowing all around you.

(Kevin Sawyer, Project Manager)

On occasion, however, respondents were able to adapt their usage of certain places such that they came to resemble collective offices. Particular hotels were known for their ambience that facilitated certain types or styles of working. Some might serve as touchdown points for impromptu meetings between team members, while others, that offered more privacy, could be used for interviews, appraisals and client meetings.

> [Hotel lobbies are good for] impromptu meetings. So where we'd decide we want to meet quickly, we can just say, 'OK, where are you this morning? Where am I this afternoon? Right, let's just find somewhere in between'. You get to know which ones are busy, which ones are quiet . . . a relaxed atmosphere for an interview candidate to come along to. And smart facilities that are busy . . . lots of business people around and it's a reasonable atmosphere . . . to debrief after we've finished a meeting with a customer.
>
> (Mike Sandicliffe, Managing Director)

Co-present travel can be used to coach colleagues and give feedback on their observed performance. Car travel offers a private cubicle of space, with little interference or disruption, that suits such interactions.

> I guess that [travelling by car with a colleague] gives us time to sort of chat about . . . what we're going to do at the next call . . . My role is to say things along the lines of, you know, 'Watch for this; look for that; when you ask that question be careful because, you know, you could be opening yourself into a minefield there; what you really need to do is to redefine it; and ask the question in such a way so you're going to get the answers that you want back'.
>
> (Roy Simms, Sales Manager)

Managing Workers on the Move

The aim of this section is to move beyond an examination of how workers on the move devise means of operating in a range of settings to a consideration of the ways in which their activities are monitored and controlled by those to whom they report. It pays particular attention to the devices workers carry, the documentation they supply to management and the disciplinary regimes under which they labour. Taken together, the trinity of devices, documents and disciplines establishes a structured network in which workers on the move are managed and long-distance control is exercised (J. Law 1986). Of particular interest are the ways in which this network corrects for the loss of workers' visibility, facilitates interaction among co-workers and others, and allows workers to avoid, subvert or defy management.

Enhancing Visibility

It is difficult for those who manage workers on the move to keep track of where they are and observe what they are doing. Managers of home-located workers face similar problems (cf Chapter 5; Felstead *et al.* 2003a), but such difficulties are more pronounced when staff work on the move since their location is variable, unpredictable and can change at a moment's notice. Workers themselves are acutely aware of the challenges this poses for management.

> I report to the Chief Executive . . . He's periodically, in fact fairly frequently, concerned at the fact that he can't pin me down. He doesn't know where I am and he would like me to be more regular in my habits – and I would. I would very much like to be more regular in my habits, just to put his mind at rest. But I can't do it because the nature of the work that I do requires me to be fairly flexible.
>
> (Richard Kew, Divisional Director)

A typical management response was to require workers to provide a documentary trace of their movements and activities, and to send these to management and others in the team. Such documents could take the form of a diary detailing where and when an individual expects to be in certain places, a forward-looking and backward-looking weekly schedule of activities, or a weekly update of highlights and achievements.

> We all share our weekly schedules and reports. So our weekly scheduling reports – what we've done last week, what we're about to do this week, and where we are – goes to our manager with cc to our colleagues . . . Everybody gets the chance to see what everybody else's doing.
>
> (Nalita Swift, Regional Manager)

Some organizations took the further step of making these documents openly accessible by posting them on intranets for colleagues to browse and consult. In these circumstances, the author of the document has no way of telling who has sought information about their whereabouts, when they did so and for what purpose (H. Miller 1995). The potential audience, therefore, becomes much larger than a circulation list of managers and colleagues, and its disciplinary power is enhanced.

Another widely used approach to managing workers on the move was to observe the outcomes of their activities, rather than attempting to measure the time they spent carrying them out. In some cases, as long as certain targets were met, the time taken to reach these goals was regarded as irrelevant.

> It's a bit like, you know, an exam at school. You can mess about at school all year, but you've got to do the exam . . . because that's what you're being judged on. On what you submit, rather than how you did it or what you did leading up to the essay or the thing you're handing in.
>
> (Stephen Drury, Middle Manager)

Managers disciplined workers' performance in other ways. Regular update telephone calls, for example, might be either fixed in the diary in advance or made without warning to monitor progress. Peers could also be used to observe how individuals performed 'in the field': for example, in front of a customer, supplier or fellow team members.

> I have regular update telephone calls that are fixed in my diary from my boss, so he tells me what's going on.
>
> (Ian Fisher, Project Manager)

> I think I've got a fantastic team [but] one of them let me down recently, just after I'd promoted him . . . I explained to him that he needed to watch what he did and what he said in a remote location because people were only too anxious to feed it back to me.
>
> (Philip Rowling, Legal Director)

Making a Presence

A week in the life of a worker on the move comprises bouts of different activities – travelling, waiting for connections, stopping *en route*, working in a variety of places before, during and after each journey. This poses a challenge for managers who have to ensure that workers on the move maintain, nurture and enhance their relations with one another, colleagues and clients. It is here that devices – mobile phones in particular – provide a 'digital umbilical cord', connecting those who work on the move into wider networks of relationships (Townsend 2001: 70).

The mobile phone greatly increases opportunities to experience 'absent presence' in one world while being 'tele-present' in another (Gergen 2002; Green 2002). A caller receives priority over others present (signalled by body movements of the recipient, such as turning away or gazing into space), who may none the less be placated by the recipient with comforting gestures and body language (such as rolling the eyes or pulling faces). In other words, the receiver is tele-present to the caller while appearing absent but physically present to those nearby. Fixed-line telephones also permit instantaneous communication between persons at a distance but mobiles free speakers from having to be at fixed geographical points to make connections (Aronson 1971; Pool 1977). The successful completion of mobile telephone calls, therefore, often demands greater delicacy when two front-stage performances are being given simultaneously – to those co-present and those on the other end of the line. While it is acceptable to be in two places at once in some settings – such as trains – it is frowned upon in others, since it is impossible to convey undivided attention while also being in a state of 'absent presence'. Issuing workers on the move with phones that they are expected to carry at all times enhances their 'tele-presence' in the organization. In most cases, refusal is not an option and it is expected that mobiles will be permanently switched on.

> Today is a period of almost instantaneous communication anywhere in the world. You've got to be able to cope with that. Not because it's necessary but because it's become almost the norm . . . I'm sure in days gone by, with no mobile phone and things like that, you could go away and people just had to wait two or three days . . . Today, in the type of business that I'm in, people don't accept that.
>
> (Adam Tully, Managing Director)

In the words of an advertising end line, workers on the move are 'always on, always ready, always connected' (PDA newspaper advert). They are rarely able legitimately to disconnect.

> If I felt that people couldn't get hold of me, or if they felt they couldn't get hold of me then . . . you shatter the illusion of availability . . . My job is a Sales Manager. So what I should be spending my time doing is selling . . . whether I'm doing it through the sales force or whatever . . . I should be accessible, so unless I'm in a meeting then I'd like to think that people can get hold of me at any time.
> (Roy Simms, Sales Manager)

As implied by this respondent, occasions on which it is regarded as legitimate to divert calls to voicemail include face-to-face interactions in which it is important to direct, and convey, undivided attention to those present. However, when it is not possible to answer immediately, those who work on the move feel under pressure to prove that suspension of their 'tele-presence' to others in the network is only temporary. Quick response to voicemail messages – especially those from more senior managers – is, therefore, a common practice. Similarly, workers on the move may account for times they are unavailable by pre-recording voice-mail messages.

> You end up playing telephone tennis sometimes, because you end up leaving messages on voicemail . . . Whatever happens I'll return calls, even if it's to just leave a message to say, 'Yeah I dealt with it', or 'Have received your message', and, you know, 'I'll get back to you'.
> (Ben Dixon, Buildings Maintenance Manager)

> I change my voicemail every day to let people know where I am.
> (Henrietta O'Rearden, Area Human Resources Manager)

Mobile phones enable managers to track the movements of subordinates and compel them to stay in contact. For example, some of those interviewed were required to make telephone calls to their line managers twice a day in order to pick up crucial information, report their whereabouts or simply flag up their presence.

> You must make sure that you've got voicemail on your mobile phone . . . And in addition, you *must* telephone the office at least once in the morning and once in the afternoon . . . It sounds sort of Big Brother-ish, but really you've got to be able to speak to people when they're roving around the country.
> (Rick Deacon, Trade Union Officer)

Managers of those who work on the move often try to engender a sense of team involvement and corporate belonging by organizing team get-togethers in convenient locations.

> We do have a monthly meeting which ends up in the pub. So we do find a degree of sociability and informality as well, but it's not like a drunken evening. It's for an hour and a half at the end of a working session.
> (Gary Atkins, Managing Director)

However, interviewees more frequently reported their own self-made disciplines – rather than those imposed by management – drove them to keep in close contact with network members. These included keeping in regular contact with colleagues by phone and synchronizing these exchanges with the rhythms of work. Such contacts constituted useful exchanges of information and provided details about developments elsewhere in the organization.

First thing in the morning and last thing at night I am often travelling, and that's when my colleagues are also travelling. So we will do a lot of our networking by phone at that time.

(Henrietta O'Rearden, Area Human Resources Manager)

You build up your own network of not just colleagues, they sort of become borderline friends . . . People phone up for a chat . . . Or they'll phone up for something to do with work that's dismissed in 30 seconds and 10 minutes later you're still gossiping . . . That's the best way of finding out what's going on.

(Amanda Squires, Relationship Manager)

In addition to establishing collegiate networks within their organizations, workers on the move strove to foster informal connections within their professions and potential clients. This frequently entailed engagement in strategically selected leisure activities and social facilities that have echoes of Oldenberg's account of 'third places': that is, settings 'beyond home and work . . . in which people relax in good company and do so on a regular basis' (Oldenberg 2001: 2). However, in these instances, leisure was mingled with the cultivation of networks related to work and career. For workers whose mobility restricted opportunities to make such connections within workplaces, voluntary associations were joined or even formed with these purposes in mind.

I'm in a couple of the old salesmen's clubs, which is where people all work together and help each other and talk about what jobs are going on . . . What you do is you meet up once a month, have a bit of lunch together, and talk about who's got what jobs . . . It is also a 'job club' . . . Ours have just got like names – name of the pub where you meet, the so-and-so club. You don't tell anyone about them.

(James Knight, Regional Sales Manager)

There are bars and cafés that I know where various organizations tend to congregate in. So I go in there and may meet them there.

(Richard Kew, Divisional Director)

Resistance

As we have seen, through the use of texts, devices and disciplines, management attempts to exercise long-distance control over those working on the move. Given the centrality of electronic technology to this process, it is appropriate to denote the networks within which work is carried out as an 'electronic envelope'. However, contrary to a recent advertising campaign which warned 'You can run but you can't hide' (technology retailer radio advert, cited in Cooper 2001), there are ways in which workers on the move can resist managerial surveillance. The modalities of this resistance are not to be found in traditional and overt forms of organizational misbe-haviour – such as unionization, strikes and work-to-rules – but in more subtle forms of subversion, such as false and incomplete compliance, feigned ignorance, engineered system failures and irony (Thompson and Ackroyd 1995; Ackroyd and Thompson 1999; Fleming and Sewell 2002).

Although many of our respondents who worked on the move were required to fill in documents – such as movement sheets and electronic diaries – indicating their whereabouts and activities to management and other team members, they could none the less thwart this exercise by failing to fill in the details in a wholly accurate or comprehensive fashion (there are parallels here with the behaviour of workers in the collective office of the Development Council, who failed to complete the details of the electronic booking system, see Chapter 4). Hence, workers on the move may make a semblance of compliance while, at the same time, evading the reach of long-distance controls.

> I evade management control by being vague and less than efficient with my electronic calendar . . . and leaving the mobile on all the time, so that I am apparently available all the time.
>
> (Richard Kew, Divisional Director)

> Nobody really knows that you are where you say you are. They trust your integrity and, if you are of that mind, you can abuse it . . . You can put some-thing on your calendar that says you're on a customer site. Nobody's going to phone you. Or if they do they're gonna phone your mobile and if your mobile's off, then you're in a meeting.
>
> (Amanda Squires, Relationship Manager)

Lack of co-presence and reliance on electronic devices to keep in touch can be used to feign ignorance of on-going events and postpone response times. Our interviews revealed a number of examples of how this prac-tice is used to dodge the reach of the 'electronic envelope'. E-mails are quick and straightforward to send, but their asynchronous nature makes them easy to ignore and the timing of their receipt uncertain. Mobile phones, on the other hand, are both synchronous and asynchronous. They allow the user to direct callers to voicemail, filter calls, playback saved messages and review the missed calls register. All of this can be done without the caller's awareness and at times unknown to the caller, thereby allowing the user to make fake claims about their knowledge of current events and need for their response.

There are always some people . . . we call them 'the black holes' . . . they just ignore their e-mails, ignore their phone calls and just do things when they want.

(Rebecca Sterling, Regional Development Manager)

Obviously there are times when you want to buy a bit of time and say, 'I'm out of the office and we'll talk about it next week'. Whereas, if you were in the office, there probably wouldn't be any excuse and you'd just have to say, 'OK we'll talk about it now'. So it [being contactable only by phone] can buy you a bit more time to think of things or do some research or whatever . . . and, I'll be honest, that does happen. I don't think I or anybody else in the organization uses it to the extent that you go somewhere to avoid having to do the work, because basically it's all there when you get back. It's just been postponed.

(Tim Winfrey, Company Director)

The 'electronic envelope' is the glue that binds staff working on the move into the organization, but the connections are stretched over long distances and are vulnerable to various sources of breakdown. As previously discussed, this makes 'presentation of the self' difficult in certain circumstances and to particular audiences. On the flipside, the same system vulnerabilities – such as battery failure and poor network coverage – can be used to engineer periodic moments of refuge from perpetual contact and, therefore, weaken managerial surveillance.

We've got one bloke who's quite renowned for when he's getting bored with a conversation – he'll say, 'Me signal's going' or 'We're going into a tunnel'.

(Rob Davies, Sales Manager)

Workers on the move are keen to overcome the suggestion that their working arrangements give them an easy life. Nevertheless, they are subject to banter and jokes implying that they spend most of their time pursuing non-work activities, visiting interesting places, eating out and working in comfortable, non-pressured environments. Although much of this was said to be 'good natured', it also constituted a source of unease for many respondents. As do home-located workers (see Chapter 5), they frequently responded by indulging in display behaviours that were intended to establish their diligence and commitment to work. These included sending e-mails and making telephone calls to get noticed, making regular visits to base, and managing people's expectations of when they will be unavailable. However, these tactics could, themselves, elicit ironic or ribald responses, which served to reinforce accusations of foot dragging and skiving. Faced with such accusations, one of our respondents described how she responds by smiling graciously and laughing, leaving accusers unsure and causing them to speculate further. Another made spoof remarks about his current activities in response to regular and detailed enquiries about his work plans. Both are examples of ambiguous and ironic forms of resistance to long-distance controls that knowingly play with negative images and cultivate joking relationships with superiors.

> The Chief Exec is always checking my electronic diary . . . He rings me up in the morning and says, 'What are you doing, I have not seen you for a week?' [laughs] . . . I tell him, 'I am lying in bed reading the paper' . . . He doesn't know whether I am joking . . . Do you have any idea how difficult it is to answer the phone plausibly while you're lying in the bath, the echo is so difficult to disguise!
>
> (Richard Kew, Divisional Director)

Conclusion

The focus of this chapter has been on those who work in a variety of places. They are among the most travelled – clocking up thousands of miles in cars, trains and planes – and spending large amounts of time in shared places that are used for a multiplicity of purposes, such as service stations, hotels, airports and cafés. The chapter has revealed how they structure their lives in order to cope with the heterogeneity of the places they pass through or stop at, and the variety of tasks they are simultaneously called upon to undertake. To give order to their uncertain worlds, workers on the move develop particular modes of self-governance or 'technologies of the self' which permit them 'to effect by their own means or with the help of others a certain number of operations on their own bodies and souls, thoughts, conduct, and way of being' (Foucault 1988:18). Simplistic advertising campaigns suggest that the efficacy of working on the move depends on the efficiency of electronic devices, particularly the mobile phone. In contrast, this chapter has argued that workers on the move have to take planned and artful action to compensate for the deficiencies of their environments as places of work, and, at the same time, mould their work activities around what is possible and acceptable in different venues. They make places work and allocate work to places. Such an analysis directs attention to the active and creative processes entailed in working on the move, and sheds light on how workers go about 'doing' or 'performing' their daily tasks.

Our research evidence reveals the innovative and ingenious ways in which workers on the move counter the heterogeneity of the contexts in which they find themselves. Workers on the move carry around as many work functions as possible, so that the trappings of the office are present whenever and wherever they are required. However, they must prioritize which functions, texts and devices are more likely to be required, in order to avoid overburdening themselves and compromising their mobility. The ability to carry out work also needs to be protected by planning for unexpected changes and delays in travelling between points in the network. Other crises – such as mislaying a document and the failure to receive a recent piece of news – may be corrected by drawing on the services of proxy workers. The chances of breakdown can be minimized by using well-trodden paths and frequented places. Once in a particular place, workers deploy a variety of tactics to strengthen their temporary claims over spaces and construct private enclaves within which to work.

While workers on the move have relatively little control over the environments they encounter, and have to make the best of those they come across, they have more say over when and where certain tasks are carried out. They aim to ensure that each task is 'fit for the place' chosen for its execution. Work tasks are segmented, and placed in particular environments, according to the nature of the operations involved and the resources they require. Workers on the move have to match the temporal requirements of tasks with the granularity of time associated with particular places and modes of travel. Similarly, the geographical space required by certain types of work has to correspond with the amount of space individuals can justly claim. Tasks also vary in level of attentiveness. Those requiring little can be carried out in places with a high likelihood of disturbance, while those requiring high concentration levels are more effectively completed in quiet, disturbance-free and comfortable environments. Interactions with others need to be appropriately framed by choosing the most fitting environmental and communication channels, otherwise there is a danger that the wrong signals will be given off unintentionally. The unpredictability of the work flow – especially via the mobile phone – has the potentiality to put workers off their stride by allocating them tasks that may be unfit for the particular time and place in which they find themselves. Call screening is therefore used to filter impositions, demands and requirements as well as to match them to particular settings. Some face work may be diaried in advance and some may be unscripted. However, seemingly accidental encounters are planned and cultivated in contexts where like-minded and career-relevant individuals are expected to 'hang out' in between appointments.

Despite the effort that workers on the move have to expend on assembly and repair, management pays little attention to easing these burdens. Instead, it seeks to frame them in networks consisting of texts, devices and disciplines that enhance workers' visibility. By these means, management endeavours to exercise long-distance control over a dispersed workforce, correcting for the loss of their visibility and presence. However, these plans are not wholly successful. Workers on the move are still able to offer false and incomplete compliance, deny knowledge of news and events when it suits, engineer system failures in order to go 'missing', and play with the uncertainty that their physical absence engenders among those to whom they report.

Given the ground level view adopted in this chapter, it is fitting that we end with the words of one of our respondents, quoted at the top of the chapter, who pithily commented that, 'I am the only constant'. This aptly sums up the uncertain and unpredictable places in which those who work on the move labour and the variability of the work they carry out. It also highlights her reliance on qualities of personal discipline and self-motivation, while her words emphasize the scale of the achievement. This chapter has sought to provide insights into the practices commonly used to chart paths and create order in such an uncertain and changeable world.

7

Conclusion

Constant revolutionizing of production, uninterrupted disturbance of all social conditions, everlasting uncertainty and agitation distinguish the bourgeois epoch from all earlier ones. All fixed, fast frozen relations, with their train of ancient and venerable prejudices and opinions, are swept away, all new-formed ones become antiquated before they can ossify. All that is solid melts into air.

(Marx and Engels 1967: 222–3)

We will not repeat here arguments that have already been summarized in Chapter 1 and rehearsed in greater detail in subsequent chapters. Instead, our objective is to highlight some of the underlying themes that run throughout the book. These all relate to aspects of change. Indeed, our title – *Changing Places of Work* – has been chosen in order to highlight the extent to which unfolding processes of socio-spatial change characterize the workscapes of contemporary managerial and professional workers. This chapter seeks to highlight the complex, multi-layered character of these transformations and their implications for all aspects of the experience of employment.

The first aspect of change concerns the types of physical spaces in which professional and managerial workers do their jobs. Robust quantitative evidence is still limited with respect to crucial aspects of these developments. Furthermore, journalists, and those with a professional axe to grind, sometimes make extravagant and heroic predictions for the future. Nevertheless, the best available statistical evidence, reviewed in Chapter 3, suggests that real and dramatic shifts are taking place. The office, as we have known it for a century or more, is being reconfigured in ways that reduce, or even in some cases eliminate, personal space. This has fundamental implications for the ways in which people work and the relationships they make with co-workers. Furthermore, work once mainly done in offices is spilling out into other locations. Prominent among these are the home, transport facilities and in-between transitional spaces that were once places of idleness. As a result, the times and spaces of work are seeping into and wrapping themselves around those that were once the preserve of non-work activities, such as leisure, family and 'down' times.

Work has broken out of the constraints of specialized locations and fixed hours (Cairncross 1997; Rifkin 2000). It is not just extending its grip on time and space, it is conquering time and space. Hence, wherever we look, drawing a line between work and non-work becomes ever more difficult.

For those involved, the experience of everyday working life is radically transformed. However, it would be simplistic to represent these changes as a 'big bang'. Rather, they are insidious, multi-dimensional and cumulative. They are insidious because they affect the minutiae of daily routines and the ordering of personal timetables. They fragment the temporal and spatial experiences of groups in the labour process and produce individualized work schedules. They are multi-dimensional in that they do not comprise a shift from one type of workplace to another; we are not, for example, witnessing a transition from working in offices to working at home. Rather, a wide range of diverse sites and locations are becoming places in which people routinely work. Homes are an important aspect of this change but represent only one site among many. The big picture comprises a shift from few to many workplaces and workstations, from singular to plural workscapes. The direction of change, therefore, is towards greater complexity and differentiation in the spaces and times of work. These changes are cumulative precisely because they do not amount to a single transformation, nor do they generate a unified way of life for all who experience their impact. They are rather a patchwork of discrete steps and transitions that advance piece by piece.

A thread of change that has run through all the chapters has been the spread of ICT and its effect in transforming where, when and how professional and managerial work can be done. Furthermore, the devices that constitute the 'electronic envelope' of work have become highly portable. In part, this is a result of a shift in the context of work from so-called 'real' time/space to the 'virtual' time/space of computers. Virtual time/space connects to real time/space at the locations in the physical world where it is possible to access computer screens and the internet, which are becoming ever more variable and ubiquitous. In addition, increasing use of electronic communication channels – principally mobile phones – instantly connects people in real time, wherever they are located. We have presented quantitative data that demonstrate the extraordinarily rapid spread of ICT throughout workplaces and beyond into the everyday lives of workers. Since professional and managerial work has become embedded in the electronic envelope, it is now possible to be engaged in productive employment in more and more locations across the globe at any time of the day or night. As a result, although workers roam across innumerable and diverse remote places, the office – conceived as a body of texts and devices, social and individual disciplines – can still be experienced as a unified entity. The office stretches to become anywhere a laptop and a mobile phone can function.

New technology does not determine the precise form that workscapes will take; it would be possible, for example, to confine the use of ICT to personal offices during nine-to-five hours. However, the driving forces of the capitalist economic system make it likely that the potentiality of ICT to revolutionize the spaces and times of work will be realized. This is because plural workscapes make it possible to lengthen the working day, intensify labour and make savings on office estates.

A further aspect of change that emerges from the substantive chapters on collective offices, working at home and working on the move – Chapters 4, 5 and 6 respectively – is that the emerging workscape of professional and managerial workers is one in which movement and mobility are institutionalized. The conduct of their work increasingly demands movement between workstations and workplaces. Plural workscapes are flows; change is the only constant. The labour processes of professional and managerial workers may be represented, therefore, as the management of transitions. Such transitions occur within collective offices between multiple types of workstations, between offices of clients and colleagues, and outside offices among a wide range of public, private and semi-private sites. Through their daily decisions, workers generate a kaleidoscope of different spaces and times in which they work, which they are responsible for assembling, repairing and reassembling over time. These shifting patterns reflect the demands of job tasks, pressures from management, technological innovations and, to some degree, workers' own personal choices. The management of transitions in the plural workscape, therefore, calls for the ability to switch personal demeanours and social performances across time and space.

Another layer of meaning implied in the title of the book is that in plural workscapes workers are increasingly required to change – that is, reconfigure – the places they temporarily occupy into locations where they are able to conduct their work. Many actual or potential workstations and workplaces are not designated, appointed and set up by an external authority, such as an employer. Rather, in moving between multiple, multifunctional and diverse locations, workers are required to change the functions, milieu and configuration of the places in which they find themselves in order to pursue their occupational tasks. They must be skilled in making places work and matching work to places. Some of the sites that make up plural workscapes are specifically designed as workstations and workplaces. Others have to be adapted by workers themselves in order to be of use. Thus, places outside the office – such as homes, cars, airports and trains – frequently have to be imagined and captured as workstations. In many different contexts, therefore, plural workscapes require workers not merely to discover but also to invent the times and spaces of work for and by themselves. The aptitudes and disciplines of assembly and repair called forth in this process are not those of 'surface acting' but rather the more profound transformations of self entailed in 'deep acting' (Hochschild 1983). Those who successfully work in plural workscapes are, in the process, changed by the experience.

Changes in places of work necessarily generate changes in the management of workers. Plural workscapes make it difficult for managers to base their supervisory strategies on the visibility and presence of the workforce. Frequently, they respond with a variety of alternative approaches, none of which is wholly successful but each of which gives managers some purchase over subordinates. Typically they deploy a range of measures, even though there may be some degree of contradiction or incompatibility between them. In the terminology of organizational learning theory, managerial responses to changing workscapes may be characterized as examples of single, double or triple loop learning (Argyris and Schon 1978; Senge 1990; Swieringa and Wierdsma 1992; Easterby-Smith 1997; Popper and Lipshitz 2000). Single-loop learning involves responding to new situations by adapting and improving existing organizational procedures and rules. This approach was manifested, in our case studies, in attempts by managers to re-establish the visibility and presence of their workforces. Here innovation was confined to fine tuning existing social technologies of regulation; for example, extending panoptical surveillance through electronic means. Double-loop learning entails fundamentally rethinking existing procedures and practices with a view to developing radically new means to achieve established objectives. Thus, some of the managers we interviewed had relinquished visibility and presence as a means of control and sought to assert authority through new channels: for example, via output management. Triple-loop learning entails questioning not only the means by which organizational goals are achieved but also the objectives that they serve. It involves rethinking the relationship between organization and environment, principles and practices. Although such fundamental shifts in perspective and purpose were few, they were apparent in some of our case study organizations. One of the striking features of these organizations was their willingness to abandon attempts to develop discrete managerial techniques for regulating specific clusters within plural workscapes, such as the home or the car. Instead, they sought to manage plural workscapes as a totality. In Cool Marketing and the Development Council, this involved a shift to culturally based systems of regulation that sought to colonize the subjectivity of workers by generating normative communities and shaping of personal subjectivities (Willmott 1993; Casey 1996; Gabriel 1999; Strangleman and Roberts 1999; Grugulis *et al.* 2000; Ezzy 2001). The point of these initiatives was not to monitor outward behavioural compliance but rather to capture inner hearts and minds. This project promised control over the whole workscape in all its diversity. Visibility and presence cease to be significant not because there are better means of exercising authority but because superficial conformity is not what is required. By inculcating a corporate identity and constructed sense of self, management aims to mould a workforce willing to mobilize their intelligence, originality and initiative in pursuit of competitive advantage for the organization (Deetz 1992; Jermier *et al.* 1994; Fleming and Sewell 2002).

In this context, changes in the aesthetic of some parts of the plural workscape become crucial. The aesthetic realm of social life is one in which values, beliefs, norms and knowledge are transmitted via embodied sensual experiences; such as sight, sound and touch. It encompasses socio-spatial relationships that communicate general principles through such channels. Aesthetic codes appeal directly to the senses, arousing emotions, symbolic understandings and intuitive identifications. The aesthetic experiences of those who occupy the clusters that make up plural workscapes are varied. When working on the move, employees often encounter neutral, bland, impersonal public and semi-public situations. When working at home they are located in the heart of an aesthetic of consumption, family and feelings that are in sharp contrast to conventional workplaces. Our interviews show that professional and managerial workers frequently construct traditional personal offices in the midst of the home, with all the aesthetic trappings that implies. In the collective office they encounter yet another, and very intense, aesthetic realm. This promotes a culture dedicated to perpetual change, observation by co-workers, serendipitous interactions and totalizing participation within informal work-based social groups. Organizations that commit them-selves wholeheartedly to the collective office can become arenas in which powerful group cultures are forged and transmitted. Moreover, experience of life in the collective office may cement employees who navigate plural workscapes – and, thereby, experience enhanced individuation and dispersal of their working spaces and times – into the unitary order of the enterprise. The aesthetic of the collective office seeks to generate an inner subjectivity that carries workers across the dispersed and fragmented sites of their working lives and binds them to the organization.

Professional and managerial workers who navigate their way around plural workscapes face unpredictability, uncertainty and ambiguity as a matter of routine. Circumstances constantly change and workers require the capacity to anticipate, accept and accommodate these developments. Assembly and repair skills, therefore, go hand in hand. However, each of the three main clusters characteristic of plural workscapes generates different sources of ambiguity and uncertainty. Each makes different demands on their participants. In the collective office, analysed in Chapter 4, uncertainty arises from the disappearance of personal space – and of space capable of being personalized – thereby sweeping away long-established patterns of managerial control, collegial interaction and worker resistance. The uncertainties of working at home, explored in Chapter 5, arise from the creation of spaces and times of employment in the midst of the private world of the household, combined with geographical remoteness from the direction and guidance of co-workers and line managers. Those who work on the move, as seen in Chapter 6, face the unpredictability that arises from the challenge of manufacturing a bubble of space/time committed to job tasks in the midst of locations that are devoted to public activities, such as leisure and travel.

Other studies of uncertainty, unpredictability and ambivalence within employment relations have concluded that these experiences are central to the work cultures that are characteristic of post-bureaucratic organizations grounded in normative forms of control. Various authors have suggested that the experience of ambivalence and uncertainty creates a psychology of dependence in individual workers, in which the employing organization is perceived as a surrogate family offering a sense of emotional security (Casey 1995, 1999; Gabriel 1999). Arguably, our case studies found at least some evidence to support this view, especially in Cool Marketing. Other research, however, suggests that there are other possible responses to the experience of ambivalence, including cynical detachment and emotional distancing (Fleming and Sewell 2002). We also encountered employees who had developed an attitude of rugged individualism – emphasizing self-sufficiency, self-motivation and self-direction – as a way of coping with unpredictability. These characteristics led us into considering the issue of resistance.

Changes in places of work and changes in strategies of managerial control call forth new forms of resistance. Notwithstanding attempts to mould their subjectivities, the potentiality remains within plural workplaces for workers to reconfigure the official space/times of employment to match their own individual or collective needs, aspirations and interests. The distinctive characteristics of plural workscapes offer many potential opportunities to subvert, evade and even defy supervisory controls by reoccupying and redefining spaces and times in ways that match workers' agendas, rather than those of management. The skills and disciplines demanded by plural workscapes, that facilitate reflexive and calculative generation of personal narratives, also potentially empower workers to create their own worlds of meaning in space and time. The balance between constraints and opportunities is complex and shifting, but the navigators of multiple workplaces should not be regarded as mere victims of circumstances, who have lost the capacity for a coherent sense of identity (cf. Sennett 1998).

There has been much debate as to whether new forms of managerial and organizational controls, grounded in cultural corporatism, have been successful in eliminating labour resistance. New forms of resistance – such as emotional detachment, over-enthusiastic compliance, equivocal affirmation, innocent disrespect or ironic collusion – have been identified (Collinson 1992a, 1992b, 1994; Gabriel 1999; Fleming and Sewell 2002; Knights and McCabe 2000). Furthermore, there is increasing recognition that compliance and resistance are not mutually exclusive but may coexist. Plural workscapes provide good illustrations of these subtleties. Stalling in collective offices is a case in point.

Stalling undoubtedly constitutes an infringement of the spirit and letter of the collective office and, if it becomes rampant, could easily undermine its effectiveness. Moreover, some stalling constitutes a deliberate refusal by staff to co-operate with the spatial principles of collective offices. However, a great deal of stalling in collective offices is motivated by a desire to achieve legitimate organizational objectives and fulfil personal productivity targets. Stalling is an attempt to reduce the uncertainty and unpredictability of collective office provisions. It may also represent an attempt to extend the intimacy and closeness generated by the aesthetic of the collective office into an unacceptable, but understandable, spatial form; that is, sitting with your mates. Furthermore, it should be remembered that in plural workscapes acceptable behaviour is purely contextual; the same behaviours that are deviant in one cluster may be highly prized in another and commonplace in a third. Thus, while stalling is non-compliant in the collective office, it is an essential skill while working on the move in a railway carriage and may be an everyday occurrence when working at home. Resistance and conformity are, thus, relational attributes of the networks that comprise workscapes. There is, then, a complex amalgam of conformity and deviance, rebellion and compliance enshrined in stalling in the collective office.

It seems fitting to close as we began, by reference to the working life of Tony Barker (Deeble 2003). It may be recalled that he commented: 'We need to rewrite the rule book for working in a mobile way'. While recognizing this remark represents a figure of speech, and in no way wishing to disagree with someone who clearly in his own life exemplifies the many layers of change that we have outlined in this book, we respectfully propose an alternative perspective. Plural workscapes make rule books redundant. Radically different ways of behaving are called for in different clusters, workplaces and workstations. Fluidity and flexibility, movement and transformation, uncertainty and ambiguity make fixed responses inappropriate and obsolete. Inasmuch they increasingly find themselves working in collective offices, at home and on the move, professional and managerial workers will be required to devise, police and reinvent their own practices and precepts by and for themselves.

Bibliography

Ackroyd, S. and Thompson, P. (1999) *Organizational Misbehaviour*, London: Sage.

Adams, J. (1999a) 'Hypermobility: too much of a good thing', University College London, November, mimeo.

Adams, J. (1999b) 'The social implications of hypermobility' in Organization for Economic Co-operation and Development (ed.) *The Economic and Social Implications of Sustainable Transportation*, ENV/EPOC/PP/T(99)3/FINAL/REV1.

Ahrentzen, S. (1990) 'Managing conflict by managing boundaries: how professional home-workers cope with multiple roles at home', *Environment and Behaviour*, 22 (6): 723–52.

Ahrentzen, S. (1992) 'Home as a workplace in the lives of women' in I. Altman and S. Low (eds) *Place Attachment*, London: Plenum.

Allan, G. and Crow, G. (eds) (1989) *Home and Family: Creating the Domestic Sphere*, Basingstoke: Macmillan.

Allan, G. and Crow, G. (1991) 'Privatization, home-centredness and leisure', *Leisure Studies*, 10: 19–23.

Allen, S. and Wolkowitz, C. (1987) *Homeworking: Myths and Realities*, London: Macmillan.

Anderson, M. (ed.) (1980) *Sociology of the Family: Selected Readings* (2nd edn), Harmondsworth: Penguin.

Anjum, N. (1999) 'An environmental assessment of office interiors from the consumers' perspective', unpublished PhD thesis, University of Dundee.

Antonelli, P. (ed.) (2001) *Workspheres: Design and Contemporary Workstyles*, New York: Museum of Modern Art.

Argyris, C. and Schon, D. (1978) *Organizational Learning*, Reading: Addison-Wesley.

Aries, P. (1973) *Centuries of Childhood* (translated by Robert Baldick), Harmondsworth: Penguin.

Aries, P. (1985) *Western Sexuality: Practice and Precept in Past and Present Times*, Oxford: Blackwell.

Aries, P. (1987) *History of Private Life*, Cambridge, Mass.: Belnap Press of Harvard University Press.

Armstrong, N. (1999) 'Flexible work in the virtual workplace: discourses and implications of teleworking' in A. Felstead and N. Jewson (eds) *Global Trends in Flexible Labour*, London: Macmillan.

Aronson, S.H. (1971) 'The sociology of the telephone', *International Journal of Comparative Sociology*, 12: 153–67.

AT&T (American Telephone and Telegraph, Inc.) (2003) *Remote Working in the Net-Centric Organisation*, http://www.att.com/emea, accessed on 9 December 2003.

Augé, M. (1995) *Non-Places: Introduction to an Anthropology of Supermodernity*, London: Verso.

Avery, G.C. and Baker, E. (2002) 'Reframing the informated household-workplace', *Information and Organization*, 12: 109–34.

Baldry, C. (1999) 'Space – the final frontier', *Sociology*, 33 (3): 535–53.

Baldry, C., Bain, P. and Taylor, P. (1998) 'Bright Satanic offices: intensification, control and team Taylorism', in P. Thompson and C. Warhurst (eds) *Workplaces of the Future*, London: Macmillan Business.

Barrett, N. (2002) *Building the Custom Home Office: Projects for the Complete Work Place*, Connecticut: Taunton.

Bauman, Z. (2000) *Liquid Capitalism*, Cambridge: Polity.

Bauman, Z. (2001) *Community: Seeking Safety in an Insecure World*, Cambridge: Polity.

Beach, B. (1989) *Integrating Work and Family Life: The Home-Working Family*, New York: State University of New York Press.

Becker, F.D. (1990) *The Total Workplace: Facilities Management and the Elastic Organization*, New York: Van Nostrad Reinhold.

Becker, F. and Steele, F. (1995) *Workplace by Design*, San Francisco: Jossey-Bass.

Becker, F., Quinn, K. and Callentine, L. (1995) *The Ecology of the Mobile Worker*, Ithaca: Cornell University IWSP.

Bedford, M. and Tong, D. (1997) 'Planning for diversity: new structures that reflect the past' in J. Worthington (ed.) *Reinventing the Workplace*, Oxford: Architectural.

Benjamin, D. and Stea, D. (eds) (1995) *The Home: Words, Interpretations, Meanings and Environments*, Aldershot: Avebury.

Bennett, T. (2002) 'Home and everyday life' in T. Bennett and D. Watson (eds) *Understanding Everyday Life*, Oxford: Blackwell and Open University Press.

Berger, J. (1972) *Ways of Seeing*, Harmondsworth: Penguin.

Bhatti, M. and Church, A. (2001) 'Cultivating natures: homes and gardens in late modernity', *Sociology*, 35 (2): 365–83.

Boden, D. and Molotch, H. (1994) 'The compulsion to proximity' in R. Friedland and D. Boden (eds) *Nowhere: Space, Time and Modernity*, Berkeley: University of California Press.

Boris, E. (1994) *Home to Work: Motherhood and the Politics of Industrial Homework in the United States*, Cambridge: Cambridge University Press.

Boris, E. and Daniels, C.R. (eds) (1989) *Homework: Historical and Contemporary Perspectives on Paid Labour at Home*, Urbana: University of Illinois Press.

Boris, E. and Prügl, E. (1996) *Homeworkers in Global Perspective: Invisible No More*, London: Routledge.

Boxer, M.J. and Quataert, J.H. (eds) (2000) *Connecting Spheres: European Women in a Globalizing World, 1500 to the Present* (2nd edn) Oxford: Oxford University Press.

Bradley, H. (1989) *Men's Work, Women's Work: A Sociological History of the Sexual Division of Labour in Employment*, Cambridge: Polity.

Brigham, M. and Corbett, M.J. (1997) 'E-mail, power and the constitution of organisational reality', *New Technology, Work and Employment*, 12 (1): 25–35.

Brock, D. (1998) *Bright Ideas: Home Offices and Studies*, London: Murdoch.

Brown, B. (2001) 'Studying the use of mobile technology' in B. Brown, N. Green and R. Harper (eds) *Wireless World: Social and Interactional Aspects of the Mobile Age*, London: Springer-Verlag.

Brown, B., Green, N. and Harper, R. (eds) (2001) *Wireless World*, London: Springer-Verlag.

Brown, B. and Perry, M. (2000) 'Why don't telephones have off switches? Understanding the use of everyday technologies: a research note', *Interacting with Computers*, 12: 623–34.

Bryden, I. and Floyd, J. (1999) *Domestic Space: Reading the Nineteenth-Century Interior*, Manchester: Manchester University Press.

Bryman, A. (1995) *Disney and His Worlds*, London: Routledge.

Bryman, A. (1999) 'The "disneyfication" of society', *Sociological Review*, 4 (1): 25–47.

Bryman, A. (2004) *The Disneyization of Society*, London: Sage.

Burchell, G. (1993) 'Liberal government and techniques of the self', *Economy and Society*, 22 (3): 266–82.

Cairncross, F. (1997) *The Death of Distance: How the Communications Revolution Will Change Our Lives*, London: Orion.

Cairns, C. (2002) 'Aesthetics, morality and power: design as espoused freedom and implicit control', *Human Relations*, 55 (7): 755–67.

Carr, A. and Hancock, P. (2003) *Art and Aesthetics at Work*, Basingstoke: Palgrave Macmillan.

Carrabine, E. and Longhurst, B. (2002) 'Consuming the car: anticipation, use and meaning in contemporary youth culture', *Sociological Review*, 50 (2): 181–96.

Casey, C. (1995) *Work, Self and Society After Industrialism*, London: Routledge.

Casey, C. (1996) 'Corporate transformations: designer culture, designer employees and "post-occupational" solidarity', *Organization*, 3 (3): 317–39.

Casey, C. (1999) ' "Come, join our family": discipline and integration in corporate organizational culture', *Human Relations*, 52 (2): 155–78.

Castells, M. (1996) *The Rise of the Network Society*, Oxford: Blackwell.

Castells, M. (2000a) *End of Millenium* (2nd edn), Oxford: Blackwell.

Castells, M. (2000b) *The Rise of the Network Society* (2nd edn), Oxford: Blackwell.

Chapman, T. and Hockey, J. (eds) (1999) *Ideal Homes? Social Change and Domestic Life*, London and New York: Routledge.

Churchill, E.F. and Wakeford, N. (2001) 'Framing mobile collaborations and mobile technologies' in B. Brown, N. Green and R. Harper (eds) *Wireless World: Social and Interactional Aspects of the Mobile Age*, London: Springer-Verlag.

Collinson, D. (1992a) 'Engineering humour: masculinity, joking and conflict in shopfloor relations', *Organization Studies*, 9 (2): 181–99.

Collinson, D. (1992b) *Managing the Shopfloor: Subjectivity, Masculinity and Workplace Culture*, Berlin: Walter de Gruyter.

Collinson, D. (1994) 'Strategies of resistance: power, knowledge and subjectivity in the workplace' in J. Jermier, W. Nord and D. Knights (eds) *Resistance and Power in Organizations*, London: Routledge.

Cooper, G. (2001) 'The mutable mobile: social theory in the wireless world' in B. Brown, N. Green and R. Harper (eds) *Wireless World: Social and Interactional Aspects of the Mobile Age*, London: Springer-Verlag.

Crabtree, J., Nathan, M. and Roberts, S. (2003) *Mobile UK: Mobile Phones and Everyday Life*, London: Work Foundation.

Craib, I. (1998) *Experiencing Identity*, London: Sage.

Crang, P. (1994) 'It's show time?: on the workplace geographies of display in a restaurant in southeast England', *Environment and Planning D: Society and Space*, 12: 675–704.

Cunningham, H. (1995) *Children and Childhood in Western Society Since 1500*, London: Longman.

Dahlbom, B. and Ljungberg, F. (1998) 'Mobile informatics', *Scandinavian Journal of Information Systems*, 10 (1/2): 227–34.

Dant, D. and Kiesler, S. (2001) 'Blurring the boundaries: cell phones, mobility, and the line between work and personal life' in B. Brown, N. Green and R. Harper (eds) *Wireless World: Social and Interactional Aspects of the Mobile Age*, London: Springer-Verlag.

Dant, T. and Martin, P.J. (2001) 'By car: carrying modern society' in J. Gronow and A. Warde (eds) *Ordinary Consumption*, London: Routledge.

Darrah, C.N., English-Lueck, J.A. and Savari, A. (1997) 'The informated households project', *Practising Anthropology*, 19 (4): 18–22.

Davidoff, L. (1990) 'The family in Britain' in F.M.L. Thompson (ed.) *People and Their Environment*, Cambridge: Cambridge University Press.

Davidoff, L. and Hall, C. (1987) *Family Fortunes: Men and Women of the English Middle Class, 1780–1850*, London: Hutchinson.

Davidoff, L., L'Esperance, J. and Newby, H. (1979) 'Landscapes with figures: home and community in English Society' in J. Mitchell and A. Oakley (eds) *The Rights and Wrongs of Women*, Harmondsworth: Penguin.

Davis, S.G. (1996) 'The theme park: global industry and cultural form', *Media, Culture and Society*, 18: 399–422.

de Boer, E. (1986) *Transport Sociology: Social Aspects of Transport Planning*, London: Pergamon.

Deeble, S. (2003) 'Upwardly mobile – my workspace', *The Guardian: Work Supplement*, 21 June, p. 27.

Deetz, S. (1992) 'Disciplinary power in the modern corporation' in M. Alvesson and H. Willmott (eds) *Critical Management Studies*, London: Sage.

DEGW and BRE (British Research Establishment) (1996) *New Environments for Working*, London: DEGW International.

Department of Trade and Industry (2000) *Working Anywhere: Exploring Telework for Individuals and Organisations* (2nd edn), London: DTI.

Department for Transport (2002) *Transport Statistics: Great Britain*, London: Stationery Office.

Dobash, R.E. and Dobash, R.R. (1992) *Women, Violence and Social Change*, London: Routledge.

Douglas, M. (1993) 'The idea of home: a kind of space' in A. Mack (ed.) *Home: A Place in the World*, New York: New York University Press.

Doyle, J. and Nathan, M. (2001) *Wherever Next? Work in a Mobile World*, London: Industrial Society.

Du Gay, P. (1996) *Consumption and Identity at Work*, London: Sage.

Duffy, F. (1990) *The Responsive Office*, London: Steelcase Strafor/Polymath.

Duffy, F. (1992) *The Changing Workplace*, London: Phaidon.

Duffy, F. (1997) *The 'New Office'*, London: Conran Octopus.

Dunbar, R. (1996) *Grooming, Gossip and the Evolution of Language*, London: Faber and Faber.

Dupuis, A. and Thorns, D.C. (1996) 'The meaning of home', *Housing Studies*, 11 (4): 485–501.

Dupuis, A. and Thorns, D.C. (1998) 'Home, home ownership and the search for ontological security', *Sociological Review*, 46 (1): 24–47.

Dwelly, T. (2000) *Living at Work: A New Policy Framework for Modern Homeworkers*, York: Joseph Rowntree Foundation.

Easterby-Smith, M. (1997) 'Disciplines and organizational learning: contributions and critiques', *Human Relations*, 50 (9): 1085–113.

Economist (2002) 'The fight for digital dominance', 11 October.

Edensor, T. (2003) 'M6 – junction 19–16', *Space and Culture*, 6 (2): 151–68.

Eldridge, M., Lamming, M., Flynn, M., Jones, C. and Pendlebury, D. (2000) 'Studies of mobile document work and their contribution to the Satchel project', *Personal Technologies*, 4: 102–12.

Elias, N. (1985) *Loneliness of the Dying*, Oxford: Blackwell.

Elias, N. (1994) *The Civilizing Process*, Oxford: Blackwell.

Eriksen, T.H. and Døving, R. (1992) 'In limbo: notes on the culture of airports', paper presented at The Consequences of Globalisation for Social Anthropology Conference, Prague, 30 August–3 September, http://folk.uio.no/gerithe/Airports.html, accessed on 22 May 2003.

Ezzy, D. (2001) 'A simulacrum of workplace community: individualism and engineered culture', *Sociology*, 35 (3): 631–50.

Feld, S. and Basso, K.H. (eds) (1996) *Senses of Place*, Sante Fe, New Mexico: School of American Research Press.

Felstead, A. (1996) 'Homeworking in Britain: the national picture in the mid-1990s', *Industrial Relations Journal*, 27 (3): 225–38.

Felstead, A. and Jewson, N. (1995) 'Working at home: estimates from the 1991 Census', *Employment Gazette*, 103 (3): 95–9.

Felstead, A. and Jewson, N. (1996) *Homeworkers in Britain*, London: HMSO.

Felstead, A. and Jewson, N. (2000) *In Work, At Home: Towards an Understanding of Homeworking*, London: Routledge.

Felstead, A., Jewson, N., Phizacklea, A. and Walters, S. (2000) 'A statistical portrait of working at home in the UK: evidence from the Labour Force Survey', *ESRC Future of Work Programme, Working Paper No. 4*, March; http://www.clms.le.ac.uk/publications/workingathome/working_paper_4.pdf.

Felstead, A., Jewson, N., Phizacklea, A. and Walters, S. (2001a) 'Working at home: statistical evidence for seven key hypotheses', *Work, Employment and Society*, 15 (2): 215–31.

Felstead, A., Jewson, N., Phizacklea, A. and Walters, S. (2001b) 'Blurring the home/work boundary: profiling employers who allow working at home', *ESRC Future of Work Working Paper No. 15*, April; http://www.clms.ac.uk/publications/workingathome/blurring_home_work.pdf.

Felstead, A., Jewson, N., Phizacklea, A. and Walters, S. (2002a) 'Opportunity to work at home in the context of work–life balance', *Human Resource Management Journal*, 12 (1): 54–76.

Felstead, A., Jewson, N., Phizacklea, A. and Walters, S. (2002b) 'The option to work at home: another privilege for the favoured few?', *New Technology, Work and Employment*, 17 (3): 188–207.

Felstead, A., Gallie, D. and Green, F. (2002c) *Work Skills in Britain, 1986–2001*, London: Department for Education and Skills. Available on: http://www.skillsbase.dfes.gov.uk/downloads/WorkSkills1986-2001.doc.

Felstead, A., Jewson, N. and Walters, S. (2003a) 'Managerial control of employees working at home', *British Journal of Industrial Relations*, 41 (2): 241–64.

Felstead, A., Jewson, N. and Walters, S. (2003b) 'The changing location of work', *ESRC Future of Work Working Paper No. 28*, June; http://www.clms.le.ac.uk/esrc/changing_place_of_work.pdf.

Felstead, A., Jewson, N. and Walters, S. (2004) 'Images, interviews and interpretations: making connections in visual research' in C. Pole (ed.) *Seeing is Believing? Approaches to Visual Research*, Oxford: Elsevier Science.

Felstead, A., Jewson, N. and Walters, S. (2005) 'The shifting locations of work: new statistical evidence on the spaces and places of employment', *Work, Employment and Society*, forthcoming.

Financial Times (2000) 'Nearly half of UK population owns a mobile phone' by Alan Cane, 6 January.

Financial Times (2002) 'A long day at home' by Alison Maitland, 21 October.

Financial Times (2003a) 'Without wires, with strings still attached' by Jonathan Moules, 4 June.

Financial Times (2003b) 'Code bans employers from snooping on workers', by Bob Sherwood and Nikki Tait, 11 June.

Financial Times (2003c) 'Drivers face bans for using mobiles' by Cathy Newman, 24 June.

Finch, J. and Mason, J. (1993) *Negotiating Family Responsibilities*, London: Tavistock/Routledge.

Fleming, P. and Sewell, G. (2002) 'Looking for the Good Soldier Svejk: alternative modalities of resistance in the contemporary workplace', *Sociology*, 36 (4): 857–83.

Ford, M. (1999) *Surveillance and Privacy at Work*, London: Institute of Employment Rights.

Foucault, M. (1977) *Discipline and Punish*, Harmondsworth: Penguin/Peregrine.

Foucault, M. (1988) 'Technologies of the self' in L.H. Martin, H. Gutman and P.H. Hutton (eds) *Technologies of the Self: A Seminar with Michel Foucault*, Amherst: University of Massachusetts Press.

Fox, K. (2001) *Evolution, Alienation and Gossip: The Role of Mobile Telecommunications in the 21st Century*; http://www.sirc.org/publik/gossip.shtml, accessed on 22 July 2002.

Frissen, V.A.J. (2000) 'ICTs in the rush hour of life', *Information Society*, 16 (1): 65–75.

Fussell, P. (1980) *Abroad: British Literary Travelling Between the Wars*, Oxford: Oxford University Press.

Gabriel, Y. (1999) 'Beyond happy families: a critical reevaluation of the control–resistance–identity triangle', *Human Relations*, 52 (2): 179–203.

Gabriel, Y. (2002) 'Glass palaces and glass cages: organizations in times of flexible work, fragmented consumption and fragile selves', Inaugural Lecture, Imperial College School of Management, 12 March 2002.

Gagliardi, P. (ed.) (1990) *Symbols and Artefacts*, Berlin: de Gruyter.

Gagliardi, P. (1996) 'Exploring the aesthetic side of organisational life' in S.R. Clegg, C. Hardy and W. Nord (eds) *Handbook of Organizational Studies*, London: Sage.

Gaventa, S. (1998) *Home Office*, London: Dorling Kindersley.

General Register Office (1956) *Census 1951, England and Wales: Report on Usual Residence and Workplace*, London: HMSO.

General Register Office (1966) *Census 1961, England and Wales: Workplace Tables*, London: HMSO.

General Register Office (1968) *Sample Census 1966, England and Wales: Workplace and Transport Tables, Part I*, London: HMSO.

Gergen, K.J. (2002) 'The challenge of absent presence' in J.E. Katz and M. Aakhus (eds) *Perpetual Contact: Mobile Communications, Private Talk, Public Performance*, Cambridge: Cambridge University Press.

Giddens, A. (1991) *Modernity and Self Identity: Self and Society in the Late Modern Age*, Cambridge: Polity.

Giddens, A. (1992) *The Transformation of Intimacy*, Cambridge: Cambridge University Press.

Gillis, J. (1974) *Youth and History*, New York: Academic.

Gioscia, V. (1972) 'On social time' in H. Yaker, H. Osmond and F. Cheek (eds) *The Future of Time*, New York: Anchor.

Gladwell, M. (2000) 'Designs for working', *New Yorker*, 11 December: 60–70.

Goffman, E. (1959) *The Presentation of Self in Everyday Life*, London: Penguin (reprinted edition).

Goffman, E. (1963) *Behavior in Public Places*, New York: Free Press.

Goffman, E. (1971) *Relations in Public: Microstudies of the Public Order*, London: Penguin.

Goldsack, L. (1999) 'Haven in a heartless world? Women and domestic violence' in T. Chapman and J. Hockey (eds) *Ideal Homes? Social Change and Domestic Life*, London: Routledge.

Goleman, D. (1998) *Working With Emotional Intelligence*, London: Bloomsbury.

Gottdiener, M. (2001a) *Life in the Air: Surviving the New Culture of Air Travel*, Lanham, Md: Rowman and Littlefield.

Gottdiener, M. (2001b) *The Themeing of America* (2nd edn), Boulder, Col.: Westview.

Graves-Brown, P. (1997) 'From highway to superhighway: the sustainability, symbolism and situated practices of car culture', *Social Analysis*, 41: 64–75.

Green, N. (2002) 'On the move: technology, mobility and the mediation of social time and space', *The Information Society*, 18: 281–92.

Gregson, N. and Lowe, M. (1994) *Servicing the Middle Classes: Class, Gender and Waged Domestic Labour in Contemporary Britain*, London: Routledge.

Gronow, J. and Warde, A. (2001) (eds) *Ordinary Consumption*, London: Routledge.

Grugulis, I., Dundon, T. and Wilkinson, A. (2000) 'Cultural control and the "culture manager": employment practices in a consultancy', *Work, Employment and Society*, 14 (1): 97–116.

Guardian (2003a) 'Rush-hour Britain slows down' by Andrew Clark, 28 March.

Guardian (2003b) 'Space oddity: staff at London's futuristic City Hall are already running out of room' by Hugh Muir, 6 June.

Guardian (2003c) 'Overcrowded GCHQ reduced to hotdesking' by David Hencke, 2 December.

Gurstein, P. (2001) *Wired to the World, Chained to the Home: Telework in Daily Life*, Vancouver: University of British Columbia Press.

Haddon, L. and Lewis, A. (1994) 'The experience of teleworking: an annotated review', *International Journal of Human Resource Management*, (1): 195–223.

Haddon, L. and Silverstone, R. (1993) 'Teleworking in the 1990s: a view from the home', Science and Technology Policy Research *(SPRU) CICT Report Series, No. 10*.

Hakim, C. (1987) 'Home-based work in Britain: a report on the 1981 National Homeworking Survey and the DE research programme on homework', *Department of Employment Research Papers, No. 60*, London: Department of Employment.

Hakim, C. (1998) *Social Change and Innovation in the Labour Market: Evidence from the Census SARs on Occupational Segregation and Labour Mobility, Part-Time Work and Student Jobs, Homework and Self-Employment*, Oxford: Oxford University Press.

Hall, C. (1982) 'The butcher, the baker, the candlestickmaker: the shop and the family in the Industrial Revolution' in E. Whitelegg, A. Arnot, E. Bartels, V. Beechy, L. Birke, S. Himmelweit, D. Leonard, S. Ruehl and M. Speakman (eds) *The Changing Experience of Women*, Oxford: Basil Blackwell.

Hannigan, J. (1998) *Fantasy City: Pleasure and Profit in the Postmodern Metropolis*, London: Routledge.

Hareven, T.K. (1982) *Family Time and Industrial Time: The Relationship Between Family and Work in a New England Industrial Community*, Cambridge: Cambridge University Press.

Hareven, T.K. (1993) 'The home and the family in historical perspective' in A. Mack (ed.) *Home: A Place in the World*, New York University Press.

Harris, C.C. (1977) 'Changing conceptions of the relation between family and societal form in western society' in R. Scase (ed.) *Industrial Society: Class, Cleavage and Control*, London: Allen and Unwin.

Harris, R. (1997) 'Real estate and the future' in J. Worthington (ed.) *Reinventing the Workplace*, Oxford: Architectural.

Harvey, D. (1989) *The Condition of Post Modernity*, Oxford: Blackwell.

Harvey, M. (1999) 'Economies of time: a framework for analysing the restructuring of employment relations' in A. Felstead and N. Jewson (eds) *Global Trends in Flexible Labour*, Basingstoke: Macmillan.

Hawkins, K. and Radcliffe, R. (1971) 'Competition in the brewing industry', *Journal of Industrial Economics*, 20 (1): 20–41.

Heath, C., Knoblauch, H. and Luff, P. (2000) 'Technology and social interaction: the emergence of "workplace studies"', *British Journal of Sociology*, 51 (2): 299–320.

Hendry, K. (1994) 'Invisible threads: from homeworkers to the high street – investigating the links in the sub-contracting chain', unpublished Masters thesis, University of Warwick.

Hepworth, M. (1999) 'Privacy, security and respectability: the ideal Victorian home' in T. Chapman and J. Hockey (eds) *Ideal Homes? Social Change and Domestic Life*, London and New York: Routledge.

Hill, E.J., Hawkins, A.J. and Miller, B.C. (1996) 'Work and family in the virtual office – perceived influences of mobile telework', *Family Relations*, 45 (3): 667–83.

Hirsch, E. and O'Hanlon, M. (eds) (1995) *The Anthropology of Landscape: Perspectives on Place and Space*, Oxford: Clarendon.

Hochschild, A. (1983) *The Managed Heart*, Berkeley: University of California Press.

Hochschild, A. (1997) *Timebind: When Work Becomes Home and Home Becomes Work*, New York: Metropolitan.

Hockey, J. (1999) 'Houses of doom' in T. Chapman and J. Hockey (eds) *Ideal Homes? Social Change and Domestic Life*, London and New York: Routledge.

Holtham, C. (2001) 'The office of the future: the most important technology will be the coffee machine', City University Centre for Virtual Work, Commerce and Learning; www.staff.city.ac.uk/~sf329/office/ec/pdf.

Holstein, J. and Gubrium, J. (2000) *The Self We Live By*, Oxford University Press.

Honsden, J. (1984) *Franchising and Other Business Relationships in Hotel and Catering Services*, London: Heinemann.

Horgen, T.H., Joroff, M.L., Porter, W.L. and Schon, D.A. (1999) *Excellence by Design: Transforming Workplace and Work Practice*, New York: John Wiley.

Hotopp, U. (2002) 'Teleworking in the UK', *Labour Market Trends*, 110 (6): 311–18.

Humphries, J. (1982) 'Class struggle and the persistence of the working-class family' in A. Giddens and D. Held (eds) *Class, Power and Conflict*, Basingstoke: Macmillan.

Huws, U. (1984) *The New Homeworkers: New Technology and the Changing Location of White-Collar Work*, London: Low Pay Unit.

Huws, U. (1993) 'Teleworking in Britain', *Employment Department Research Series, No. 18*, London: Department of Employment.

Independent on Sunday (2003) 'Change your life: commute to the end of the garden' by Clare Francis, 3 November.

ITU (International Telecommunication Union) (2003) 'Key global telecom indicators for the world telecommunication service sector'; http://www.itu.int/ITU-D/ict/statistics/at_glance/KeyTelecom99.html, accessed 20 March 2003.

Iyer, P. (2000) *The Global Soul: Jet-Lag, Shopping Malls and the Search for Home*, London: Bloomsbury.

Jacobs, J. (1965) *The Death and Life of Great American Cities*, Harmondsworth: Penguin.

Jamieson, L. (2002) *Intimacy: Personal Relationships in Modern Societies*, Cambridge: Polity.

Jensen, A. and McKee, L. (2003) *Children and the Changing Family: Between Transformation and Negotiation*, London: Routledge Farmer.

Jermier, J.M., Knights, D. and Nord, W.R. (1994) (eds) *Resistance and Power in Organizations*, London: Routledge.

Joyce, P. (1987) *The Historical Meanings of Work*, Cambridge: Cambridge University Press.

Katz, J.E. and Aakhus, M. (2002) (eds) *Perpetual Contact: Mobile Communications, Private Talk, Public Performance*, Cambridge: Cambridge University Press.

Knights, D. and McCabe, D. (2000) '"Ain't misbehaving"?: Opportunities for resistance under new forms of "quality" management', *Sociology*, 34 (3): 421–36.

Knights, D. and Morgan, G. (1991) 'Selling oneself: subjectivity and the labour process in selling life assurance' in C. Smith, D. Knights and H. Willmott (eds) *White-Collar Work*, London: Macmillan.

Laing, A. (1997) 'New patterns of work: the design of the office' in J. Worthington (ed) *Reinventing the Workplace*, Oxford: Architectural.

Laing, A., Duffy, F., Jaunzens, D. and Willis, S. (1998) *New Environments for Working*, London: BRE and DEGW.

Lankshear, G., Cook, P., Mason, D., Coates, S. and Button, G. (2001) 'Call centre employees' responses to electronic monitoring: some research findings', *Work, Employment and Society*, 15 (3): 595–605.

Lasch, C. (1977) *Haven in a Heartless World: The Family Besieged*, New York: Basic.

Lash, S. and Urry, J. (1994) *Economies of Signs and Space*, London: Sage.

Laslett, P. (1979) *The World We Have Lost*, London: Methuen.

Laurier, E. (2001a) 'Notes on dividing the attention of a car driver', TechEthno-Online, 1 (1): 1–17; http://www.teamethno-online.org/issue1/Laurier/gooddriv.html, accessed on 21 July 2003.

Laurier, E. (2001b) 'The region as a socio-technical accomplishment of mobile workers' in B. Brown, N. Green and R. Harper (eds) *Wireless World: Social and Interactional Aspects of the Mobile Age*, London: Springer-Verlag.

Laurier, E. (2001c) 'Why people say where they are during mobile phone calls', *Environment and Planning D: Society and Space*, 19: 485–504.

Laurier, E. and Philo, C. (1999) '"Meet you at junction 17": a socio-technical and spatial study of the mobile office', *ESRC End of Award Report*, R000222071, Swindon: ESRC.

Law, A. (1999) *Creative Company: How St Luke's Became 'The Ad Agency to End All Ad Agencies'*, New York: John Wiley.

Law, A. (2001) *Open Minds: 21st Century Business Lessons and Innovations from St Luke's*, New York: Texere.

Law, J. (1986) 'On the methods of long distance control: vessels, navigation and the Portuguese route to India' in J. Law (ed.) *Power, Action and Belief: A New Sociology of Knowledge*, London: Routledge and Kegan Paul.

Law, J. and Hassard, J. (eds) (1999) *Actor Network Theory and After*, Oxford: Blackwell.

Lefebvre, H. (1991) *The Production of Space* (translated by D. Nicholson-Smith), Oxford: Basil Blackwell.

Letherby, G. and Reynolds, G. (2003) 'Making connections: the relationship between train travel and the processes of work and leisure', *Sociological Research Online*, 8 (3); http://www.socresonline.org.uk/8/3/letherby.html, accessed on 12 September 2003.

Lindsay, C. (2003) 'A century of labour market change: 1900 to 2000', *Labour Market Trends*, 111 (3): 133–44.

Ling, R. (1997) '"One can talk about common manners!" The use of mobile telephones in inappropriate situations' in L. Haddon (ed.) *Communications on the Move: The Experience of Mobile Telephony in the Late 1990s*, COST 248 Report, Farsta: Telia.

Lyon, D. (1994) *The Electronic Eye: The Rise of Surveillance Society*, Cambridge: Polity.

Lyon, D. (2001) *Surveillance Society*, Buckingham: Open University Press.

Mack, A. (ed.) (1993) *Home: A Place in the World*, New York: New York University Press.

McKendrick, N. (1962) 'Josiah Wedgewood and the factory discipline', *Historical Journal*, 4: 30–5.

Madigan, R. and Munro, M. (1996) 'House beautiful': style and consumption in the home', *Sociology*, 30 (1): 41–57.

Madigan, R., Munro, M. and Smith, S.J. (1990) 'Gender and the meaning of home', *International Journal of Urban and Regional Research*, 14 (4): 625–47.

Mäenpää, P. (2001) 'Mobile communication as a way of urban life' in J. Gronow and A. Warde (eds) *Ordinary Consumption*, London: Routledge.

Magee, J.L. (2000) 'Home as an alternative workplace: negotiating the spatial and behavioural boundaries between home and work', *Journal of Interior Design*, 26 (1): 35–47.

Marglin, S. (1976) 'What do bosses do?' in A. Gorz (ed.) *The Division of Labour*, Brighton: Harvester.

Markus, T. (1993) *Buildings and Power: Freedom and Control in the Origins of Modern Building Types*, London: Routledge.

Marx, K. and Engels, F. (1967) *The Communist Manifesto*, Harmondsworth: Penguin.

Mason, D., Button, G., Lankshear, G. and Coates, S. (2002) 'Getting real about surveillance and privacy at work' in S. Woolgar (ed.) *Virtual Society? Get Real!* Oxford: Oxford University Press.

Massey, D. (1995) 'Rethinking radical democracy spatially', *Environment and Planning A, Society and Space*, 13: 283–8.

Michelson, W. and Linden, K.P. (1997) 'Home and telework in Sweden', paper presented at the Gender and Teleworking Conference, National Resource Centre for Women (NUTEK), Stockholm, Sweden, 14 March.

Miller, D. (ed.) (2001) *Home Possessions: Material Culture Behind Closed Doors*, Oxford: Berg.

Miller, D., Jackson, P., Thrift, N., Holbrook, B. and Rowlands, M. (1998) *Shopping, Place and Identity*, London: Routledge.

Miller, H. (1995) 'The presentation of self in electronic life: Goffman on the Internet', paper presented to the Embodied Knowledge and Virtual Space Conference, Goldsmiths' College, University of London; http://ess.ntu.ac.uk/miller/cyberpsych/goffman.htm, accessed on 7 July 2003.

Mirchandani, K. (2000) ' "The best of both worlds" and 'Cutting my own throat": contradictory images of home-based work', *Qualitative Sociology*, 23 (2): 159–82.

Mitterauer, M. and Sieder, R. (1982) *The European Family: Patriarchy to Partnership from the Middle Ages to the Present*, Oxford: Blackwell.

Moore, J. (2000) 'Placing home in context', *Journal of Environmental Psychology*, 20: 207–17.

MORI/Vodafone. (2003) *The British Mobile Communications Survey*, London: MORI (Market Opinion and Research International); http://www.mori.com/polls/2002/vodafone.shtml, accessed on 16 June 2003.

Morris, M. (1988) 'At Henry Parks Motel', *Cultural Studies*, 2: 1–47.

Myerson, G. (2001) *Heidegger, Habermas and the Mobile Phone*, Cambridge: Icon.

Myerson, J. and Ross, P. (1999) *The Creative Office*, London: Lawrence King.

Nathan, M. and Doyle, J. (2002) *The State of the Office: The Politics and Geography of Working Space*, London: Industrial Society.

Newby, H. (1977) *The Deferential Worker: A Study of Farm Workers in East Anglia*, London: Allen Lane.

Newby, H. (1979) *Green and Pleasant Land? Social Change in Rural England*, London: Hutchinson.

Nickson, D., Warhurst, C., Witz, A. and Cullen, A.M. (2001) 'The importance of being aesthetic: work, employment and service organization' in A. Sturdy, I. Grugulis and H. Willmott (eds) *Customer Service: Empowerment and Entrapment*, Basingstoke: Palgrave (now Palgrave Macmillan).

Nickson, D., Warhurst, C., Cullen, A.M. and Watt, A. (2003) 'Bringing in the excluded? Aesthetic labour, skills and training in the "new" economy', *Journal of Education and Work*, 16 (2): 185–203.

Nippert-Eng, C. (1996) *Home and Work: Negotiating Boundaries Through Everyday Life*, Chicago: University of Chicago Press.

Office Angels (2001) 'Office rituals make workers more productive', Office Angels press release, April 2001.

O'Hara, K., Perry, M., Sellen, A. and Brown, B. (2001) 'Exploring the relationship between mobile phone and document activity during business travel' in B. Brown, N. Green and R. Harper (eds) *Wireless World: Social and Interactional Aspects of the Mobile Age*, London: Springer-Verlag.

Oldenberg, R. (1991) *The Great Good Place: Cafés, Coffee Shops, Community Centres, Beauty Parlors, General Stores, Bars, Hangouts, and How They Get You Through the Day*, New York: Paragon House.

Oldenberg, R. (2001) *Celebrating the Third Place: Inspiring Stories About the 'Great Good Places' at the Heart of Our Communities*, New York: Marlowe.

ONS (Office for National Statistics) (2000) *Editing and Imputation for the 2001 Census*; http://www.statistics.gov.uk.census2001/pdfs/ag0013.pdf, accessed on 26 November 2003.

ONS (Office for National Statistics) (2003a) *Census 2001: National Report for England and Wales*, London: Stationery Office.

ONS (Office for National Statistics) (2003b) 'National Travel Survey: 2002 provisional results', ONS press release, 18 December; http://www.dft.gov.uk/pns/, accessed 18 December 2003.

OPCS (Office of Population Censuses and Surveys) (1974) *Census 1971, England and Wales: Workplace and Transport to Work Tables, Part 1 (10% Sample)*, London: HMSO.

OPCS (Office of Population Censuses and Surveys) (1982) *Labour Force Survey 1981*, London: HMSO.

OPCS (Office of Population Censuses and Surveys) (1984) *Census 1981: Workplace and Transport to Work, England and Wales*, London: HMSO.

OPCS (Office of Population Censuses and Surveys) (1994) *1991 Census: Workplace and Transport to Work, Great Britain*, London: HMSO.

Parker, M. (1995) 'Working together, working apart: management culture in a manufacturing firm', *Sociological Review*, 4 (3): 518–47.

Pelegrin, E. (1996) *The Office*, Paris: Flammarion.

Perry, M., O'Hara, K., Sellen, A., Brown, B. and Harper, R. (2001) 'Dealing with mobility: understanding access anytime, anywhere', *ACM Transactions on Computer–Human Interaction*, 8 (4): 323–47.

Phizacklea, A. and Wolkowitz, C. (1995) *Homeworking Women: Gender, Ethnicity and Class at Work*, London: Sage.

Plant, S. (2001) *On the Mobile: The Effects of Mobile Telephones on Social and Individual Life*; http://www.motorola.com/mot/documents/0,1028,333,00.pdf, accessed on 27 July 2003.

Pollert, A. (1981) *Girls, Wives, Factory Lives*, London: Macmillan.

Pool, I. (1977) (ed.) *The Social Impact of the Telephone*, Cambridge, Mass.: MIT Press.

Pooley, C.G. and Turnbull, J. (1999) 'The journey to work: a century of change', *Area*, 31 (3): 281–92.

Popper, M. and Lipshitz, R. (2000) 'Organizational learning: mechanisms, culture and feasibility', *Management Learning*, 31 (2): 181–96.

Raymond, S. and Cunliffe, R. (1997) *Tomorrow's Office: Creating Effective and Humane Interiors*, London: E. and F. Spon.

Reid, D.A. (1976) 'The decline of Saint Monday', *Past and Present*, 71: 76–101.

Rifkin, J. (2000) *The Age of Access: How the Shift from Ownership to Access is Changing Capitalism*, London: Penguin.

Ritzer, G. (1999) *Enchanting a Disenchanted World: Revolutionizing the Means of Consumption*, Thousand Oaks, Cal.: Pine Forge.

Roberts, E. (1984) *A Woman's Place: An Oral History of Working Class Women, 1890–1940*, Oxford: Basil Blackwell.

Rorty, R. (1980) *Philosophy and the Mirror of Nature*, Oxford: Blackwell.

Rose, N. (1990) *Governing the Soul: The Shaping of the Private Self*, London: Routledge.

Ross, P. (1995) *The Cordless Office*, London: Morgan Lovell.

Rybczynski, W. (1988) *Home: A Short History of an Idea*, London: Heinemann.

Salmi, M. (1996) 'Finland is another world: the gendered time of homework' in E. Boris and E. Prügl (eds) *Homeworkers in Global Perspective: Invisible No More*, New York: Routledge.

Salmi, M. (1997) 'Autonomy and time in home-based work' in T. Heiskanen and L. Rantalaiho (eds) *Gendered Practices in Working Life*, London: Macmillan.

Saunders, P. (1990) *A Nation of Homeowners*, London: Unwin Hyman.

Schivelbusch, W. (1986) *The Railway Journey: The Industrialization of Time and Space in the Nineteenth Century*, Berkeley: University of California Press.

Schwartz, H.S. (1987a) 'Anti-social actions of committed organizational participants: an existential psychoanalytical perspective', *Organization Studies*, 8 (4): 327–40.

Schwartz, H.S. (1987b) 'On the psychodynamics of organizational totalitarianism' *Journal of Management*, 13 (1): 45–54.

Scott, J. (2000) *Social Network Analysis: A Handbook* (2nd edn), London: Sage.

Segalen, M. (1983) *Love and Power in the Peasant Family*, Oxford: Basil Blackwell.

Senge, P.M. (1990) *The Fifth Discipline: The Art and Practice of the Learning Organization*, London: Century Business.

Sennett, R. (1998) *The Corrosion of Character: The Personal Consequences of Work in the New Capitalism*, London: W.W. Norton.

Sewell, G. and Wilkinson, B. (1992) ' "Someone to watch over me": surveillance, discipline and the just-in-time labour process', *Sociology*, 26 (2): 271–89.

Silva, E.B. and Bennett, T. (eds) (2003) *Contemporary Culture and Everyday Life*, Durham: sociologypress.

Silverstone, R. and Hirsch, E. (eds) (1992) *Consuming Technologies: Media and Information in Domestic Spaces*, London: Routledge.

Smith, P. and Kearney, L. (1994) *Creating Workplaces Where People Can Think*, San Francisco: Jossey-Bass.

Sorokin, M. (1992) *Variations on a Theme Park: The New American City and the End of Public Space*, New York: Noonday.

Sparke, P. (1995) *As Long As It's Pink: The Sexual Politics of Taste*, London: Pandora.

Spears, T.B. (1995) *100 Years on the Road: The Travelling Salesman in American Culture*, New Haven: Yale University Press.

Standen, P. (1997) 'Home, work and management in the Information Age', mimeo, Department of Management, Edith Cowan University.

Steward, B. (2000) 'Changing times: the meaning, measurement and use of time in teleworking' *Time and Society*, 9 (1): 57–74.

Stimson, G.V. (1986) 'Place and space in sociological fieldwork', *Sociological Review*, 34 (3): 641–56.

Stone, L. (1977) *The Family, Sex and Marriage in England, 1500–1800*, London: Weidenfeld and Nicolson.

Stone, P.J. and Luchetti, R. (1985) 'Your office is where you are', *Harvard Business Review*, March-April.

Strangleman, T. and Roberts, I. (1999) 'Looking through the window of opportunity: the cultural cleansing of workplace identity', *Sociology*, 33 (1): 47–67.

Strati, A. (1996) 'Organizations viewed through the lens of aesthetics', *Organization*, 3 (2): 209–18.

Strati, A. (1999) *Organization and Aesthetics*, London: Sage.

Strati, A. and de Montoux, G.P. (2002) 'Organizing aesthetics', *Human Relations*, 55 (7): 755–67.

Suchman, L. (1987) *Plans and Situated Actions: The Problem of Human–Machine Communications*, Cambridge: Cambridge University Press.

Suchman, L. (1999) 'Reconstructing technologies as social practice', *American Behavioural Scientist*, 43 (3): 392–408.

Sullivan, C. (2000) 'Space and the intersection of work and family in homeworking households', *Community, Work and Family*, 3 (2): 185–204.

Swieringa, J. and Wierdsma, A. (1992) *Becoming a Learning Organization*, Wokingham: Addison-Wesley.

Taylor, R. (2002a) *Britain's World of Work – Myths and Realities*, Swindon: Economic and Social Research Council.

Taylor, R. (2002b) *Managing Workplace Change*, Swindon: Economic and Social Research Council.

Taylor, S. (2002) 'Overcoming aesthetic muteness: researching organizational members' aesthetic experience', *Human Relations*, 55 (7): 755–67.

Thompson, E.P. (1967) 'Time, work-discipline and industrial capitalism', *Past and Present*, 38: 56–97.

Thompson, P. and Ackroyd, S. (1995) 'All quiet on the workplace front? A critique of recent trends in British industrial sociology', *Sociology*, 29 (4): 615–33.

Thompson, T. (1997) 'Supporting organizational change' in J. Worthington (ed.) *Reinventing the Workplace*, Oxford: Architectural.

Thrift, N. (1990) 'Owners' time and own time: the making of a capitalist time consciousness 1300–1800' in J. Hassard (ed.) *The Sociology of Time*, London: Macmillan.

Thrift, N. (1996) *Spatial Formations*, London: Sage.

Tietze, S. and Musson, G. (2002) 'When "work" meets "home": temporal flexibility as lived experience', *Time and Society*, 11 (2/3): 315–34.

Tilly, L.A. and Scott, J.W. (1978) *Women, Work and the Family*, London: Holt, Reinhart and Winston.

T-Mobile (2003) 'Starbucks and T-Mobile expand wireless offering in the UK', T-Mobile press release, 6 March 2003; http://www.t-mobile.co.uk, accessed 5 July 2003.

Townsend, A.M. (2001) 'Mobile communications in the twenty-first century city' in B. Brown, N. Green and R. Harper (eds) *Wireless World: Social and Interactional Aspects of the Mobile Age*, London: Springer-Verlag.

Turner, G. (1997) *The Changing Government Workplace*, Leicester: De Montfort University Press.

Turner, G. and Myerson, J. (1998) *New Workspace, New Culture*, London: Design Council/Gower.

Urry, J. (2000a) 'Mobile sociology', *British Journal of Sociology*, 51 (1): 185–203.

Urry, J. (2000b) *Sociology Beyond Societies: Mobilities for the Twenty-First Century*, London: Routledge.

Urry, J. (2002) 'Mobility and proximity', *Sociology*, 36 (2): 255–74.

Urry, J. (2003) 'Social networks, travel and talk', *British Journal of Sociology*, 54 (2): 155–75.

Valentine, G. (1999) 'Eating in: home, consumption and identity', *Sociological Review*, 47 (3): 491–524.

Vincent, J. (2003) 'Emotional attachment to mobile phones – an extraordinary relationship', paper presented to the Fourth Wireless World Conference, Digital World Research Centre, University of Surrey, 17–18 July.

Warhurst, C. and Nickson, D. (2001) *Looking Good, Sounding Right*, London: Work Foundation.

Warren, T. (2003) 'Class and gender-based working time? Time poverty and the division of domestic labour, *Sociology*, 3 (4): 733–52.

Westwood, S. (1984) *All Day, Every Day: Factory and Family in the Making of Women's Lives*, London: Pluto.

Westwood, S. (2002) *Power and the Social*, London: Routledge.

Wiberg, M. and Ljungberg, F. (2001) 'Exploring the vision of "anytime, anywhere" in the context of mobile work' in M. Wiberg (ed.) 'In between mobile meetings: exploring seamless ongoing interaction support for mobile CSCW', unpublished PhD thesis, Department of Informatics, Umeå University, Umeå, Sweden.

Wiesner-Hanks, M. (2000) 'Women's work in the changing city economy, 1500–1650' in M.J. Boxer and J.H. Quataert (eds) *Connecting Spheres: European Women in a Globalizing World, 1500 to the Present* (2nd edn), Oxford: Oxford University Press.

Willmott, H. (1993) 'Strength is ignorance, slavery is freedom: managing cultures in modern organizations', *Journal of Management Studies*, 30 (4): 515–52.

Witz, A., Warhurst, C. and Nickson, D. (2003) 'The labour aesthetics and the aesthetics of organization', *Organization*, 10 (1): 33–54.

Wolf, W. (1996) *Car Mania: A Critical History of Transport*, London: Pluto.

Woodward, I., Emmison, M. and Smith, P. (2000) 'Consumerism, disorientation and post-modern space: a modest test of an immodest theory', *British Journal of Sociology*, 51 (2): 339–54.

Woodward, K. (2002) *Understanding Identity*, London: Arnold.

Worrall, L., Cooper, C. and Campbell, F. (2001) 'The new reality for UK managers: perpetual change and employment instability', *Work, Employment and Society*, 14 (4): 647–68.

Worthington, J. (1997) *Reinventing the Workplace*, Boston: Architectural.

Zaretsky, E. (1976) *Capitalism, The Family and Personal Life*, London: Pluto.

Zelinsky, M. (1997) *New Workplaces for New Workstyles*, New York: McGraw-Hill.

Zelinsky, M. (2002) *The Inspired Workplace: Designs for Creativity and Productivity*, Gloucester, Mass.: Rockport.

Zimmerman, N. (2003) *Home Workspace Idea Book*, Connecticut: Taunton.

Zuboff, S. (1988) *In the Age of the Smart Machine: The Future of Work and Power*, Oxford: Heinemann.

Subject Index

Author Index